The Definitive Guide to Oracle FDMEE

Tony Scalese

Published in 2016 by P8tech, an imprint of Play Technologies (England) Limited

Copyright © Play Technologies (England) Limited

ISBN: 978-0-9929105-2-5

P8Tech has endeavoured to provide trademark information about all the companies and products mentioned in this book by the appropriate use of capitals. However, P8Tech cannot guarantee the accuracy of this information.

P8Tech
6 Woodside
Churnet View Road
Oakamoor
ST10 3AE

www.P8Tech.com

To my wife, without you this book never would have
been possible. I love you.

*

*"Give a man a fish and you've fed him for a day.
Teach a man to fish and you've fed him for a lifetime."*

"Knowledge isn't power, sharing knowledge is power."

Acknowledgements

I would like to acknowledge and thank everyone that has helped me in writing this book - not only the task of creating this volume but for helping me get to the point where I have been able to undertake this. To all the people that have contributed to my creation of this book, I want to recognize so many of you. The order below in no way represents a ranking, please know that I am eternally grateful to each of you.

First and foremost, I want to thank my wife. Anna, your unwavering support of me is something I simply cannot thank you enough for. Through all of the challenges of my professional life, you have been a constant source of advice, support and learning. Thank you for the countless nights and weekends when you took over the responsibilities of our household so that I could chase my muse.

To my daughter, thank you for all of the time over the course of me writing this book when you have given up daddy daughter time. You're too young to yet understand why papa works so hard but know that it is for you. You have made me a better person and I cannot thank you enough for that.

To my mom, thank you for all that you have done to help me get to where I am today. Your hard work and dedication have been instrumental in me growing into the man I am today.

To my editor and publisher, James. Thank you for the support over the course of this project. Your editing of my sometimes lackluster grammar is appreciated by not only me but surely by the readers of this book.

To my best friend, John. Thank you for the help through the contracts process and more so for being a great friend even while I have been MIA throughout the course of this project.

To Wayne, thank you for everything that you have taught me over the years. Thank you for the tremendous ability and dedication that you bring to the team. You are a rock star and I can't imagine a team that doesn't have you on it.

To Seema, thank you for being the FDM ninja. Your quiet demeanor has always been a balance to my "enthusiastic" style. Like Wayne, I never want to imagine a team that doesn't include you.

To my team, thank you all for being the best in the business. I am so incredibly proud of each of you and I couldn't be happier with what our team has become.

To Robin and Chris, thank you for the support to write this book and the opportunity to grow in my career.

To Peter, thank you for the opportunity to enter the consulting world so many years ago. Your leadership and mentorship has meant the world to me.

To Chris, thank you for the introduction to the world of Hyperion so many years ago. Thank you for the constant support over the course of my career.

To Mike and Kumaresh, a sincerest of thank yous for all of the support over the years. Your willingness to partner has empowered me and my team and I am incredibly grateful for that.

To Jeff Jones, John Pak and Matt Meyerhoff, thank you for all of the support and knowledge that you shared so many years ago when I first started to dive into the world of FDM. Your commitment to customers has set a model to which all organizations should strive.

Tony

About This Book

Oracle Hyperion Financial Data Quality Management, Enterprise Edition, (FDMEE) is a critical component within the Oracle Hyperion Enterprise Performance Management (EPM) suite of products.

While the value and use of products like Hyperion Financial Management (HFM) and Hyperion Planning is readily apparent to their target audience, the value of FDMEE is one that is often misunderstood or underestimated. In this book, I provide a deeper dive into many of the foundational metadata elements in an effort to provide an administrator with a better understanding of each component as well as their interdependencies. Additionally, this book will provide information about how to effectively own and manage the application by exploring such topics as: integrating new data sources, unlocking overlooked user interface features, and troubleshooting. This book will empower an administrator and in doing so provide an opportunity to realize an even great return on your FDMEE investment.

This book is not intended to be a replacement for formal product training or the administrator guide provided by Oracle. Instead this book is a supplement and assumes a certain level of knowledge about FDMEE. Functionality described in this book is assumed for the 11.1.2.4.000 release of the product except where otherwise noted.

Leading Practices

Throughout this book I will make reference to best/leading practices for settings, design and build concepts, and product usage. One of the most valuable things I have read was a discussion about best practices. The author, Peter Fugere, described the use of the term best practices as a hammer because it is so often used to shut down discussion about a topic. I fully agree that the term best practice is overused and allows a person to be lazy. Instead of offering context and explanation for why something should be done, they can easily default to "best practice says to do it this way".

Throughout this book I will make recommendations based on having been involved in dozens of implementations. These recommendations are not absolutes and as such I like to refer to them as leading practices. A leading practice fully acknowledges that there are instances where deviation is not only possible but necessary.

About The Author

Tony Scalese is an industry-recognized expert for the Oracle Hyperion Financial Data Quality Management product suite – FDM Classic as well as FDMEE. He is an Oracle ACE, recognized specifically for his expertise in both products.

Tony has a wealth of experience in the Oracle Hyperion space. He started his career as an administrator of Hyperion Pillar in 2000 for a Fortune 500 medical device manufacturer. He soon added the role of Hyperion Enterprise administrator supporting the global consolidation and reporting for management reporting. In this role he was part of the team that implemented Upstream. Fast forward several years and Tony was part of the global implementation of Hyperion Planning. Soon after this project, Tony realized that he wanted to continue implementation work and decided to join the consulting ranks. Tony's experience "sitting on the other side of the table" consistently reminds him to remember the challenges faced on a daily basis by the customer that eventually needs to own and administer the solutions that he and his team develop.

As a consultant, Tony was initially part of the HFM practice of Vertical Pitch. Prior to the growth of FDM/FDMEE within the Oracle Hyperion stack, it was common for HFM consultants to also be versed in FDM Classic because it was the de facto mechanism to load data into HFM. As part of this practice Tony became skilled in HFM and became certified in both the System 9 and Fusion 11 editions of HFM. Tony's experience with many of the products in the Oracle Hyperion stack enabled (and continues to enable) him to design and implement solutions efficiently and effectively.

Vertical Pitch was subsequently acquired by Edgewater Ranzal, creating the first Oracle Hyperion partner that offered deep expertise in the product pillars of Essbase, Hyperion Planning and HFM. As the years progressed, Tony began to focus more heavily on the FDM product, eventually becoming 100% dedicated to this product. As that personal progression happened, the product was also evolving and the industry was embracing it more for Essbase and Hyperion Planning implementations – albeit to a much smaller degree than HFM. As the product usage continued to grow, Edgewater Ranzal identified the opportunity to further differentiate itself by creating a separate integration practice dedicated to the Oracle Hyperion data integration products.

Today, Tony is the head of the integration practice at Edgewater Ranzal, an Oracle Platinum partner that focuses solely on the Oracle Hyperion product suite. Edgewater Ranzal is one of the largest providers of Oracle Hyperion consulting services in the United States but also has an office in London, UK and presences in South America and Asia. Edgewater Ranzal is a full service provider offering consulting services across all of the Oracle Hyperion product suites including Financial Close & Consolidation (HFM, FCM, ARM & SDM), Enterprise Planning (Essbase, Hyperion Planning & HSF), Business Intelligence (OBIEE & Endeca), Infrastructure, Data Governance (DRM & DRG) and Integration (FDM Classic, FDMEE & ODI). In addition, Edgewater Ranzal offers Advisory, Education and Managed Services.

Tony and his team are dedicated solely to the Oracle Hyperion products of FDMEE, FDM Classic and Oracle Data Integrator (ODI). He and his team deliver world class solutions, many of which have been adopted as industry leading practices.

History of FDMEE

It is important to understand the history of FDMEE to gain a better appreciation of what the product is and why it is so valuable to an organization. The product FDMEE was first branded in the 11.1.2.3 release of the Oracle Hyperion stack which was released April 30, 2013[1]. However, the core foundation of the product has existed for over a decade. As noted in the author bio, FDM Classic became the de factor mechanism to load data into HFM; however that wasn't always the case.

Prior to HFM, there was a product called Hyperion Enterprise. Hyperion Enterprise included a tool called LedgerLink which was used to transform/map data and load to Enterprise. LedgerLink was a fat client solution meaning that it needed to be installed locally onto each administrator's PC. LedgerLink was also single user meaning that the program and its mapping tables could only be accessed by a single person at a given time. While LedgerLink did its intended job there was a lot of opportunity for improvement.

As with any technology gap, something always fills the void and in this case that was Upstream. Upstream was a fundamental game changer. The product allowed multiple people to load data into Hyperion Enterprise concurrently. This represented a paradigm shift; end users could now take control of their data mapping and load cycle. The product was easy to use and the company that created the product was incredibly customer focused. It was not uncommon for a customer to request an enhancement to the product and the functionality would be delivered within a matter of days. Lastly and perhaps most importantly, the product provided an extremely high level of auditability. Companies could now

---

[1] http://www.oracle.com/us/corporate/press/1941317

prove to their internal and external auditors the source of information that made up their financial results. All of this critical information was stored in the Upstream product. The result was a game changer especially in the face of bankruptcies from companies like Enron that spurred the Sarbanes-Oxley regulation.

The Upstream product eventually became Upstream Weblink which provided a web interface for the end user. Also, support for Enterprise level RDBMS platforms like Microsoft SQL Server and Oracle eventually became the standard. The product was growing and maturing. Most importantly, it was penetrating the market and customers loved it. On April 20, 2006, Hyperion Solutions acquired Upstream Software[2].

Prior to the Upstream acquisition, Hyperion previously licensed Vignette Software and branded it Hyperion Application Link (HAL). HAL was the standard that Hyperion promoted for the extract, transform and load (ETL) process within the Corporate Performance Management (CPM, now known as Enterprise Performance Management or EPM) stack. HAL was incredibly powerful but its fatal flaw, especially in the Hyperion Solutions stack, was that it was anything but easy to use or understand. Hyperion software was designed with the accounting & finance communities in mind. The products were intended to be run with minimal or no IT support other than maintaining a server or two. HAL flew in the face of this. Few accounting and finance professionals were able or interested in embracing this tool as it was viewed as far too "technical". The acquisition of Upstream now provided the Hyperion community (consulting as well as customers) with a data management tool that aligned with the value proposition of Hyperion software – empowering the accounting and finance communities.

After the acquisition, Hyperion rebranded Upstream Weblink to Hyperion Financial Data Quality Management or FDM. The "Q" was intentionally dropped as most of the acronyms in the Hyperion stack were 2-3 characters. While Hyperion made some investment into the FDM product including a cleaned up user interface (UI), the product core was maintained. In my opinion, this was a brilliant decision by Hyperion. Customers of FDM loved the product and any attempts to rehaul it could have been disastrous if poorly executed.

On March 2, 2007, Oracle acquired Hyperion Solutions[3]. This acquisition was a critical point in the evolution of FDM. Oracle is one of the world's largest providers of Enterprise Resource Planning (ERP) applications in the world. With

---

[2] http://www.computerworld.com/article/2554564/business-intelligence/hyperion-to-acquire-data-quality-vendor-upstream-software.html

[3] http://www.nytimes.com/2007/03/02/business/02oracle.web.html?_r=0

the acquisition, Oracle had the ability to provide customers with a source system and a best-in-breed EPM reporting solution (Hyperion). They also had, in FDM, an end user-friendly tool to move the data between those systems.

As with all acquisitions, the integration of two companies takes some time. The acquirer needs to more fully vet what they bought and how they can use it to grow their business and differentiate themselves from the competition. As part of this, Oracle realized that FDM provided them with an opportunity. Oracle knew their source systems like eBusiness Suite (EBS) and PeopleSoft very well. They knew exactly where the data is stored. More importantly, they had the ability to modify those systems. Oracle looked to leverage this advantage and provide even more value to their customers by creating a product known as ERP Integrator (ERPi).

ERPi was introduced in the 11.1.1.3 version of Oracle Hyperion. ERPi provided two new pieces of functionality – prepackaged direct connections into EBS and PeopleSoft, and drill through from Hyperion to those source ledger systems. Now an HFM or Planning user that wanted to understand a variance had the ability to simply right click a cell in SmartView and drill through back to FDM and eventually the live GL source, not a staging table where data had been loaded. The drilling user would eventually be in the actual ERP application leveraging all of the functionality available to them from that application. This represented a major step forward for data integration.

The introduction of ERPi surfaced a lot of questions from customers as well as the partner community. Is ERPi a replacement for FDM? Can I use FDM with ERPi? What is the best practice for using FDM and ERPi? The direction that I shared with my team and our customers was to use them in concert with one another. In doing so we created a best-of-breed solution by using each tool for what it is best intended. ERPi was used to manage the data extraction and drill through capabilities while FDM was used for data mapping, integration with Oracle Hyperion targets, and the guided workflow. This strategy proved very effective but complicated the overall integration landscape since two tools were now involved in the integration process. This resulted in duplicate maintenance for things like the period control tables as well as multiple points of potential failure.

Oracle continued to iterate the ERPi product over the 11.1.2.0, 11.1.2.1 and 11.1.2.2 releases but realized that the FDM and ERPi products needed to eventually merge into a single product. Starting with the 11.1.2.3 release, ERPi and FDM Classic functionality was combined into a single product and branded as FDM, Enterprise Edition (or FDMEE). The product known as FDM was rebranded as FDM Classic. At the same time Oracle made its intentions clear,

11.1.2.3 would be the terminal release of FDM Classic and FDMEE was defined as the strategic focus.

In the 11.1.2.3 release, FDM Classic continued to exist and could be used in concert with FDMEE similar to how FDM was used with ERPi in earlier releases; however, the proverbial writing was on the wall. Migrating to FDMEE was an eventuality. As of the writing of this book, 11.1.2.4 is the latest release of FDMEE and FDM Classic no longer exists.

As we head into the future with FDMEE, one core tenet that made Upstream so successful remains – a hyper focus on customers. Over the years I have heard people criticize Oracle for the bugs in its software and what they perceive to Oracle's ambivalence to the frustration it causes customers. To those criticisms I offer this. Oracle is mammoth and provides software solutions that are run globally across multiple platforms. This is a herculean undertaking and one that inevitably will have bugs. I equate this to Microsoft Windows. Windows revolutionized personal computing. It runs across literally thousands of hardware platforms, it is easy to use and there are millions of programs that are able to run on it. The trade-off is that not everything is going to work perfectly the first time, every time. However, I can assure you that Oracle's teams that are responsible for FDMEE have an unyielding commitment to their customers. I have witnessed product management and development join conference calls to address customer issues, develop one off patches to provide critical fixes, and share information with customers and partners freely. This level of commitment will ensure that the product that we knew and loved in FDM will only be better in FDMEE.

Errata

Despite best efforts, mistakes can sometimes creep into books. If you spot a mistake, please feel free to email us at errata@p8tech.com (with the book title in the subject line). The errata page for the book is hosted at *www.P8tech.com/FDMEE*

Table of Contents

Chapter 11 – Application Care and Feeding

1
Settings Explained

In this chapter we explain the System, Application and User settings that are available in Oracle Hyperion Financial Data Quality Management, Enterprise Edition (FDMEE). Understanding each of these settings and their impact upon different application components is critical to ensuring application integrity as well as an optimal end user experience.

System Settings

System settings define the behavior of the application globally. All settings in System settings are applied to all integrations and users unless specifically overridden at the application or user level. System settings are grouped into four major categories:

Category	Purpose
File	Controls file system interaction
POV	Controls the point of view
ODI	Connection information for FDMEE application to relational store
Other	Catch all grouping of settings not associated with other categories

Each of the settings below is optional unless otherwise specified.

File Settings

System File Settings control how the FDMEE application interacts with the file system component of the application architecture. FDMEE data storage is a combination of the relational database (RDBMS) and a file system. All financial data is stored in the FDMEE RDBMS however other items are stored on a file system. For example, the file system is used to store scripts, logs and data files imported to and exported from FDMEE.

Application Root Folder

The application root folder is the top level file system directory where FDMEE will create subdirectories that are used to store the aforementioned file system objects. This setting must be specified for the application to function properly.

It is highly recommended to specify the application root directory using a universal naming convention (UNC) path. Once the path is specified, click the Create Application Folders button to create the default subdirectories within the FDMEE root directory.

Figure 1-1: Application Root Folder

Specify the Application Root Folder (box 1) using a UNC path and then click Create Application Folders (box 2). The resulting application subfolders are created in the path specified.

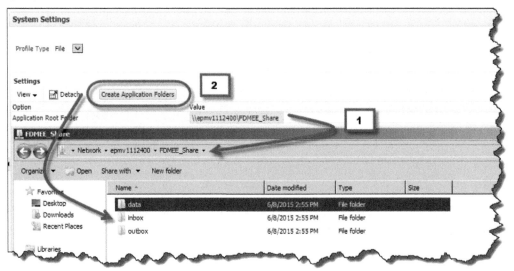

Create Location Folder

The Create Location Folder setting controls if a subfolder is created within the Inbox for each location added to the application. Most customer implementations set this to Yes to enable the application UI to apply filtering security to the dialogue box presented for uploading and downloading information.

Figure 1-2A: Location Folder Filtering

The below image shows how the application web interface filters the location folders from which an end user can import data based on locations to which the user has access.

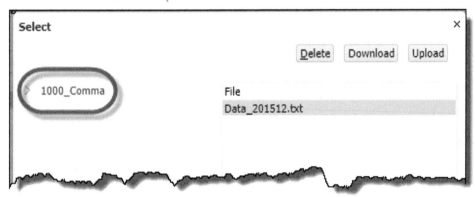

Figure 1-2B: Location Folder

List of all location subfolders within the inbox from which an end user can import data.

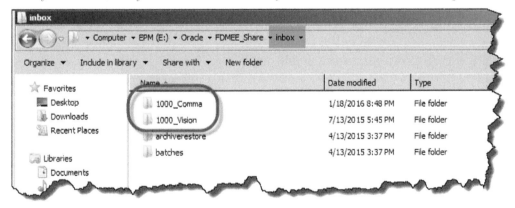

Archive Mode

The Archive Mode setting is used to control the creation of copies that are processed through the application. There are three settings that can be applied.

Setting	Behavior
Copy	Data file is copied from source directory into the data subdirectory of the application root folder. Original file is maintained in the source directory.
Move	Data file is moved from the source directory into the data subdirectory of the application root folder. The original file no longer exists in the source directory.
None	Data file is neither moved nor copied to the data subdirectory of the application root folder.

When the file is moved or copied to the data subdirectory, it is renamed based on a system generated number which is a combination of the process ID and the period key to which the data is associated. This is the file that is used to enable the Open Source Document feature. The choice to use Copy or Move will be customer-specific; some customers prefer to see the actual data file in the inbox (Copy) while others do not want to duplicate file storage (Move). Using the option None will prevent the Open Source Document feature from functioning as no data file will exist in the data subdirectory.

Excluded File Upload Wild Cards

Excluded file upload wild cards is a comma delimited list of file extensions that prevents particular files from being uploaded during the FDMEE import workflow step. This setting prevents users from unknowingly or unwittingly uploading a file that could include malicious or damaging code.

Common extensions to exclude are:

- .exe
- .cmd
- .bat
- .sql

Figure 1-3: Excluded Extensions

Example excluded extensions setting

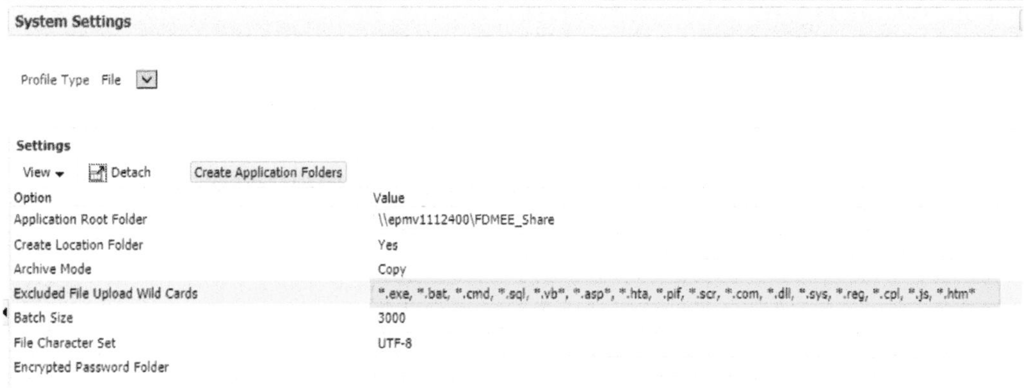

System Settings

Profile Type   File   ☑

Settings

View ▾   Detach   Create Application Folders

Option	Value
Application Root Folder	\\epmv1112400\FDMEE_Share
Create Location Folder	Yes
Archive Mode	Copy
Excluded File Upload Wild Cards	*.exe, *.bat, *.cmd, *.sql, *.vb*, *.asp*, *.hta, *.pif, *.scr, *.com, *.dll, *.sys, *.reg, *.cpl, *.js, *.htm*
Batch Size	3000
File Character Set	UTF-8
Encrypted Password Folder	

Batch Size

The Batch Size setting controls how the application holds data rows in memory before committing them to the database during the import stage. This setting is a function of the amount of memory (RAM) as well as the number of concurrent users expected. The optimal level is one that will be found through extensive testing and refinement. A realistic starting point is between 1,000 and 5,000 records.

A good testing strategy is to test the import with the largest data file in your application when no other users are using the application. Monitor the RAM utilization and also review the process logs to determine the performance times. Find the optimal level for the batch size setting and then test again – simulating the highest expected level of concurrency to ensure that enough memory is available to support concurrent processes.

File Character Set

The File Character Set setting is used to instruct the application which encoding is expected in the data files to be processed. The overwhelming majority of data files will be able to be handled using the UTF-8 setting. UTF-8 supports Unicode encoding of all characters including double byte Unicode alphabets like Japanese Kanji. There are instances where UTF-8 may not apply and in these cases the setting can be overridden either at the System or User setting level.

Encrypted Password Folder

The Encrypted Password Folder setting is used to specify the directory where the file with encrypted passwords is stored. This file is created by the encryptpassword utility (.bat or .sh) found in the
`\Middleware\EPMSystem11R1\Products\FinancialDataQuality\bin directory`

For additional information on encrypted passwords refer to the Oracle provided Administrator's Guide section **Working With Batch Scripts**.

POV Settings

Default POV

The point of view (POV) settings control the default location, period and category that a user will have in the POV when first logging into the application.

Figure 1-4: Point-Of-View

*A sample point of view within the application. Location is set to **1000_Vision**, Period is **Dec – 2014** and Category is **Actual**. These defaults can be specified by the Default POV setting.*

Setting the default location at the System level is rare. Setting a default period and category at the System level is most common when managing integration to only a single target. In instances where multiple targets are defined, the choice of setting a default period or category will depend on the usage of the product.

For example, if you are integrating into three Planning applications – Workforce, Expense and GL – as well as a single HFM target, you may set the default category at the System level to Forecast. You may make this choice because more targets are dependent on this setting. If you choose to set the category at the System level then you may consider setting the default category for the HFM application to Actual under the Application Settings. Additional information about Application Settings can be found below.

Global POV Mode

The Global POV Mode setting controls if a non-administrative user is able to change the Period or Category in the POV. When set to Yes, the POV for Period and Category is considered locked and cannot be changed by an end user.

Figure 1-5: Global POV

When the Global POV mode is set to Yes, an end user will see the locked icon next to the period and category selection boxes when opening the POV dialogue box.

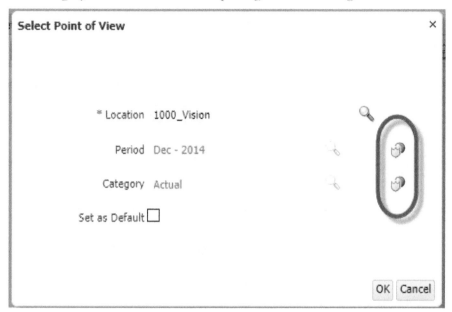

Setting the Global POV mode to Yes is usually determined by the number of targets within the FDMEE application. When integrating into a single target this setting can be useful to ensure prior periods are not modified or inadvertently processed. However when integrating into multiple targets, the use of the global POV can become challenging as the category and time periods that end users need to process may vary based on the target application to which data will be loaded.

ODI Settings

Oracle Data Integrator (ODI) is the underlying data engine of FDMEE. All information related to the application is stored in the Master and Work repositories of ODI. This settings section specifies the connection parameters. All ODI settings are mandatory and generally should not be modified after the initial installation except in the instance of a new database server or a scheduled updated to the ODI master or work repository passwords.

Figure 1-6: ODI Connection Information

Below is a sample set of ODI connection information.

Upon initial installation, or following any changes to the ODI settings, the Check ODI Connection button should be used to confirm connectivity between the FDMEE application and the underlying RDBMS which houses the application data.

Figure 1-7: Check ODI Connection

Click the Check ODI Connection button to check the ODI connection parameters that are specified. An information dialogue will show the status of the connection.

ODI User Name and Password

The ODI User Name and Password setting specifies the credentials to connect to, and access, the ODI master repository. The default user name is SUPERVISOR and is specified during installation.

ODI Execution Repository

The ODI Execution Repository specifies where the execution scenarios are stored within the ODI repository. The execution scenarios are pseudo-compiled code that Oracle delivers as part of the FDMEE product. The scenarios provide core functionality like loading data to HFM or sourcing data from EBS. This setting is configured by default upon installation and generally is not modified.

ODI Work Repository

The ODI Work Repository specifies the repository where execution of the aforementioned scenarios occurs. As with the Execution Repository, this setting is configured by default upon installation and generally is not modified.

ODI Master Repository Driver

The ODI Master Repository Driver is a selection box used to specify the driver that the FDMEE application will use to connect to the ODI Master Repository. The driver can be either for an Oracle or SQL Server RDBMS. This setting should *never* be changed.

ODI Master Repository URL

The ODI Master Repository URL is used to specify the technical connection parameters used to connect the FDMEE application to the ODI repository. Information included in this URL will vary based on the RDBMS provider but will, in general, refer to the database server and port where the database/schema is hosted for the application.

The information in this setting should only change in the event of a change in the database server such as a new server being commissioned.

ODI Master Repository User and Password

The ODI Master Repository User specifies the login credentials to the relational repository. In Oracle terms, this is the schema/user, while for SQL Server this is the database login. The user name is generally not modified after the initial installation; however, the password can be updated as necessary to account for password changes as required by internal policies and procedures.

Other Settings

The Other settings are a collection of other system controls which cannot be grouped as per the above, but which include several important settings.

Figure 1-8: Other Settings

The below image shows the other system settings

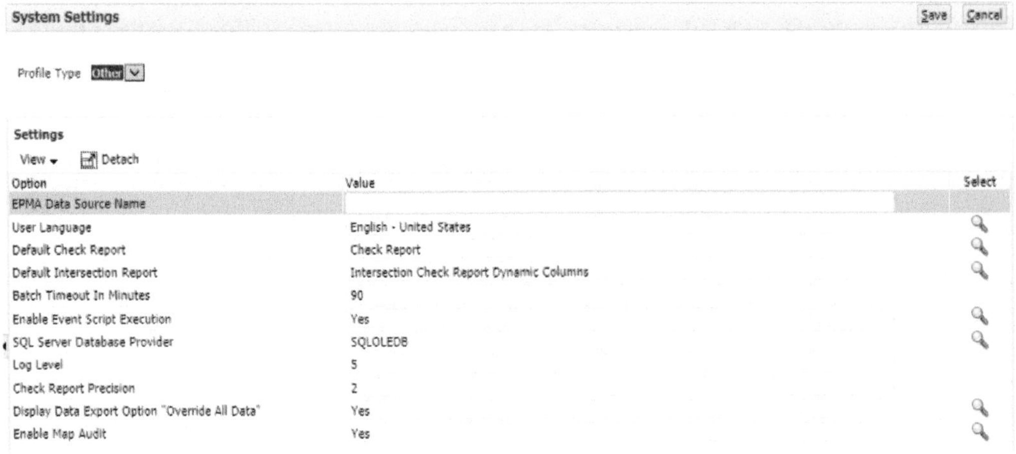

EPMA Data Source Name

The EPMA Data Source Name is used to specify the name of the EPMA data source that can be used to integrate metadata and data for the EPMA interface tables. Given the direction of EPMA for data synchronization – i.e., being phased out in favor of FDMEE – this setting is usually populated only if integrating metadata through FDMEE. This should match the Data Source name specified in an EPMA import profile.

User Language

The User Language is used to control the language in which UI (including reports) will be displayed. It is generally recommended to set the System language to the language of the region where the application server is hosted. End users can override this setting individually within User Settings. In the instance where a given local language is not available, the recommended setting is English – United States.

Default Check Report

The Default Check Report setting is used to specify the report that should be used during the Check workflow step. Additional information about the Oracle delivered check reports can be found in the administrator guide under the **Setting System Level Profiles** section.

Default Intersection Report

The Default Intersection Report is used in HFM integrations to produce the Intersection Validation report that alerts a user when a mapped intersection will be rejected by HFM due to a number of conditions including metadata settings, locked data, no input rules or no access due to security. The Intersection Check Report Dynamic Columns is recommended for any HFM target which does not have 12 dimensions (i.e., 4 customs).

Batch Timeout In Minutes

The Batch Timeout In Minutes is a setting that specifies the number of minutes a batch job can run before being automatically terminated by the application. This setting will depend heavily on the frequency of scheduled data loads as well as workflow performance times due to mapping complexity and data file size.

For example, if there exists a file that has 10M records and which takes 75 minutes to import, validate and export, you would not want to set the batch timeout to 60 minutes because the batch would never complete before being terminated by the application. In another example, if you have a batch scheduled every hour, you likely do not want the timeout to be set to 90 minutes as you could create overlapping executions. As with the batch size setting under the File settings, this timeout will be determined based on testing.

Enable Event Script Execution

Enable Event Script Execution is used to globally enable or disable the execution of event scripts throughout the workflow process. More information about Event Scripts can be found in the scripting chapter.

In my opinion, this setting should always be Yes in the System settings. The enabling/disabling of event scripts can be managed at the application level or within the script code itself. As with anything technology related, nothing is an absolute; however in the majority of use cases, this will address the majority of needs to limit event script execution.

SQL Server Database Provider

SQL Server Database Provider is used to specify the MS SQL Server connection version that will be leveraged the Visual Basic API. Prior to release 11.1.2.4 it was also used by the HFM adaptor. SQLNCLI is for SQL Server 2005, SQLNCLI10 is for SQL Server 2008 and SQLOLEDB is for SQL Server 2000. Oracle intends to add SQLNCLI11 which supports SQL Server 2012. SQLOLEDB will eventually be sunset.

Log Level

The Log Level setting controls how verbose the process logs are. A setting of 5 provides the most detailed information for debugging purposes including the SQL statements that are executed as part of the different scenario executions. A log level of 5 is recommended for new development and testing but in production this can be reduced to 4 or less. Below is a table of the log levels from most to least verbose and the application event type at which information will be written to the process log.

Log Level	Event/Script	Interpretation
5	logDebug	All events are logged
4	logInfo	Fatal events, errors, warnings as well as general information that is useful for debugging and performance tracking are logged
3	logWarn	Fatal events, errors and any warnings or areas for additional investigation are logged
2	logError	Fatal events as well as errors through the process are logged
1	logFatal	Only fatal events that cause a process to fail are logged

As an example, if the Log Level is set to 3, any events associated with info or debugging would not be logged but any warnings, errors or fatal events would be captured and written to the log. In a stable production environment, log level 4 meets most needs for auditing and debugging.

Check Report Precision

The Check Report Precision setting is used to specify the number of decimal places that will be used to determine if a check rule fails or passes. For example, if a check rule is created that tests if the balance sheet balances, and a given entity has an out of balance of 0.0000015, the check rule would fail if the Check report precision were 6. However, if the check report precision were set to 2, the check rule would pass validation. The majority of implementations have a Check Report Precision of 2.

Display Data Export Option "Override All Data"

The Display Data Export Option Override All Data is a setting that is specific to Essbase and Planning integrations. When loading data to an Essbase database, Essbase provides the option to clear all data (for all intersections) when performing a data load.

In my opinion, there are very limited instances where one would want to enable this option. My recommendation is to leave this option set to No unless a very specific use case is presented for which no other option is available.

Enable Map Audit

The Enable Map Audit setting is used to control if the application will track changes made to the mapping table. This functionality is available in 11.1.2.4.100. When set to Yes, the application will track any changes to the maps made through the web interface, excel and text based imports as well as Life Cycle Management (LCM) imports.

This option should always be set to Yes as the overhead associated with this being enabled is not significant enough to justify disabling it.

Application Settings

Application Settings allow an administrator to override one or more global/system settings for each of the applications registered. This concept was discussed briefly under the default POV section of System Settings. Below is an example that helps to illustrate how Application Settings can be used to better manage end users' use and interaction with the system.

Managing Default POVs with Multiple Target Applications

As FDMEE continues to grow as an integration solution within the EPM stack, more implementations will include multiple target applications. In these instances it would not be uncommon to have an HFM target as well as a Planning target. The HFM target may only load through the Actual category where the Planning target could load through both the Actual and Forecast category. In this example, setting the default scenario to Actual as well as global POV mode to Yes at the application level would force the POV category to Actual whenever an end user selects a location which is associated with the HFM target.

Figure 1-9: Application Settings

The below image shows application settings specific to the Comma (HFM) target application. The default category has been set to Actual and global POV mode has been set to Yes.

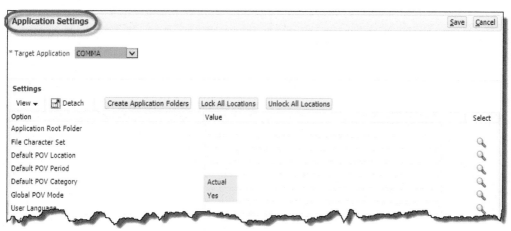

To continue this example, assume that the default category for the Planning target is set to Forecast but the Global POV mode is blank and/or No. In this instance, there are several possible outcomes.

Let's assume an end user (Mike) has access to a location to load data to HFM as well as a location to load data to Planning. Mike has set his default location to the HFM location since he uses this one more frequently (more information on user settings follows). Mike logs into FDMEE and his category is set to Actual since this is the default specified for the HFM application. Mike then changes his location to the Planning associated location. The category remains as Actual even though the default category set for the Planning application is Forecast. The reason is that Planning application settings do not have Global POV enabled so the change to the category is not forced. In an instance when the Global POV setting was Yes, Mike's location change would have changed the category from Actual to Forecast. Importantly, Mike would not be able to select Actual for any Planning associated location with the Global POV enabled.

Let's change the scenario slightly. Mike has set his default location to the Planning location. When Mike logs into FDMEE, his category is set to Forecast. When Mike changes his location to the HFM location, his category is changed to Actual due to the Global POV setting being enabled for the HFM application.

As you can see, there are a number of combinations that are possible. The right combination of Application settings to address specific needs can usually be found through testing with native users.

Application Root Folder

The application root folder allows you to create a separate directory that is specific to the target application. This can be a subdirectory within the Application Root Folder specified in System Settings or a stand-alone directory at the same root level.

Figure 1-10: Application Root Folder

The below image shows the application root folder being set for the Comma target application. After specifying the application root folder and clicking the Create Application Folders button, an information dialogue box is displayed.

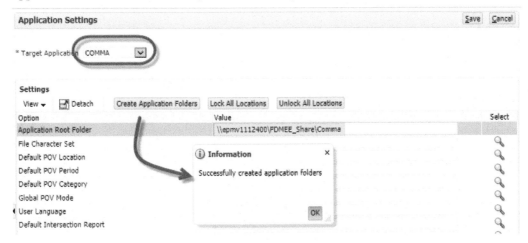

The primary subdirectories – Data, Inbox, Outbox – are created within the application specific folder.

Figure 1-11: Application Directory

The below image shows the application-specific directory being created in the root directory specified in system settings. The below is an extension of figure 1-10.

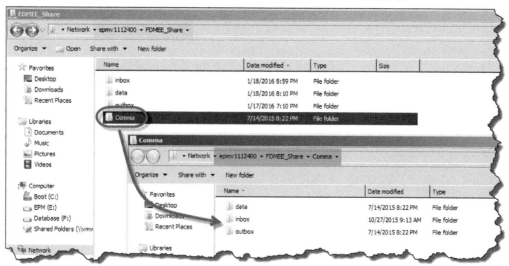

There are pros and cons to utilizing an application-specific root folder. One benefit is that all of the files and folders associated with that application are isolated as opposed to being comingled with other target applications when no application specific root folder is defined. A drawback to this approach is that any scripting assets would not be able to be shared across other applications. While this is fine for import scripts (since there is usually little to no overlap) event and custom scripts are often applicable to multiple targets. When each application has its own root folder, multiple copies of the script would need to be maintained. In general I avoid using an application-specific root folder unless there is a clear need and there is little to no overlap of scripting assets to be used by the different target applications.

Other Application Settings

The remaining application settings simply override the System setting and should be updated/specified only if the application needs to differ from the System setting defined.

Lock All Locations

Point of view locking is functionality that prevents additional data processing through a given point of view. This is critical to ensuring that data is not changed once it is considered final in the target application. Many customers question why POV locking within FDMEE is needed if a target application like HFM has the ability to lock and/or promote data.

Auditability and drill through are the key considerations for FDMEE POV locking. By preventing changes to the data stored in FDMEE (through either applying new maps or importing new source data) you preserve the integrity of the drill through. Drilling through to FDMEE essentially runs a query against the FDMEE data and returns the records that match the POV initializing the drill. If new maps are applied to existing records there is a chance that a previously loaded intersection will have been modified to a new intersection and as a result the drill through will fail.

If a new data file is imported with potentially different values the drill through would work because the query runs on the member names and not the data value itself; but the integrity of the drill is compromised since the target system value does not match the value in FDMEE. In either of these scenarios the auditability of the data is also compromised. The ability to use FDMEE to prove to internal or external audit the source of the data is a key value proposition of the software. POV locking ensures that this capability is preserved.

POV locking was a core component in FDM Classic but was not included in the initial release of FDMEE. Oracle reintroduced POV locking to FDMEE in the 11.1.2.3.520 release and enhanced the functionality. In FDM Classic, a single POV could be locked or all locations could be locked for a given period and category. In FDMEE the ability to lock a single POV still exists but the locking of a category and period combination is now specific to a given target application.

This enhancement has removed the need to either manually lock/unlock locations that were not applicable to the FDM Classic Lock All Locations execution. For example, all of the locations associated with the HFM application can be locked once the statutory close is complete but the Essbase locations used to load actual data to the management reporting cube can remain open.

Figure 1-12: Lock All Locations

To lock all locations select the target application (Comma) under application settings and click the Lock All Locations button. A dialogue box will open to specify the period and category for which all locations should be locked. Set the POV and click OK.

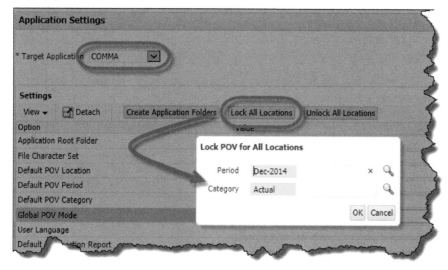

As with FDM Classic, individual points of view can be unlocked in FDMEE. Locking/Unlocking a POV is as simple as clicking on POV and choosing the Lock/Unlock POV check box.

Figure 1-13: Unlock Single POV

In the below image, the point of view for 1000_Comma, Dec–2014 Actual is locked as indicated by the lock icon (circled). To unlock a single point of view, click the location name from the POV bar. Check the box next to the option to Unlock POV and click OK

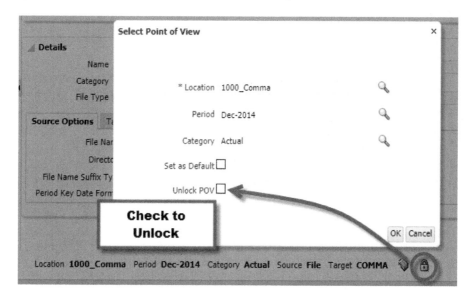

User Settings

System and Application settings are generally managed at the administrator level. User settings, however, empower a user to control settings that will make their use of the application more efficient and familiar. The user settings that are most commonly specified are:

- **File Character Set**: Defined when non-standard file encoding is provided by the source system from which the user will be loading data

- **Default POV Location**: Set when a user has access to multiple locations but uses a certain location more often.

- **User Language**: Set when a user has a native language that differs from the System or Application language

Figure 1-14: User Settings

The below image shows the user settings that can be specified by an end user. The most frequently modified options are highlighted in yellow.

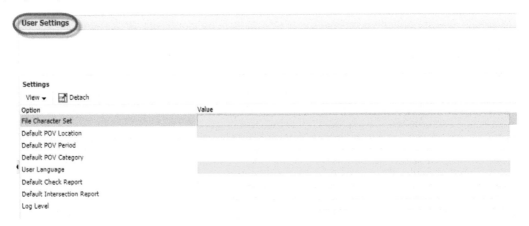

The ability for an end user to modify their settings is controlled through security. An administrator can enable or disable the User Setting on a 'user by user' or 'group by group' basis. More information about security is contained in Chapter 8.

Settings Precedence

For the three settings – System, Application and User – there is a precedence that exists. The System setting is the global setting that will be used for all target applications and users unless specifically overridden at either the Application or User Level.

If a user specifies an override for a given setting, that takes precedence over an application or system setting except in the case of the POV (Period or Category) when Global POV is enabled at either the System or Application level. For example, the

System setting for the User language is English – United States because the application is administered and hosted in the United States. A Planning application for a European headquarters based in France is one of the registered targets and the user language for this target application is set to French - France. A user of this target Planning application is based in Germany so she sets her User Language (in User Settings) to German – Germany. When this user runs a reports, the report displays in German. If a user in the United States runs a report for the same POV and does not have a language set at the user level, the report displays in French because the language for the Planning application is set to French - France. If that same user runs a report for a POV associated with a different target application, the report displays in English.

The interaction of these three groups of settings allows for a highly customizable end user experience.

Summary

In this chapter we explored in detail the System, Application and User Settings. An administrator should now have a better appreciation for leading practices for each setting, and a greater understanding for how each of these settings can control the user interface. In turn, the precedence of each setting and its impact on the end user experience should also be more fully understood.

In the next chapter we will explore the core FDMEE metadata including source and target systems, import formats, locations and data load rules and how they are interrelated.

2

Metadata Dependencies Explained

In this chapter, we unravel the relationship between a source system, target application, import format, location and data load rule. While each of these metadata elements may be understood, this chapter will provide additional context as well as explain the interdependency between these elements.

Source Systems

In the world of integration, a source system is a term that is often assumed. It is taken for granted that an FDMEE administrator understands what an Enterprise Resource Planning, or ERP, system is. It has become clear to me over the years that taking this information for granted is a mistake. Since this information is often assumed, some will fail to ask the questions needed to better educate themselves about these systems for fear of exposing their lack of knowledge. This section will not provide a deep dive into the architecture and design of an ERP system but will offer high level context and terminology to ensure that the terminology used throughout this and future chapters is clear.

Enterprise Resource Planning (ERP)

Enterprise Resource Planning system is a term that was coined in the 1990s. The vision was to provide a suite of systems that allowed a company (enterprise) to manage their assets (resources) more efficiently. Obviously this is a very simplified definition but it paints the picture of these systems – massive, highly complex and supposedly highly integrated. Data is intended to flow between each of the applications easily, due to a common architecture.

Within an ERP there are a number of subsystems including inventory management, payroll and accounts receivable – to name a few. These sub systems are where millions of transactions can be input either by a human or an automated process on a daily basis. The center of the financial universe is the module known as the general ledger or G/L. This is the system that collects and aggregates data from a multitude of subsystems.

Enterprises realized over the 1990s and 2000s that while ERP systems were critical to day to day operations, the ability to translate the data housed in these systems into actionable business intelligence was extremely limited. As the market was confronted with this realization, two core technologies experienced rapid growth – data warehousing and corporate performance management. Hyperion grew as a world class CPM software vendor that allowed organizations to unlock the wealth of information stored in the ERP through applications like Essbase and HFM.

With the growth of what is now known as EPM came a need to integrate data from the ERP. The ERP and specifically the G/L in the early days of Hyperion had become a source system instead of the center of the data universe. Today the G/L remains a core source especially for HFM. However the advance of technology has enabled Oracle Hyperion systems to consume and process larger volumes of data. Subsystems within the ERP can also be integrated into the Oracle Hyperion suite of products and FDMEE is a very viable option for these integrations.

FDMEE Source Systems

Historically, the ERP was considered the primary source system for FDM Classic. The introduction of FDMEE and specifically the data synchronization functionality in 11.1.2.4, saw the definition of source system expanded to include a myriad of systems including ERPs, data warehouses and even the Oracle Hyperion stack itself. Before we delve into the various source systems in detail, let's explore why the FDMEE has expanded this definition.

First and foremost, FDMEE is architected using 21st century technology. FDM Classic was a 32 bit application and performance was constrained by .NET technology (.NET would only allow an FDM process to consume 2 GB of RAM). Any very large datasets would fail processing when more than 2 GB of RAM was needed. FDMEE, in contrast, is a 64 bit application and in theory each process could consume up to 16 TB of RAM. In practice, FDMEE is generally configured to consume 6 GB of RAM. This additional memory allows much larger data sets to be processed.

As a result of FDMEE being able to process larger data sets, the definition of what can be considered a source system has grown. Summarized G/L balances that were most commonly the source for Hyperion applications can be exploded to include such detailed information as daily sales activity or project detail. Data warehouses that collect and cleanse a variety of detailed information are another viable source system.

Importantly, FDMEE has enabled Oracle Hyperion applications to be considered a source system for one another. For over a decade the 'dirty' secret of Hyperion technology is that it did not share data easily between the core products of Essbase and HFM. The reason for this is simple: the Oracle Hyperion stack of products grew as a result of acquisition. HFM was the next generation of the product Hyperion Enterprise. Hyperion Enterprise was the Windows version of the product Microcontrol which was developed by IMRS. IMRS rebranded itself Hyperion Software. Essbase was a technology developed by Arbor. In 1998 Hyperion Software and Arbor merged to form Hyperion Solutions[1].

Essbase is considered online analytic processing, or OLAP technology, with a cube architecture. HFM on the other hand is considered relational online analytic processing or ROLAP. ROLAP uses a relational database to house its data and simulates a cube architecture at the application tier. Given the two very different data storages, moving data between these technologies was cumbersome and often required a significant amount of custom coding. While these core technologies remain different, FDMEE has provided a standardized mechanism that is accessible through a web user interface and in doing so expanded the definition of a source system.

File

The single most common source system is a flat file. The term system appears to be a misnomer as it relates to a file. A better definition would be a flat file extract from any source system can be used as a source which FDMEE has the ability to process. A flat file is any file that can be opened with a text editor like Notepad and is able to be viewed intelligibly.

Figure 2-1A: Valid Flat File

Example of a valid flat file opened in Notepad. Notice how the text is easily understandable.

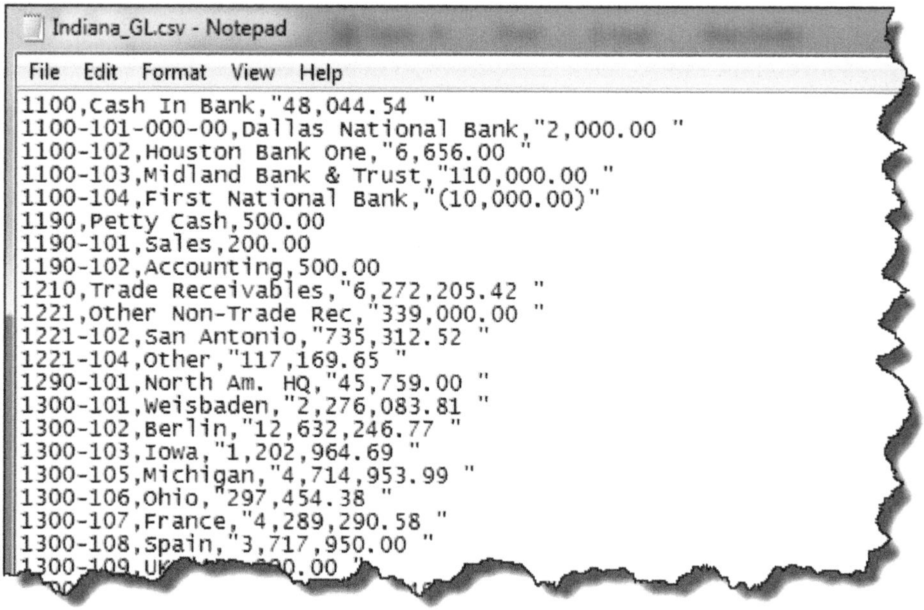

```
Indiana_GL.csv - Notepad
File  Edit  Format  View  Help
1100,Cash In Bank,"48,044.54 "
1100-101-000-00,Dallas National Bank,"2,000.00 "
1100-102,Houston Bank One,"6,656.00 "
1100-103,Midland Bank & Trust,"110,000.00 "
1100-104,First National Bank,"(10,000.00)"
1190,Petty Cash,500.00
1190-101,Sales,200.00
1190-102,Accounting,500.00
1210,Trade Receivables,"6,272,205.42 "
1221,Other Non-Trade Rec,"339,000.00 "
1221-102,San Antonio,"735,312.52 "
1221-104,Other,"117,169.65 "
1290-101,North Am. HQ,"45,759.00 "
1300-101,Weisbaden,"2,276,083.81 "
1300-102,Berlin,"12,632,246.77 "
1300-103,Iowa,"1,202,964.69 "
1300-105,Michigan,"4,714,953.99 "
1300-106,Ohio,"297,454.38 "
1300-107,France,"4,289,290.58 "
1300-108,Spain,"3,717,950.00 "
1300-109,UK           .00 "
```

---

[1] https://en.wikipedia.org/wiki/Oracle_Hyperion

Figure 2-1B: Invalid Flat File

Example of a file that is not considered a flat file that has been opened in Notepad.
Notice how the text of the file contains special characters and is illegible. This is an
Excel document which is not a valid flat file.

There are two flat file formats – delimited and fixed width.

Delimited Flat Files

A delimited flat file is one whose fields are separated or delimited by a specific
character. Technically, nearly any character can function as a delimiter; however, due to
real world limitations the most common delimiters are:

- Comma (,)
- Pipe (|)
- Exclamation (!)
- Semi-colon (;)
- Colon (:)
- Tab; also known as horizontal tab or char(9) in the ASCII character map

With a delimited flat file the length of each field is irrelevant. The length of the field can
be variable since the delimiter determines the start and end position of a field.

Figure 2-2: Delimited File Example

The below example shows a comma delimited flat file. Notice that the first field is variable length where the first record is four digits while the second record is 15 digits.

```
Indiana_GL.csv - Notepad

File   Edit   Format   View   Help
1100,Cash In Bank,"48,044.54 "
1100-101-000-00,Dallas National Bank,"2,000.00 "
1100-102,Houston Bank One,"6,656.00 "
1100-103,Midland Bank & Trust,"110,000.00 "
1100-104,First National Bank,"(10,000.00)"
1190,Petty Cash,500.00
1190-101,Sales,200.00
1190-102,Accounting,500.00
1210,Trade Receivables,"6,272,205.42 "
1221,Other Non-Trade Rec,"339,000.00 "
1221-102,San Antonio,"735,312.52 "
1221-104,Other,"117,169.65 "
1290-101,North Am. HQ,"45,759.00 "
1300-101,Weisbaden,"2,276,083.81 "
1300-102,Berlin,"12,632,246.77 "
1300-103,Iowa,"1,202,964.69 "
1300-105,Michigan,"4,714,953.99 "
1300-106,Ohio,"297,454.38 "
1300-107,France,"4,289,290.58 "
1300-108,Spain,"3,717,950.00 "
1300-109,UK        0.00 "
```

Fixed Width Flat Files

A fixed width flat file is a file where each field is a set number of characters. If the field length is fewer characters than the width of the field then spaces will follow the field value.

Figure 2-3: Fixed Width Flat File

In the below example the first field (Account) is 15 characters. The first data record (1100) is only four digits but the second field (Cash in Bank) starts in the exact same position as the second record where field 1 (1100-101-000-00) is 15 digits.

```
gltbrp.p                              25.15.4 Trial Balance Summary                    Date: 02/2/03
Page: 1                               Texas Automotive Systems, Inc.                   Time: 15:42:50

Texas xxxxxxxx                         Reporting Currency:   USD
                                       Exchange Rate:


                           Beginning Balance    Period Activity    Ending Balance
Account      Description     12/31/02                                1/31/03        Adjustments  Balance
-----------  -----------   ----------------    ---------------    --------------   -----------  -------
1100             Cash In Bank            283,767.29     135,722.75cr        48,044.54
1100-101-000-00  Dallas National Bank      2,000.00           .00          2,000.00
1100-102         Houston Bank One          9,986.39       3,330.39cr        6,656.00
1100-103         Midland Bank & Trust           .00     110,000.00        110,000.00
1100-104         First National Bank      50,000.00      60,000.00         10,000.00cr
1190             Petty Cash                  500.00           .00            500.00
1190-101         Sales                       200.00           .00            200.00
1190-102         Accounting                  500.00           .00            500.00
1210             Trade Receivables       158,857.30   6,113,348.12      6,272,205.42
1220             Tooling & Prototype Rec  71,087.28      71,087.28cr            .00
1221             Other Non-Trade Rec           .00     339,000.00        339,000.00
1221-101         N/T Rvbl Dallas          93,145.54      93,145.54cr            .00
1221-102         San Antonio             712,693.72      22,618.80        735,312.52
1221-103         United Banks          50,817.31      50,817.31              .00
```

Pre-Built Source Systems

One of the key differentiators of FDMEE is the delivery of prebuilt connections to a variety of ERP systems. These prebuilt source system connections are often referred to as adaptors. Adaptors are available for a variety of Oracle branded ERP systems as well as SAP. The below table shows the prebuilt source system connections currently available:

System	Vendor
eBusiness Suite (11 and 12)	Oracle
PeopleSoft Financials 9	Oracle
PeopleSoft Human Capital Management (HCM) 9	Oracle
Fusion Applications	Oracle
JD Edwards Enterprise One	Oracle
Fusion Budgetary Control	Oracle
SAP (R3 and ECC)	SAP
SAP Business Warehouse	SAP

Adaptors provide two fundamental advantages. First, the extract code needed to retrieve data from these source systems is developed by Oracle (or its partner in the instance of SAP). This approach ensures a standardized extract methodology that is reliable and auditable. Oracle has also reduced the time to deploy a solution by providing an adaptor. Secondly, in developing adaptors, Oracle also enabled a second very valuable piece of functionality known as 'drill through' by enabling or leveraging handlers in the source system that accept a web drill through request.

Drill Through

Drill through is the functionality that allows an end user to move seamlessly between different Oracle Hyperion systems and source systems when investigating a balance. Drill through is usually initiated from a target application like HFM either in a web grid or through a SmartView ad hoc retrieval. The user will drill through to FDMEE where they are presented with the source system balances that have been mapped to the particular intersection that is being investigated. If the user needs additional information then the user can drill through to the system from which the balance was sourced.

Once the user drills from FDMEE to the source system they are logged into the source system and the full functionality of the source system is available to the end user including the ability to drill into subsystems.

Drill through represents a key differentiator over other software vendor offerings and empowers an end user to better understand the financial data and its path into the reporting application from which it is most often consumed.

Source Adaptors

The prebuilt connections to Oracle eBusiness Suite, Fusion and PeopleSoft are the most commonly used adaptors due to the extensive install bases that these ERP systems enjoy. As a result the adaptors are built into FDMEE as out-of-the-box functionality and do not require any additional configuration. Other prebuilt adaptors including JD Edwards and anything SAP-related must be configured and are controlled within the Source Adaptor section of the Setup tab. Configuration of these adaptors is outside the scope of this book.

Other Source Systems

Out-of-the-box, the Others source system type refers to the Open Interface Adaptor or OIA. Others can be used to identify custom ODI packages that have been developed to provide custom integrations to other source systems.

Open Interface Adaptor

The Open Interface Adaptor is a prebuilt generic adaptor that provides a framework to source data from the `AIF_OPEN_INTERFACE` staging table within the FDMEE repository when the import workflow process is run. This staging table can be populated by a custom extract procedure, an ODI package or the `BefImport` event script.

The OIA when combined with the `BefImport` event script can connect directly to a relational data source using the JAVA protocol of JDBC and populate the `AIF_OPEN_INTERFACE` staging table with the balances that will be processed through the application. More information on the Open Interface Adaptor is contained in Chapter 5: FDMEE Scripts.

Figure 2-4: Data Movement Using Open Interface Adaptor

The below shows a high level view of the movement of data between a source system and FDMEE when using OIA.

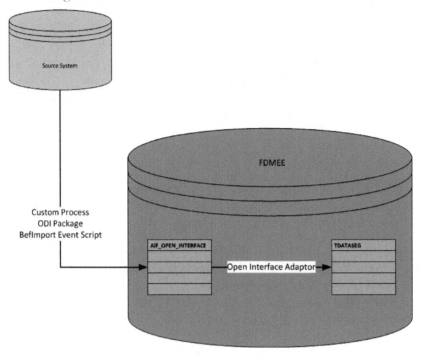

The open interface source adaptor is generic and can be duplicated and modified for multiple sources. Duplicating the adaptor is optional but recommended if renaming the source columns, modifying the parameters or utilizing the drill URL. While multiple drill URLs can be specified for a given open interface source adaptor, maintaining a 1:1 relationship is a good practice. This is a simply a safeguard to prevent a drill URL being attached to data that was not sourced from the system to which that drill URL is associated. This certainly can be achieved through mindful administration but this is a more failsafe way to prevent that situation.

Source Accounting Entities

Source Accounting Entities are only applicable when integrating Fusion Financials, Oracle eBusiness Suite or PeopleSoft using the prebuilt adaptors. Essentially the Source Accounting Entity is a mechanism to activate a Fusion Financials or eBusiness Suite Set of Books/Ledger or a PeopleSoft Business Unit for processing through FDMEE.

Entity Groups

Entity groups allow two or more Fusion Financial/eBusiness Suite Sets of Books/Ledger or PeopleSoft Business Units to be grouped together for processing. As with any technology the use of Entity Groups has pros and cons.

One of the key benefits of entity groups is the ability to create less FDMEE metadata. When using an Entity Group you can have a single location and data load rule to load multiple source accounting entities. This is good from an end user interactive processing perspective as there are fewer points of view to process.

Conversely, a single location has several impacts to consider. First is the impact to workflow performance. When creating an entity group, the execution of the workflow for each source accounting entity is forced into a serial execution. This means that if an entity group contains three source accounting entities then data is extracted for the first then the second and finally the third. This also means that all data is processed through a single point of view in FDMEE. The effect is two-fold.

Serial processing is less efficient than parallel processing. Parallel execution allows multiple smaller streams of data to be processed through FDMEE concurrently. I always describe it this way. If I have 100 journal entries to book at the end of the month, which is going to be more efficient: 10 accountants processing 10 journals each or one accountant processing all 100 journals? The answer is obviously that the 10 accountants will finish before the single accountant. The same applies to FDMEE. By using an entity group you are forced into a single processing thread for the source accounting entities contained within the Entity Group.

Besides the lack of parallelism, an Entity Group also creates a larger dataset. FDMEE needs to evaluate each record in the dataset to apply the appropriate mapping and perform the data quality checks associated with the workflow. While it is true that the application will need to do this for all records regardless, a larger dataset can often mean greater utilization of system resources (in particular, memory) and as a result can slow the workflow process. Thinking back to the accountant example, the ability to spread the workflow across multiple threads and smaller datasets is more efficient for FDMEE since a process for a smaller dataset can complete faster and therefore release memory.

The second major impact to consider when using an Entity Group is data security. FDMEE security is far less granular than the majority of target applications. Target applications have the ability to apply security at a cell level. While security to this level is unwieldy to manage, it is common to have security at the entity level. FDMEE, by contrast, only supports data security at a location level. This means that if multiple target system entities are processed through a single location, any user that has access to that location will have access to all of the data for each of the entities processed through that location.

Figure 2-5: Data Security with Entity Groups

In the below image you can see information that was imported into FDMEE using an Entity Group containing two eBS ledgers. In yellow is a record from a different ledger than the others on the screen. You can also see in green and pink different legal entities/companies being contained in not only the second ledger (Brazil) but also within the same ledger (Operations). Foregoing the use of Entity Groups will address the data security issues associated with the yellow and pink highlights; however the green highlight remains an issue that can be addressed by a data load rule filter and is covered later in this chapter.

The decision of when and how to use entity groups, given the limited ability of FDMEE to filter data using security, should be carefully considered based on a blend of maintenance, performance and data security requirements.

Target Applications

A target application is simply any system to which FDMEE provides transformed data. In the world of FDM Classic, a target application was almost always an Oracle Hyperion application. The tax adaptor for FDM Classic, as well as custom scripting, allowed FDM Classic to provide data files to other non-Oracle Hyperion systems but this use case was much more limited. With FDMEE the conceptual definition of a target system has expanded. While Oracle Hyperion applications continue to be the primary target for FDMEE, Oracle eBusiness Suite and PeopleSoft are now available as a target for the write-back functionality.

Write-back is functionality that allows data to be processed through FDMEE and loaded to the ERP interface tables. Data is not written directly to the general ledger but a post load process can be developed that creates and posts the journals to the general ledger from the interface table.

In the context of this chapter, target application refers to the target application types that can be registered within the target application screen. These are:

- Planning
- HFM – including Hyperion Tax Provisioning (HTP)
- Essbase

- Account Reconciliation Manager (ARM)

- Hyperion Profitability and Cost Management (HPCM)

- Custom Application

All of the above, with the exception of the custom application target, are Oracle Hyperion applications. A custom application is used to provide a mechanism to leverage application functionality while combining scripting. This approach can further extend the capabilities of FDMEE.

Target Application Dimensionality

When a new target application is registered the dimensionality of the target application is automatically associated with a corresponding FDMEE data column. Without delving too deep into the database structure of FDMEE, each data record stored in the FDMEE repository has a source and target (mapped) field. These FDMEE fields are associated to the target application dimensions so when the account field is populated, FDMEE will load to the account dimension of the target application.

Figure 2-6: Target Application Dimensionality

In the below image, target application dimensionality (in this case HFM) is highlighted in yellow. The dimension class type, as defined by the target application, is in pink. The dimension class is almost always populated correctly by the system and rarely needs to be updated. The FDMEE dimension to which the target dimension is associated is highlighted in green. For HFM applications, the CustomX fields should align to the UDX FDMEE dimension/data column name. For other target applications, the UDX fields can be reassigned as needed. The sequence column is used to control the order in which the dimension is processed during the execution of maps. More information about the sequence is provided in Chapter 4.

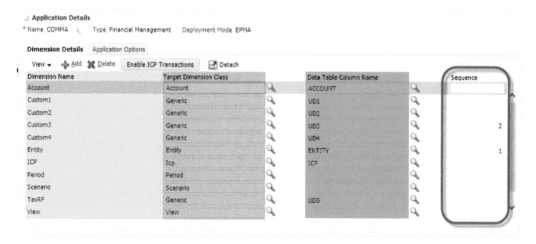

Application Options

Application options enable an administrator to control how FDMEE interacts with a target application like HFM. Options are specific to each application type with which FDMEE interacts. This section will not cover each of the application options for each target application type but instead focus on leading practice settings for the most common application targets.

Hyperion Financial Management (HFM)

HFM integrations including HTP have several settings that are defaulted to values that do not align to most real world usage.

Check Intersections

HFM has the ability to restrict intersections where data can be populated in the application through the use of metadata settings, rules, security and data locking. FDMEE can proactively detect when a mapped intersection violates any of the HFM valid intersections and alert the end user with a report during the Validate workflow stage.

Figure 2-7: Invalid Intersection Report

The below shows a representative Invalid Intersection report. The report's color coding helps to identify the reason why HFM will reject the record(s).

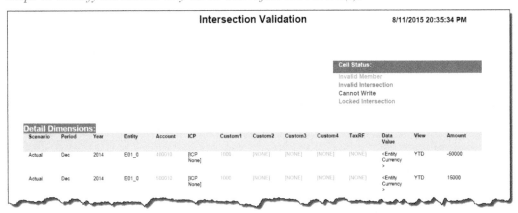

By default, Check Intersection is set to No but should be updated to Yes.

Consolidation Type

FDMEE has the ability to launch an HFM consolidation following a successful data load. The default setting of Impacted aligns with most customer needs as it launches an HFM Consolidate action. All with Data equates to the HFM Consolidate All With Data while All equates to the Consolidate All action of HFM. While this book is not intended to outline HFM best practices, in general, Consolidate All/All is avoided as it can lead to data explosion in HFM.

Enable Force Calc

When FDMEE is configured to execute a calculation or consolidation after a successful data load, the Enable Force Calc option should be set to Yes to ensure that the calculation of the HFM entity is successful.

Enable Force Translate

When FDMEE is loading to a multicurrency HFM application, the Enable Force Translate option should be set to Yes to initialize an HFM translation following a successful data load.

This option works in conjunction with the **Translation Level** setting to determine the currency into which the entity should be translated.

Data Protection

Data protection provides key value add functionality to HFM integrations. Before we discuss data protection, let's take a moment to level-set on HFM terminology and default application behavior. An HFM application has at least 10 dimensions that can be classified into two categories:

Dimension	Category
Scenario	Page
Year	Page
Period	Page
View	Page
Value	Page
Entity	Page
Account	Subcube
ICP	Subcube
Custom1	Subcube
Custom2	Subcube
Custom*X*	Subcube

There are two core methods by which data can be loaded into HFM – **Replace** (also Replace by Security) and **Merge**. There is a third method of **Accumulate** but it is so rarely used that it is not included in this discussion.

During a data load using the Replace methodology, data across all intersections of the subcube is cleared from HFM for each distinct intersection of the page dimensions contained within the file being loaded. For example, if a data file contains July 2015

Actual data for Entity A & Entity B then all intersections of account, ICP, Custom1-*X* are cleared from HFM and the new data records are loaded.

During a data load using the Merge methodology, intersections in HFM are updated based upon the data contained in the data file. Any intersections contained in the data file that currently exist in HFM will be updated with the value in the data file. Any new intersections contained in the data file will be loaded to the application. Importantly any intersections currently in HFM but not contained in the data file will be preserved.

The difference between Replace and Merge can be summarized this way. If HFM has three existing intersections of data for July 2015 Actual data for Entity A and a new data file for the same page intersection contains two records – both of which provide updates to the existing balances in HFM – when loading using replace, HFM would have two records reflecting only the balances contained in the data file. If the same file were loaded using merge, then HFM would have three records and two of the records would have updated balances while the third would remain unchanged.

This explanation of the load methods available in HFM is critical when considering how FDMEE will integrate data. In general, data should be loaded using the replace method. This ensures that any data that has been reclassed in the source system will be fully removed from HFM. The challenge that most customers face with using replace mode for all data loads is that there may be multiple data sources for a given page intersection. For example, Entity A has general ledger data that is loaded through FDMEE but also a secondary data feed for statistical information which is also loaded through FDMEE but at a later time. If the statistical data feed is loaded using the replace method then the general ledger data previously loaded would be removed from HFM. Likewise, if the general ledger data needs to be reloaded after the statistical information has been loaded then statistical information would be removed from HFM. This situation creates a need to load one or more data feeds using the merge functionality.

FDMEE's data protection functionality provides an out-of-the-box mechanism to enable data loads to always be executed using the replace methodology. This functionality preserves data in HFM that is not identified as being provided from the data source from which the data is being loaded. To properly leverage this functionality there needs to be coordination between the HFM metadata design as well as the FDMEE target application integration options and maps.

How Data Protection Works

FDMEE's data protection functionality, while extraordinarily valuable, is incredibly simple. Data protection executes during the Export workflow step. Following the generation of the data file from the mapped data, FDMEE data protection extracts data from HFM based on criteria defined in the data protection settings. The extracted data is then appended into the FDMEE generated data file as additional records. The data file is loaded using Replace and all of the intersections are cleared from HFM based on the logic described above. However since the "protected" data was extracted and appended to the data file, the data that is not part of the mapped data set which FDM is loading is preserved/protected.

HFM Metadata

FDMEE's data protection works in concert with HFM metadata. A leading practice in HFM metadata design is to create a custom Data Type dimension. This custom is used to identify the source of data not only from an input perspective but also in terms of calculations including intercompany eliminations. The use of this dimension is powerful not only for reporting purposes but it is paramount for FDMEE data protection.

Figure 2-8: Sample Data Type Dimension

*In the below image, the HFM member **GL** is used to capture data that is loaded from the general ledger while the **Stat** member is used to capture data from a secondary source.*

There are three target application integration option settings that are used to enable data protection.

Enable Data Protection

To activate data protection this setting must be Yes.

Data Protection Value

The Data Protection Value represents the HFM dimension member that will be used to determine which data to protect. This can be any member in any dimension; however, it is strongly recommended to create a data type dimension member specifically to support the use of data protection.

Data Protection Operator

The data protection operator works in conjunction with the data protection value to determine which records to extract from the HFM application. There are two values – Equals (=) and Does Not Equal (<>). The choice of which to use will be determined by individual requirements. A walk through the data protection settings required to address the previously outlined scenario is detailed in the data load rule section of this chapter.

Essbase

There are several options to consider when integrating with Essbase (and by default Planning since Essbase is the underlying data repository to which FDMEE is loading data).

Load Method

There are two methods which FDMEE can use to load data into an Essbase target application – File or SQL. The file method will function similarly to HFM integrations where FDMEE will generate a flat file and then load to Essbase. The SQL load method will not generate a flat file but instead use an Essbase SQL load rule to query data from the FDMEE repository and load to Essbase.

SQL is generally preferred as the load method due to better performance that results from not having to write data to the disk.

Load Rule Name

The Load Rule Name option works in conjunction with the load method option. This setting is optional. When no load rule name is specified, the application will generate an Essbase load rule on the fly during the Export workflow step. This load rule is automatically regenerated during each data load so any modifications to the system generated load rule are lost during the next data export to Essbase.

If a custom data load rule is defined in Essbase then it should be specified in this option value. Native Essbase load rules have the ability to perform additional transformation and /or data manipulation; however, it is strongly discouraged when using with FDMEE. First and foremost, transformation performed in the Essbase load rule will impact the ability to drill on the data since the drill query is against the transformed data within FDMEE. Secondly, and as importantly, maintaining all transformations in a single tool is strongly recommended as it makes maintenance and auditability far easier.

Drill Region

The Drill Region option is used to control if FDMEE will generate a drill region that will enable an end user to drill from a target application through to the FDMEE repository. When set to No, drill through is essentially disabled. When drill through is required, this value should be set to Yes.

Global User For Application Access

The Global User is especially useful for Essbase integrations because otherwise each end user executing loads to the Essbase application would potentially need security filters that allow them to execute calculation scripts. This security maintenance can become unwieldy as well as open – providing security rights that an end user otherwise would not require.

Specifying a Global User enables FDMEE to use the security credentials of that user when interacting with the Essbase application including loading data and executing calculation scripts.

Calculation Scripts

When using FDMEE to load data to Essbase, the application provides a framework to execute calculation (calc) scripts at different stages of the workflow process. Calc scripts can be executed by the application before a load, after a load, before the check step and after the check step. This approach is nothing new to Essbase administrators who have been creating MAXL scripts for years that update substitution variables, run a clear calc, execute an Essbase load rule and then run an aggregation calc script.

With FDMEE and its calculation mechanism, there is no longer the need to create and maintain custom MAXL scripts. By creating an Essbase calc script that utilizes run time substitution variables, FDMEE is able to intelligently execute calc scripts based on the data being loaded without the need for MAXL scripts.

Run Time Substitution Variables

Essbase run time substitution variables or RTSV allow a dynamic variable to be leveraged in an Essbase calculation script. RTSV receive the member during execution. I often describe these as being similar to run time prompts in the old Planning Business Rules. Since the RTSV gets the member name to substitute at execution, the value is never stored in Essbase and therefore does not need to be updated. This allows FDMEE to execute clear. It also allows aggregation scripts to be dynamic as well as execute concurrently across different slices of the Essbase cube.

Figure 2-9: Sample Calculation Script Using RTSV

The below sample clear calc script defines four run time substitution variables as highlighted in yellow. The RTSV are then used in the calc logic for the FIX and CLEARBLOCK statements.

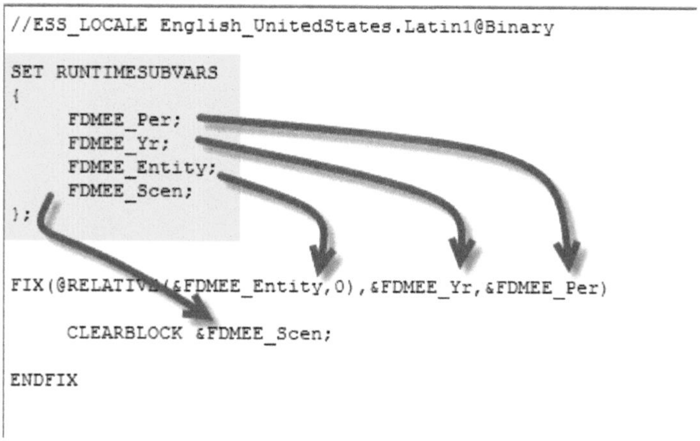

```
//ESS_LOCALE English_UnitedStates.Latin1@Binary

SET RUNTIMESUBVARS
{
    FDMEE_Per;
    FDMEE_Yr;
    FDMEE_Entity;
    FDMEE_Scen;
};

FIX(@RELATIVE(&FDMEE_Entity,0),&FDMEE_Yr,&FDMEE_Per)

    CLEARBLOCK &FDMEE_Scen;

ENDFIX
```

FDMEE Calculation Script Setup

Once the calc scripts have been created in Essbase, FDMEE will automatically recognize the run time substitution variables. FDMEE also provides default functions that allow member names to be passed to the RTSV based on the point of view being processed. Additionally, FDMEE allows location and data load rule integration options as well as static values to be specified as RTSV members.

Figure 2-10A: FDMEE Calculation Scripts

In the below image the clear calc script (FDMEECLR) was specified to run before a data load. Clicking the Calculation Script Parameter pencil opens a screen to add the run time substitution variables. Clicking Add on the new screen and then clicking the magnifying glass opens the list of RTSV available in the calc script.

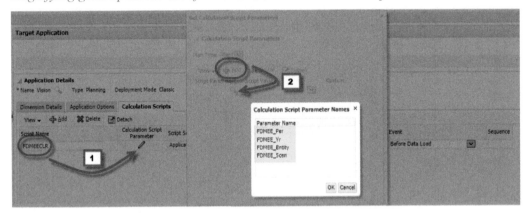

Figure 2-10B: FDMEE Parameters

The below image shows the completed run time substitution variables based on FDMEE parameters including the POV and metadata settings.

When the clear is executed, the year, time period and scenario will derive from the FDMEE point of view while the entity will be passed from the text specified in integration option 1 of the data load rule.

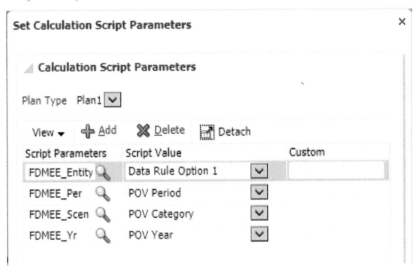

FDMEE's ability to execute targeted clears and aggregations of the Essbase cube provides a significant level of flexibility. In doing so, FDMEE allows an administrator to challenge the legacy approaches to Essbase data integrations. The idea that an entire dataset needs to be loaded is no longer dogma. More discussion on this topic will follow in Chapter 6: Best Practices for Integrating New Data Sources.

Import Formats

FDMEE is different from other integration tools in that it stores the data processed within a relational repository. Import formats are used to instruct the application how to extract data from a source system and import it into the FDMEE relational repository for subsequent transformation (mapping) and target system data load.

An import format is directly related to the source system from which data is loaded. This chapter guides you through a more traditional import format where data is extracted from a source system for loading to an Oracle Hyperion target. More information about intra-Hyperion data movement through FDMEE's data synchronization can be found in the Oracle supplied administrator guide.

Each import format has two components – details and mappings. The details section is used to instruct the application how to extract data from the source system while the mappings section is used to associate source system chart fields to the dimensionality of a target system which has been associated to the import format.

The details section of the import format is easily standardized based on the source system from which data is being integrated; however, the mappings section will vary not only for every source system but sometimes even for each business unit within that source system. This chapter is not intended to be a step by step guide of how to define the import format mappings but instead highlight functionality native to the application that can be utilized to build efficient and powerful import formats.

Flat File Import Format Definitions

Prior to the introduction of FDMEE, flat file import formats were the most common import format used. While there has been greater adoption of direct interfaces using Oracle source adaptors for systems like eBusiness Suite, PeopleSoft, JD Edwards and SAP as well as the open interface adaptor, flat file import formats still continue to be a very important component of the FDMEE data integration process. There are two flat file formats, delimited and fixed width, as noted in the source system section above.

When defining an import format the below information needs to be specified:

Field	Delimited	Fixed Width
Name	Varies; see Chapter 6 for naming conventions	
Description	Optional	Optional
Source Type	ERP	ERP
Target Type	EPM	EPM
Source	File	File
Target	Target application to which data should be loaded	
File Type	Delimited	Fixed
File Delimiter	Varies depending on file format	N/A
Drill URL	Optional; can use used to define the query parameters to be combined with the drill URL specified in the source system definition	

Import Format Builder

Delimited flat file import formats are the easiest to create since the file can be easily interpreted visually. Fixed width file formats are generally a bit more challenging since counting the number of spaces in a field is tedious and can be prone to error. The Import Format Builder can be used in either instance to speed the development of the import format.

Figure 2-11A: Import Format Builder

Once the details of the flat file import format have been defined and saved, click the **Build Format** *button under the mappings section. Select the flat file from which the import format needs to be built. Select the portion of the flat file that needs to be associated with a given target system dimension and click* **Assign Dimension***.*

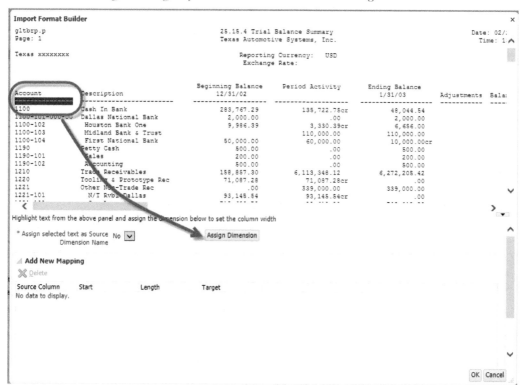

Figure 2-11B: Associate Chart Field to Dimension

In the image below, the source chart field is identified as the GL account and is associated to the target system Account dimension. The source dimension name is the text that is displayed on the Workbench. If no text is entered, the field displays the target dimension name.

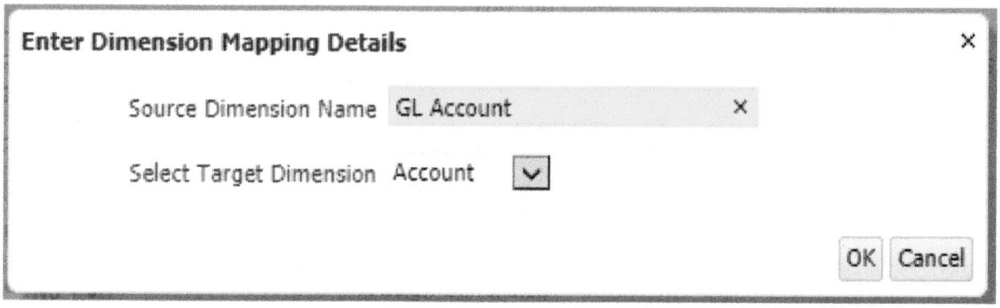

Figure 2-11C: Completed Import Format

The below image shows the import format builder completed for the Account and Entity dimensions as well as the description and amount fields. Additional work to finalize the import format mappings is required; however, the import format build was used to efficiently parse the relevant information from the data file.

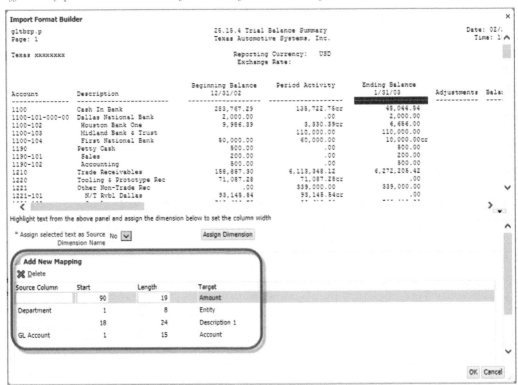

Figure 2-11D: Completed Import Format

The next image shows the completed import format. The fields in yellow were manually entered and the expression field was used to specify a hard coded value that will be the source value to be mapped. The expression field highlighted in green is assigned an import expression to parse the credit balance indicator.

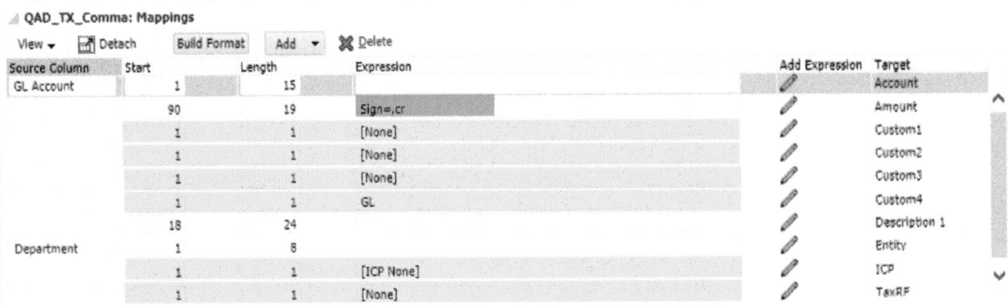

Import Expressions

FDMEE includes native functionality to address the most common chart field modifications that are needed when importing flat files. These expressions are only available to flat file sources. The table below outlines the functionality available.

Expression	Use	Dimension	Amount
Fill	Used to append characters to the end of the field being imported. This makes the field a fixed number of characters which can be useful for wildcard mapping. Can also be used for the amount field to convert European number format to US conventions.	✓	✓
FillL	Same as Fill except text is prepended to the source field	✓	✓
DRCRSplit	Only applicable to fixed width files. Used to specify the amount field midpoint; left of the value specified is the debit balance while right is the credit balance	✗	✓
Sign	Used to handle non-standard number conventions	✗	✓
Factor	Used to scale the amount field by a factor	✗	✓
NZP	Used to instruct FDMEE *not* to suppress zero value records when importing; use with caution!	✗	✓
Column	Used to instruct FDMEE to read data values across multiple columns; used for multi-period loading	✗	✓

Chapter 2

Import Expression Examples

The below provides examples of how import expressions can be used.

Expression	Setting	Raw	Expression Applied
Fill	Fill=0000	A32	A320
Fill	Fill=0000	A321	A321
Fill	Fill=EuroToUS	10.000,00	10,000.00
FillL	FillL=0000	123	0123
DRCRSplit	DRCRSplit=10	1,500.00 1,000.00	500
Sign	Sign=D,C	1200D	1200
Sign	Sign=,CR	500CR	-500
Column	Column=5,16	N/A	N/A

Import Scripts

Import scripts can also be leveraged in flat file import formats only. A deeper discussion of import scripts is contained in Chapter 5: FDMEE Scripts.

Open Interface Adaptor Import Format Definitions

The Open Interface Adaptor enables direct connectivity to a relational data source. An open interface adaptor import format leverages a combination of an **Others** type source system and the **Open Interface** source adaptor.

When creating a new OIA import format, the following details should be specified:

Field	Value
Name	Varies; see Chapter 6 for naming conventions
Description	Optional
Source Type	ERP
Target Type	EPM
Source	Source system associated with Open Interface source adaptor
Target	Target application to which data should be loaded
Accounting Entity	N/A

Field	Value
Source Adaptor	Select from list of source adaptors
Concatenation Character	Only applicable if two or more mapping records for a single target dimension are added to the mapping section. It is recommended to avoid using underscore (_) since underscore is a SQL wildcard character and could impact mapping results.
Drill URL	Select from drill URL(s) defined in the source adaptor

Once the import format is defined, the mappings between the columns within the OPEN_INTERFACE_TABLE and target system dimensionality can be specified. It is important to note that there are no import expressions available when utilizing the open interface adaptor. Any modification to the source data that would normally be handled through an import expression needs to be addressed by the mechanism to populate the OPEN_INTERFACE_TABLE, an event script or data load mapping.

Once the import format is defined be sure to click the Regenerate ODI Scenario button. Failure to complete this step will result in an error when attempting to integrate data under this import format.

Figure 2-12: Regenerate ODI Scenario

When defining or modifying an import format that uses a source adaptor, you must regenerate the ODI scenario associated with the import format after saving. An import format needing ODI scenario regeneration is noted by the yellow status icon.

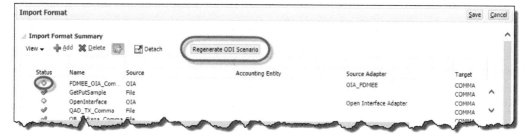

Pre-Built Source System Import Format Definitions

When defining an import format that is associated with a pre-built source system like eBusiness Suite or PeopleSoft it is important to activate a source accounting entity that contains a chart of accounts whose chart fields can be used to map to target system dimensions.

When creating a new pre-built source system import format, the following details should be specified:

Field	Value
Name	Varies; see Chapter 6 for naming conventions
Description	Optional
Source Type	ERP
Target Type	EPM
Source	Source system associated with the connection to the ERP
Target	Target application to which data should be loaded
Accounting Entity	Select accounting entity with representative chart fields/chart of accounts
Source Adaptor	N/A
Concatenation Character	Only applicable if two or more mapping records for a single target dimension are added to the mapping section. It is recommended to avoid using underscore (_) since underscore is a SQL wildcard character and could impact mapping results.
Drill URL	N/A – defined at the source system level

Once the details of the import format are defined, the mapping of the chart fields to target system dimensions can be completed.

Figure 2-13: Import Format Mapping Chart Fields to Target Dimensions

The below image shows a sample completed import format mapping from eBusiness Suite chart fields to HFM dimensions. Notice that there are two rows for HFM Custom1 where the eBS Account and Department are used to define the source Custom1. The second Custom1 row was added to the import format mappings by clicking the Add button.

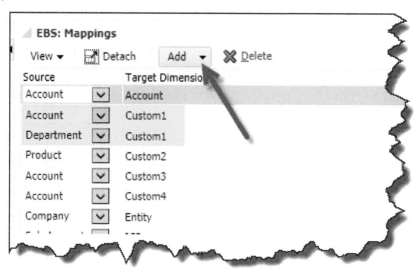

Locations

A location in FDMEE is simply a container of data. A location is used to segregate data within the application. While a location has a one-for-one relationship with a target system, the decision to create one or more locations for a given target is driven by several factors.

The primary reason to create multiple locations is the need to have unique mapping based on the business usage of the source system's chart of accounts. While multiple business units may share the same source system, how each uses the chart of accounts can sometimes differ. As a result, the mapping for each business unit would be different and generally dictates different locations since mapping is generally associated with a location. Some may argue that the introduction of data load rule specific mapping rules eliminates the need for multiple locations. I will address this functionality and its limitations in Chapter 4: Data Load Mapping Explained.

Another key consideration in determining the need for multiple locations is data security. As noted in the Entity Group section, under Source Systems, FDMEE data security is limited to locations only. There is no ability to dynamically filter and/or ignore data within a given location based on the target system's dimensional security model. Unless a global user is specified for application access within the target application options, a user will not be able to load to target dimension members to which they do not have security access. As a result, multiple locations will often be created to replicate the dimensional data security of the target application. In general this is usually associated with the target system entity dimension but in the event that more granular security is required for another data slice (e.g., product data) then multiple locations would also need to be created.

Security is important to consider for the workflow process but even more so when considering drill through. If multiple legal entities were loaded through a single location then any user that has access to that location for drill through purposes would have access to all of the data in that location regardless of their target system entity security. As a result, multiple locations can also be created to ensure that users with drill through access to the data in FDMEE are limited to the data sets to which they should have access.

The final major consideration for the creation of locations is performance and concurrency. A workflow process can only be executed for a given POV by a single user. This applies to both interactive processes where a user is executing the workflow within the FDMEE web interface, as well as lights out batch automation processes. Creating multiple locations enables multiple streams of data to be processed concurrently. This usually means that smaller data sets are being processed through each POV and as a result the workflow process is more efficient. Multiple locations are required to support concurrency.

When creating a location, there are only two required fields which are location name and import format. The remaining fields on the location details tab are optional and will be discussed in greater detail in Chapter 6: Best Practices for Integrating New Data Sources.

With locations, often overlooked functionality resides in the Integration Options tab. Integration options are akin to the user defined fields that are available in applications like HFM and Essbase. Integration options are used to store information that can be used for calc script execution run time sub variables, scripting or report purposes. These fields are free text.

Figure 2-14: Location Integration Options

In the below image, integration option specifies the company that will be used in place of the RTSV for the clear calc script.

Location Details	**Integration Option**	
Integration Option 1 C_1000		Integration Option 2
Integration Option 3		Integration Option 4

Data Load Rules

Data Load Rules (DLR) are a new concept in FDMEE. They are considered the fourth dimension of the point-of-view where Location, Time Period and Category are the other three. DLRs are specific to a single location and category but a location can have multiple DLRs assigned to it.

Data load rules can be executed from the Data Load Rule screen or the Data Load Workbench. When executing from the Workbench, the name of the data load rule appears in the FDMEE point-of-view.

Figure 2-15: FDMEE POV

The below image shows the DLR for the current Workbench POV.

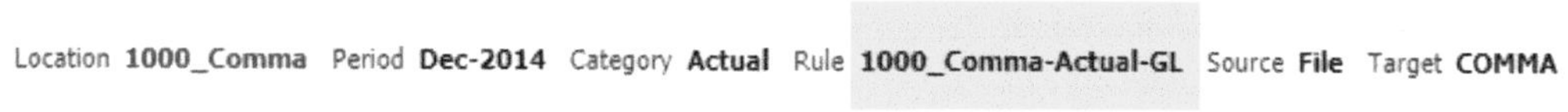

Location **1000_Comma** Period **Dec-2014** Category **Actual** Rule **1000_Comma-Actual-GL** Source **File** Target **COMMA**

Data Load Rules provide additional flexibility when designing integrations. For example, when integrating with Essbase the data view of the core financial statements often varies. Income statement data is usually loaded as periodic activity while the balance sheet data is usually loaded as year or life to date. When integrating data directly from a source system like SAP, which does not have the ability to specify different data views for income statement and balance, the use of two DLRs allows a single FDMEE location to be used to process a full trial balance since the data view extract method can vary for each DLR created.

Flat File Data Load Rules

The below settings should be considered when defining flat files data load rules.

Setting	Description
Target Plan Type	Only applicable to Essbase/Planning integrations. Select the Plan Type/Essbase database to which data should be loaded.
File Type	Used to control the execution of the data load rule. More information is below.
Import Format	Optional; the DLR uses the import format assigned to the location by default. Allows override for different source system formats. Cannot be used to integrate other source system types like Open Interface.

File Type

The file type setting is used to control how the DLR processes the data file. There are five options currently available:

- Single Period Load
- Multi-Period Text File (Contiguous Period)
- Multi-Period Text File (Non-Contiguous Period)
- Multi-Period Excel File (Contiguous Period)
- Multi-Period Excel File (Non-Contiguous Period)

Selecting the Single Period load file type enables the data load rule to be run from the Data Load Workbench as well as the Data Load Rule screen. If a file whose import format has been created to enable multiple periods of data to be processed is executed from the Workbench with the DLR file type set to Single Period Load then the data column will be parsed based on the import format field settings. As such it is paramount to update the file type when creating an import format and data load rule that will be used to load multiple periods of data.

The Multi-Period file types are used to denote files that have multiple data columns. DLRs that use this file type can only be executed from the Data Load Rule screen. Simply selecting one of the multi-period file types is not sufficient to enable multi-period file processing. The Column import expression must also be assigned to the amount field of the import format assigned to the location or the DLR.

A multi-period DLR can be executed for a range of periods that is less than or equal to the number of periods defined by the Column expression in the import format. It is important to note that the range of periods for which the DLR is executed cannot exceed the number of columns specified in the Column import expression. For example, if the column expression indicates nine data columns and the DLR is run for January through December, execution of the DLR will fail.

Figure 2-16: Multi-Period Import Format

The below import format has the Column import expression assigned to the Amount data row and indicates that data is in columns 3 through 6.

Non-Contiguous Multi-Period File Types

The Non-Contiguous Multi-Period file type is used to identify files that have multiple data columns but which are not in calendar order. For example, if integrating budget information that is only available in a quarterly view, assuming a single year of data, then the data file would have four data columns. Let's assume that the target application has a 12 input level period representing January through December. In this example, a Non-Contiguous Multi-Period DLR would be created and the mapping of the columns to the respective FDMEE time period, through which data should be processed, would then be specified. It is important to note that this Source Periods mapping would need to be maintained for future executions where the data column to time period relationship would likely shift.

Figure 2-17: DLR Source Period Mapping

In the below image, a Multi-Period Non-Contiguous file type was selected. The data columns are then mapped to the respective FDMEE time periods.

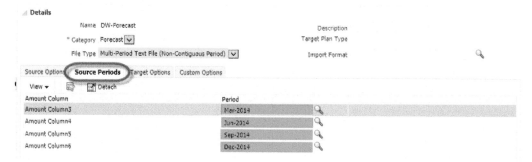

Source Options

Specifying the source options for a flat file is optional but can aid in streamlining the workflow process as well as any batch automation. Source options are used to specify the name of the file that should be processed by the data load rule. This is particularly useful when a production process exists that will output a data file to a specific directory. Once the file exists in the target directory then an interactive user or a lights out batch process can execute the workflow process.

Any subdirectory to the application root directory specified in System settings can be defined. The easiest way to populate this directory is to select a file from the directory where the DLR should import data. If this directory is not populated, the application assumes the application root directory.

To ensure that the DLR is dynamic and does not need to be updated for each time period, the file name suffix can be applied. There are two options for the file name suffix – the FDM period name (e.g., Dec – 2014) or a Period Key. When selecting the period key option, the period key format must be input using **JAVA SimpleDateFormat** conventions.

If a file name suffix is going to be leveraged, then the file name specified must not include the file name because the application will automatically append the suffix to the file name when searching for the file to import. For example, if the file name is specified as Data_20141201.txt and the file name suffix is set as Period Key with a format of yyyyMMdd then FDMEE would attempt to locate a file named Data_2014120120140601 when processing June 2014. In this example, the file name would need to be specified as Data_.txt.

Figure 2-18: Source Options

In the below example, the data file name has been specified. The application will import from the 1000_Comma location folder within the Inbox. The file names will be suffixed with the period in yyyyMMdd format. Based on the data in the directory, the DLR can be run for March, June, September or December 2014.

When the DLR is executed for September 2014, the application imports the Data_20140901.txt file.

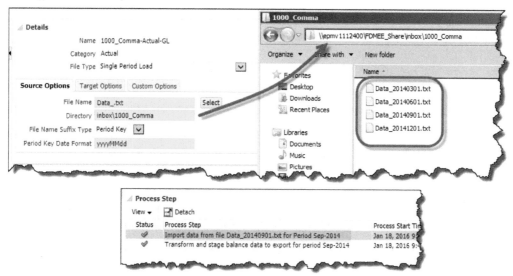

Non-Flat File Data Load Rules

As noted in the foreword, this book is not intended to replicate the Oracle-provided administrator guide. While this book assumes 11.1.2.4 functionality, many of the concepts discussed are core to the product and as such it is expected that the conceptual discussion of the topic will continue to be relevant to future releases. The source options assigned to source adaptor based DLRs are an exception to this expectation as the source adaptors are consistently evolving. The most up-to-date information about the source options for adaptor-based DLRs can be found in the Oracle administrator guide under the **Defining Data Load Rule Details** section.

A discussion of the Period Mapping Type, Calendar and Include Adjustment Periods settings of an adaptor-based data load rule can be found in Chapter 3: Other Metadata Explained.

Data Protection Example

We previously discussed data protection in the HFM target application options. To give additional context as to how data protection can be leveraged in a real world implementation, let's walk through an example and explore how data load rules can be used to address a common integration requirement.

For a given business unit, trial balance/general ledger information and statistical information is stored in two separate source systems and is available at different times throughout the close cycle. To keep this example simple, let's assume that the file layout is identical so a single import format can be used. The mapping for these two sources can be shared so a single FDMEE location can be used.

The last metadata component to consider is data load rules. In this example, we create two data load rules. The first will be used to load the general ledger balances and will use default target application integration options for data protection which is to protect any member that does not equal GL. This means that any input level record in HFM that does not include a member GL will be extracted from HFM, appended to the FDMEE generated mapped data file and then loaded into HFM. The result is that any data already loaded to the Stat member is protected.

The second data load rule differs from the first only in that the target options are modified to override the application level integration options specified. In this instance, the data protection will protect any member not equal to Stat. This DLR-specific setting will protect the general ledger data loaded by the reciprocal general ledger DLR.

Through the use of multiple data load rules and DLR-specific target application options, all data is able to be loaded to HFM using the replace method while still ensuring data completeness and quality.

Figure 2-19: Data Load Rule Target Option Overrides

In the below image, the protection value has been overridden to Stat. The application natively highlights (in yellow) any setting which is modified from the global setting defined in the target application integration options. This setting change will apply only when this DLR is executed.

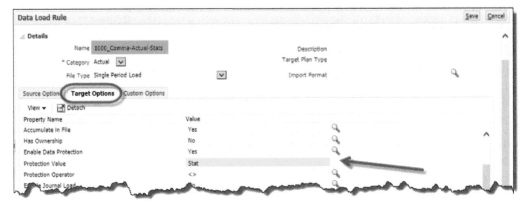

Summary

In this chapter we discussed source systems including a brief overview of the ERP. We explored the different target applications with which FDMEE integrates. We learned how an import format is used to populate the FDMEE repository. We highlighted the role of the Location and finally the Data Load Rule.

Let's recap and bring it all together. Every FDMEE integration requires a source and target system. Data is extracted from a source system and loaded to a target system. The import format is used to manage the extraction of data from the source system to populate the FDMEE database. The location is the subset of data while the data load rule or rules are the individual datasets associated with the location. The point-of-view defined as Location, Data Load Rule, Time Period and Category houses the transformed source data that is loaded to the target system.

Another way to bring the components together is to think about it from the most granular level and work backwards. The data load rule is the individual component that allows a single data set to be loaded. Every DLR is assigned to a location. Every location requires an import format. Each import format is associated to exactly one source system and one target system.

Figure 2-20: Metadata Dependency

The below image shows each of the components of a data integration and their interdependence.

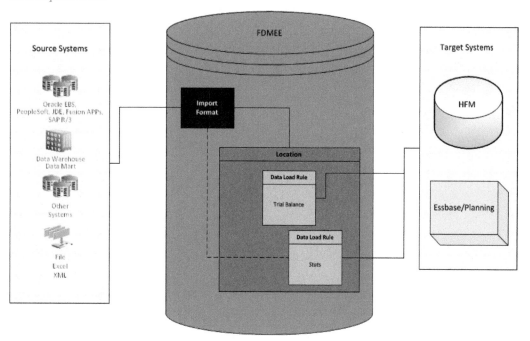

In the next chapter we will explore Period and Category mappings as well as application components including Check Rules, Check Entities and Logic Groups that can be used to streamline and enhance the data integration cycle.

3
Other Metadata Explained

In this chapter, we examine the remaining application metadata. We discuss how to properly maintain period and category mapping as well as understand how to enrich the data integration process through the use of optional but powerful features.

Period Mapping

FDMEE period mapping is used for several purposes. First, time periods are an important component of the point-of-view. While the location functions as the overall superset container of data, the period functions as a 'slice of data' container. On the FDMEE table where data is stored, a given location can have data for multiple periods. The period key is a filter used to identify the records that should be processed for the current POV.

The second and most relevant purpose, in terms of this chapter, of FDMEE periods is to create a mapping relationship between the FDMEE time period and the source and target system time periods as well as years. Period mapping allows a single FDMEE time period to interact with source and target systems that have varying time period and year formats. For example, the year dimension of an HFM target applications requires the year to be in the YYYY format (e.g., 2016) while Essbase and Planning generally follow the FYYY (e.g., FY17) convention. Period mapping ensures that FDMEE is able to load to the different target applications.

Another way to think about period mapping is to consider it a globally mapped dimension. Every integration has a time period measure so the period and year dimensions have been moved from the individual mapping tables to a global mapping relationship. This also applies to the category mapping which will also be discussed in this chapter.

This chapter will focus on the most common calendar format where the month is the most granular time period in the target application. For calendars with a more granular frequency (like weekly or daily) additional information can be found in the Oracle-supplied administrator guide under the section Defining Period Mappings.

Period Global Mapping

Global period mapping is used to establish the aforementioned slice of the data container. Global period mapping is used as the default target system time period and year mapping when a mapping is not specifically defined in the application period mapping tab.

Period Key

The period key upon which all other period mapping is based is defined in the global mapping. The period key is most often defined in a MM/DD/YYYY format. In FDM Classic, the convention when defining a period key was to utilize the last day of the month – for example, 12/31/2015. This convention has since changed in FDMEE. The standard convention, now, is to utilize the first day of the month – for example, 12/1/2015. This shift is largely due to the FDMEE product development team and their extensive experience with Oracle eBusiness Suite where the period key is most often defined by a start and end period. The start period is usually the first day of the month. I too encourage this approach since the actual period key is never visible to the end users of the application. The period description which is described below is what is displayed in the POV bar, reports, and most other application interfaces with which an end user would interact.

Figure 3-1: Period Key

The below images shows a sample global period mapping using the MM/01/YYYY format.

Some organizations that run on non-calendar-based fiscal periods such as a 4-4-5 will sometimes attempt to define the FDMEE time periods based on these time periods. I caution against this as FDMEE is not a transactional system. I encourage an organization to adhere to the convention of the calendar month that corresponds to the reporting period when defining the period key. For example, if the fiscal year runs from April through March, when defining period one (P1) utilize period key 4/1/YYYY.

Finally, when establishing period keys to enable a load of beginning balances, I recommend the convention of the day-1 from the period key of the first period of the year. For example, when establishing a normal calendar, the beginning balance period key would be 12/31/YYYY. In the prior example of an April-March calendar, the beginning balance period key would be 3/31/YYYY.

Figure 3-2: BegBalance Period Key

The below image shows a sample beginning balance period key. Notice the year of the period key differs from the year defined in the Period Name and Year Target fields.

Prior Period Key

I have noticed a fair amount of confusion regarding the prior period key. The prior period key is not intended to be the last day of the date range associated with the time period. Very simply, the prior period key should match the period key of the prior FDMEE period. For example, if my period key is 4/1/2015, my prior period key should be 3/1/2015.

Figure 3-3: Prior Period Key

The below image displays the relationship between the prior period key and the period key.

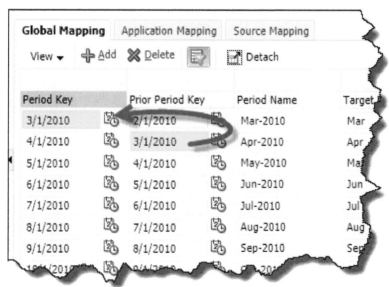

Period Name

The period name defines the FDMEE point-of-view period that will be the label displayed to the end user. The period name is free form. While a common convention of the period name is MMM-YYYY this can be customized as needed for business purposes. Returning to the previous example of the April-March calendar, the period name format for period key 4/1/2015 could be defined as P01-FY15 (P*MM*-FY*YY*). The key when defining the period name is to make it easily understandable to the end user community because, again, this is the FDMEE POV member with which they will interact.

It is strongly recommended to avoid using spaces in the period name. For any command line execution of FDMEE processes, spaces are an illegal character. Additionally, when integrating with PBCS, spaces in member names are not support by the file transfer utility (now deprecated) or EPMAutomate.

Target Period

As previously noted, this chapter focuses on the most common integration which is loading to a target application where the most granular time period is a month. In this instance, the **Target Period Month** column should be completed with the period format from the target application.

In the event that FDMEE integrates with multiple Hyperion target systems (e.g., Essbase & HFM), I generally recommend to specify the Target Period Month in the format of the target application for which the most target applications need to be registered. For example, if integrating with HFM whose time periods are full month names as well as three Essbase applications that utilize a three digit month abbreviation, the Target Period Month should follow the three digit month abbreviation format. I recommend this since the Global period mapping is used in the absence of a specifically defined Target Application Period Mapping.

Figure 3-4: Target Period Month

The below image shows the Target Period Month utilizing the Essbase three digit month abbreviation format.

Finally, I do not recommend completing the Target Period Quarter, Year or Day fields for a standard month-based calendar. These fields are not used in this instance and completing them is superfluous.

Year Target

As with the Target Period, the Year Target field should be completed utilizing the format of the target application for which the most target applications are registered. In the event of Planning and Essbase this is FYYY while HFM requires the YYYY format.

Period Application Mapping

Application mapping is used to build an association to the time period and year dimensions of a target application for which the global mapping does not apply. For example, when defining the global period mapping in Essbase format, an application mapping is required for the HFM application.

I have noted different behavior in how period mapping functions across different versions of the product. In some versions, I have observed all functionality work as expected without an explicit mapping for each target application – essentially defaulting to the global mapping. In other instances, I have observed certain functionality not work as expected unless an application mapping was specifically defined for each target application. As such, I strongly recommend defining an application mapping for each target application.

To add an application mapping, a global period must first be defined. Once all global periods are created, the application period mapping can be established. Navigate to the Application Mapping tab and select the target application for which the period mapping needs to be defined. Click the Add button. A dialogue box with the global mapping defined period keys will display. Select a time period and select OK. Complete the remaining fields as outlined in the global period mapping but apply the target system time period and year formats appropriately. Repeat this process for each target application registered.

Figure 3-5: Application Period Mapping

The below image shows an application mapping for a target HFM application. Notice the Year Target column is specified in the YYYY format.

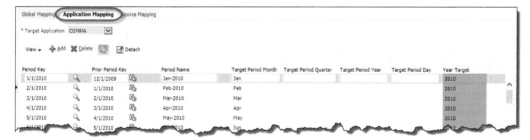

Period Source Mapping

As noted in the global period mapping section, FDMEE period keys are not recommended to be established in the format of the source systems from which they will source data. When you consider the purpose of FDMEE – to integrate multiple disparate systems – attempting to emulate the period key of the source system is unrealistic. As such, source period mapping is used to establish the relationship between the FDMEE time period and the time period of the source system from which FDMEE is integrating data.

Source period mapping is only required when integrating with a source system through a prebuilt connection (eBS or PeopleSoft) or when using a source system adaptor like the Open Interface Adaptor, J.D. Edwards, or SAP.

Much like application mapping, source mapping is defined per source system. Click the Source Mapping tab and then select the source system for which a period mapping is required. Click Add. Select the global period key for which the map needs to be populated. Complete the remaining input fields; this will vary depending on the system from which data is being sourced. Repeat this procedure for all periods and source systems.

Figure 3-6: Source Period Mapping

The below image shows a sample source system period mapping. In this example, the global period key is established for an April-March calendar. The global period key 4/1/2010 is mapped to the Fiscal eBS period of Apr-10 which represents period 1 of fiscal year 2010.

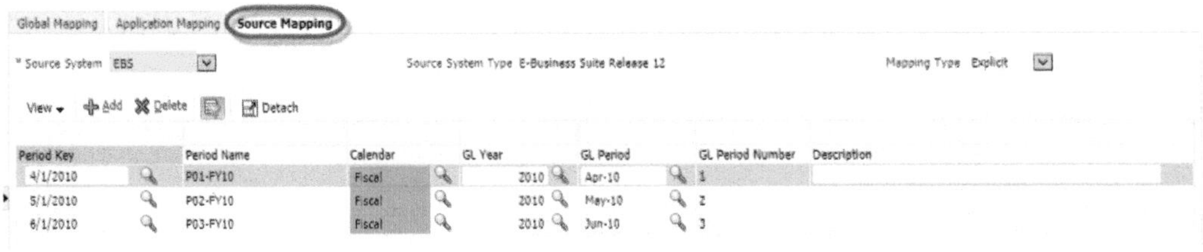

Category Mapping

Similar to Period Mapping, category mapping is used for multiple purposes. Category is an integral component of the point-of-view and acts as yet another slice of the data container. As with the period key, data is further identified on the data table by the category key. The category key is the numeric indicator of the category name that is displayed on the POV bar. Unlike the period key, the category key is auto-generated by the application when a new category is added.

Similar to the period mapping, the category is used to define the relationship between the FDMEE category member and the target application Scenario. A slight tangent but one that will add context. One might wonder why the FDMEE component is referred to as a Category when it always has an association with an Oracle Hyperion application dimension named Scenario. This is a legacy of the product's history. When Upstream was first developed, it was created to integrate with Hyperion Enterprise. Hyperion

Enterprise did not have Scenarios, it had Categories. While the product now known as FDMEE has experienced significant changes over the years, this one legacy component persists.

Category Global Mapping

Global category mapping is used to establish the aforementioned slice of the data container. Global category mapping is used as the default target system scenario mapping when a mapping is not specifically defined in the application category mapping tab.

Category

Category is the field in which the category members that are available to be selected in the FDMEE point-of-view are defined. While the category key is auto-generated, the category is what will display in the POV bar.

In my opinion, the categories created should represent a superset of the Scenarios of the target application to which FDMEE will load data. Understanding that Essbase applications often have multiple scenarios that are used for analysis and reporting purposes (e.g., `Actual_at_BudgetFX`), the categories created in FDMEE should reflect only those scenarios to which FDMEE will actually load data. Additionally, the superset of categories should reflect the unique scenario types. For example, if the HFM scenario for actual data is **ACT** and the Essbase scenario is **Actual**, a single Actual category is needed in FDMEE. The mapping of the FDMEE category to the target application scenario should be managed with category application mapping.

Description

This field is optional. The category description is not used in any FDMEE process except, potentially, reporting.

Frequency

As noted at the beginning of this chapter, the overview of the period mapping focuses on the most often used calendar where month is the most granular time period. The Frequency designation for an FDMEE category controls the target period field that FDMEE will utilize when retrieving the target period member when loading through a given FDMEE time period.

If a target application has a time period dimension that is more granular than month, the FDMEE categories will require the corresponding frequency to be defined. As well, the period mapping will require the appropriate column to be completed.

Figure 3-7: Category Frequency

The below image shows that Actual and Forecast categories are both established with a Monthly frequency. This means that the Target Period Month column in the Period Mapping will be used by FDMEE when loading data when the FDMEE POV category is Actual or Forecast.

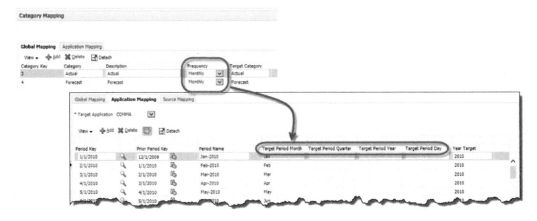

Target Category

Target category represents the target application scenario to which data will be loaded when a data load is executed. As with the period mapping, the target category defined on the global mapping is often associated with the scenario of the target application *type* (e.g., Essbase) for which multiple targets are registered.

Figure 3-8: Sample Category Mapping

The below image shows an example global category mapping. Notice the FDMEE category is exactly aligned with the Target Scenario name.

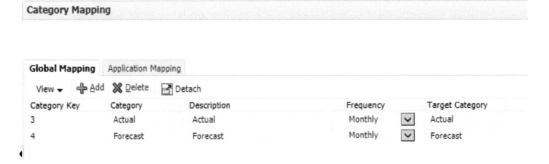

Category Application Mapping

Similar to application period mapping, application category mapping is used to build an association to the scenario dimension of a target application for which the global category mapping does not apply. As with period mapping, I strongly recommend defining an application category mapping for each target application.

To add an application mapping a global category must first be defined. Select the Application Mapping tab and select the target application for which the category mapping needs to be defined. Click the Add button. Select the category to map from the drop down. While the column is labelled Target Category, you are selecting a member from the Scenario dimension of the target application by using the magnifying glass. Repeat this process for each category and each target application registered.

Figure 3-9: Category Application Mapping

The below shows an example category mapping for the COMMA application.

Logic Groups

Logic groups are an optional component of the application. Logic groups are assigned to an FDMEE location which means that they are applied to any data load rule associated with the location. Logic groups execute during the import workflow stage as well as anytime a point-of-view is recalculated. Logic groups do require additional processing and, as such, add time to the workflow execution. They should be used sparingly.

Logic groups can be leveraged for a variety of reasons including loading a single source data point to multiple intersections in the target application, creating a supplemental source record that can be used when mapping other records or performing allocations. While each of these is a possible use case, I strongly caution against the last scenario. One of the key messages that I share with customers is to use the right tool for the job. While FDMEE can perform allocations using logic groups, there are better systems – HFM, Essbase or Hyperion Profitability and Cost Management (HPCM) - to perform those calculations. FDMEE is not the right tool for the job.

The most common use case for logic groups, that I have seen across various implementations of FDM Classic and FDMEE, is to duplicate a source system data point so that it can be loaded to multiple intersections in the target application. For example, let's assume that a source system produces a trial balance with revenue accounts. One of the fields in the data file represents the product. Now let's consider the target application and assume it is HFM. In this particular application there is the standard account dimension which includes the financial statement account hierarchies for Income Statement and Balance Sheet. There is a supplemental section in the account dimension for Statistical and Reporting accounts. Within this supplemental section is a set of Revenue by Product accounts since a custom dimension was not allocated to product as it is used on a limited basis. A logic group can be utilized to enable the source data file with a single data point for revenue to be loaded simultaneously to the trial balance and supplemental accounts.

As there are a myriad of uses for logic groups, this section will not provide an overview of each field of a logic group but instead offer useful tips for how to utilize certain fields effectively. Additional detailed information about each field including the Value/Expression field and its function can be found in the Oracle-supplied administrator guide.

Simple Logic Groups

A simple logic group is one in which the logic group performs its operation based on the source account and does not evaluate any other source dimensions. The key field in a simple logic group is the **Item**. The item dictates the source account value that will be generated by the logic group.

I generally recommend that the Item specified follow the convention of `L-TargetSystemAccount` where L- indicates that the source value was generated as a result of a logic group and the Target System Account is the actual member in the target application to where the data will be loaded. By using this convention you can also create a Like map (L-* maps to *) and the logic group generated records are simply passed through.

Figure 3-10: Simple Logic Group

In the below image the Item is specified as L-Revenue. When the simple logic group creates duplicate records for those records where the account is like 400010 the resulting source account will be L-Revenue. The lower portion of the image shows the result of the logic group running against the source data.

Complex Logic Groups

A complex logic group is one in which the logic group can perform its operation across one or more source dimensions. For example, a complex logic group can evaluate the source account and cost center to generate an additional record. Complex logic groups are slightly more difficult to create, initially, but once you are familiar with different fields and how each is used their creation becomes much less daunting.

When using a complex logic group in the same manner as described in the simple logic group section above, the key field to consider is the **Group By** field in the Criteria Values. Leverage this field in a similar manner to the way the **Item** field was utilized in the simple logic group.

Figure 3-11A: Complex Logic Group Criteria

In the below image, the account and UD1 (Cost Center) values are used to determine which records need to be impacted by the logic group. The Entity dimension was added to the criteria in order to specify the Group By value of L-Corporate.

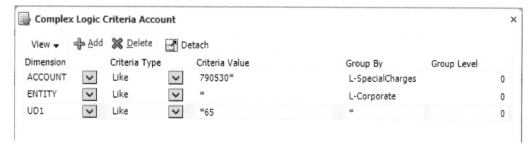

Figure 3-11B: Complex Logic Group Result

The below image shows the result of the above complex logic group. When the account is 790530 and the cost center ends in 65 then an additional record is created with a source account of L-SpecialCharges, a source cost center equal to that of the record which was duplicated and a source entity of L-Corporate. The amount on the logic group created record was also multiplied by negative one. Utilizing a series of L-* to * maps allows the logic group records to pass through the values specified in the Criteria Value Group By field.

Check Rule and Check Entity Groups

The final step in the workflow process – Check – while optional, is a powerful way to enhance the data integration cycle. By utilizing Check report functionality, the end user is able to immediately see a snapshot of the data in the application which FDMEE has loaded. The user is presented with key metrics and key data validation points which allows them to quickly assess the quality of the data that has been loaded.

The Check workflow step is controlled by the intersection of the Check Rule and Check Entity Groups. While the Check Entity group is optional, the Check Rule, when assigned to a location, results in the Check step being executed.

Check Rule Groups

Check rule groups establish the intersections of data that should be displayed on the Check Report as well as the data intersections that should be interrogated for data quality. Check rules can be used to retrieve balances from the target application that have been calculated and/or consolidated. Check rules can pull not only base level intersections but also parent level intersections.

The check rule definitions execute for each target entity in the data set or for each entity defined within the check entity group assigned to the location for which the On Report field is checked.

Check Rules have two basic sections – list and rules. The list section of the Check Rule is used to specify intersections of data that should simply be displayed to the end user. The values in the list section of the Check Rule are not evaluated for data quality. They are simply a reported value. For example, the list section of the Check Rules may retrieve key financial statement metrics like Total Revenue, Gross Margin, Net Income or Total Assets. The list section of the check rule would not evaluate if the asset balance is positive.

The rules section is used to establish data quality measures. In this section of the report, data is actually compared against administrator-defined metrics which determine if the data passes or fails the Check workflow step. When loading trial balance information, one of the most common check rules is determining if the balance sheet is in balance.

For each rule in the rule section the result must return a Boolean (True/False) value. As an example, a rule that checks if the balance sheet balances within $100 would return a true or false value. A rule that simply checks the value of Assets minus Liabilities and Equity would not return a Boolean result and would not be valid for the rule section.

When the check rule is executed, any failure of any rule within the rule section for any entity for which the check rule is executed will result in the Check workflow step failing. This means that all rules must pass for all entities in order for the Check workflow step to pass.

It is important to note that when a location fails the check workflow step there is no out-of-the-box functionality in FDMEE that will delete the data from the target application. This can be accomplished with FDMEE scripting but that is outside the scope of this book.

Check Rule Conventions

The following are the conventions that I consider leading practices when creating a check rule definition. The Title should always be the first item in the check rule. Next I begin the List section of the report. In this section I like to include at least one subtitle to inform the end user about the type of information that section contains.

The list section then contains the intersections that should be retrieved. The sequence number in this section should increment by five for each new item. This allows additional items to be inserted, later on, without having to reorder all of the existing items. Once the list section is complete, the rule section can begin. I like to set the rule section sequence to a very large number relative to the list section. 500 is a number that will allow you nearly 100 list items assuming an increment of five. The rule section should be established in a similar fashion as the list section. Lastly I include an "End of Report" subtitle to clearly delineate the data for each entity. This subtitle is assigned a large sequence number to ensure it is always displayed last. Finally, I do not recommend making any check rule item Category-specific unless absolutely necessary.

As I mentioned in the Foreword, these conventions are my leading practices. They are not absolutes and will need to be adapted for each deployment and its needs.

Figure 3-12A: Sample Check Rule

The below image shows a simple check rule. Notice the conventions noted above are represented in this example.

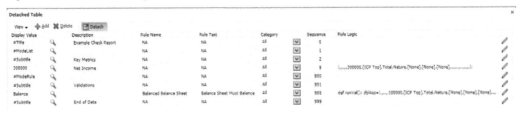

Figure 3-12B: Sample Check Report

The below image shows the resulting check report based on the check rule.

Example Check Report

Location: ABC_Comma
Category: Actual
Period: 2014-12-01

Validation Group: Comma

Pass
E01_0

Key Metrics

Account	Value
300000 - Net Income	35,000.00

Validations

	Rule Name	Rule Definition	Value
Ok	Balanced Balance Sheet	Balance Sheet Must Balance	0.00

End of Data

Check Entity Groups

Check Entity group is an optional component that can be associated with a location. When used, the Check Entity group serves two purposes. First and foremost, it controls which entities are calculated or consolidated in the target application during the Export workflow step. Secondly the Check Entity Group can be used in conjunction with the Check Rule Group to execute the Check workflow step for specific entities.

Check Entity Consolidation

The use of the Check Entity group for consolidation further streamlines the data integration cycle. By enabling FDMEE to execute a consolidation as part of the data load operation, the entire process is more efficient since the user no longer needs to be burdened with logging into multiple EPM applications simply to load and consolidate data.

When populating the Check Entity group for calculation/consolidation purposes, it is important to consider the hierarchy of the target application. The sequence (order) in which entities will be calculated or consolidated is especially important for HFM target applications as calculating a child after a parent will render the calc status of the HFM parent as **CN** (Consolidation Needed). This means that multiple consolidations in order to get an **OK** calculation status would be unnecessarily needed as a result of specifying an inappropriate sequence to the Check Entity.

Figure 3-13A: Entity Hierarchy

The below shows an example entity hierarchy. E01_0 is the child of E01.

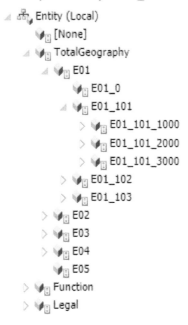

Figure 3-13B: Check Entity Group Sequence

When specifying entities in the entity group it is important to calculate the children before consolidating the parents. For example E01_0 should have a sequence number less than the sequence number for E01.

Target application options should be considered when determining if the Consolidate check box should be checked. For example, with HFM integrations, technically the entities below a parent do not need to be flagged for consolidation if the Force Calculate option is set to Yes; however, there is no harm in checking the Consolidate box.

Finally, it is important to note that the Parent field is critical when creating a check entity group for an HFM target application. The parent tells HFM which node (parent.child) to calculate/translate/consolidate when a given entity rolls up under one or more alternate hierarchies. It is also important for determining the parent currency when FDMEE initializes the translation of an entity. If the top of the house entity, for example **TotalGeography**, is to be calculated, simply specify it in both the parent and entity fields.

There is a known bug in 11.1.2.4.000 where this field does not display when the check rule group is first selected. To display this field, select another target application and then re-select the HFM target application for which the Check Entity needs to be created.

When determining which parent entities to consolidate through the check entity group, be mindful of the potential for repetitive consolidations and/or impact to parent entity calculation status as a result of loads from another location. For example, consider the entity hierarchy in Figure 3-13A. If location A loads to entity E01_0 while location B loads to entity E01_101_1000 then including entity E01 in the Check Entity group for either location A or location B would mean that Entity E01 would be consolidated multiple times. This may be acceptable but it should be evaluated to determine if it is necessary. This is especially important to consider when consolidation times are lengthy.

Check Entity for Check Reports

As noted above, Check Entity can also be used to control which entities are evaluated against the Check Rules when the Check report is executed. This option is useful for including or excluding a given entity from the Check Rule evaluation.

Figure 3-14A: Check Entity Including Parent

The below image shows the check entity definition modified to also include the parent entity on the report.

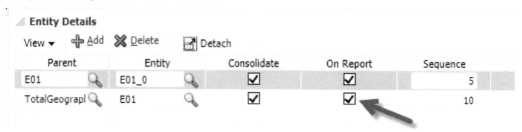

Figure 3-14B: Updated Check Report

The below image shows the check report with both the base and parent entities from the Check Entity Group.

Example Check Report

Location: ABC_Comma
Category: Actual
Period: 2014-12-01

Validation Group: Comma

Pass
E01_0

Key Metrics

Account	Value
300000 - Net Income	35,000.00

Validations

	Rule Name	Rule Definition	Value
Ok	Balanced Balance Sheet	Balance Sheet Must Balance	0.00

Pass
E01

Key Metrics

Account	Value
300000 - Net Income	35,000.00

Validations

	Rule Name	Rule Definition	Value
Ok	Balanced Balance Sheet	Balance Sheet Must Balance	0.00

Determining which entities should be included for display on the check report will vary for each application. It will be driven largely by which users have access to which data in the target application. You would not want to display a parent entity on the check report when the users provisioned to the FDMEE location to which that check entity group is assigned do not have access to the parent in the target application.

Summary

In this chapter we explored critical metadata items including period and category mapping. We explained how global, application, and source period mapping is used throughout the application. We also highlighted the key – optional but powerful – metadata components of logic groups, check entity groups, and check entity rules. In reading this chapter you should have gained a better understanding of how these components can be used to address specific data requirements as well as streamline the data integration cycle and ensure data integrity.

In the coming chapter we will explore data load mapping. Mapping is one of the pillars of the application. I will highlight capabilities as well as discuss strategies for designing efficient, easy to maintain and, most importantly, accurate maps.

4
Data Load Mapping Explained

In this chapter, we will explore one of the most critical components of an FDMEE application – data load mapping or simply mapping. At the end of this chapter you will have gained a better understanding of the different mapping capabilities of the application as well as insight into the impact of your mapping design decisions. The goal of this chapter is to provide you with the knowledge necessary to design and build maps that are first and foremost accurate while providing a balance of performance and maintainability.

Defining Mapping

Similar to the discussion about source systems in chapter two, I believe that the understanding of mapping is taken for granted. In light of that, let's take a very brief moment to define what mapping means as it relates to FDMEE.

Transformation (the T in ETL (Extract, Transform, Load)) is the technical term for mapping – the process of transforming a source system chart field element to a target system dimensional member. Even more simply, transformation is the act of changing. So mapping is transforming/changing a source system item into a target system item. For example, the natural account for cash in the ERP maybe 10010 while in HFM the account dimension has a member named *Cash*. A map can be used to transform the source system natural account 10010 to the HFM Cash account.

FDMEE is not a true ETL tool; however, it has many ETL-like functions and mapping is one of the key functions of the application.

Parent Mapping

Mapping is defined at an individual location and even at the data load rule level. This allows each location to have a unique set of transformations even when sharing a single source system. This is useful when the business units that share a source system do not use the chart of accounts in the same manner or when a source system has multiple charts of accounts.

However, multiple business units are often encompassed in a single source system and each share a common chart of accounts. Let's assume that each business unit is created as a unique location in FDMEE for the reasons outlined in Chapter 2. While FDMEE allows each of these locations to have an individual set of maps, it is far more efficient to use a parent map location in FDMEE.

A parent map location is a location which is used to define and store the mapping definitions that can be used by all locations that share that source system and chart of accounts. To be clear, the parent location is not a hierarchical relationship, it is simply the location from which the mapping definitions are inherited when data is processing through a different location.

The key benefit of a parent mapping location is the elimination of duplicate map maintenance. The maps only need to be created once during the initial build of the integration regardless of the number of locations needed to support integrating the source system. Any additions, changes, or deletions to the maps in the future are automatically applied to all of the locations utilizing the parent map. And, just as importantly, by utilizing a parent map, data consistency and quality is assured since a single definition is shared across all of the locations.

The key risk to parent locations in a distributed mapping model (one in which each location owner also has the ability to modify maps) is that any update made to the mapping table will be affected across all of the locations that share the parent. This too can impact data quality and, as such, the usage of parent maps, training of end users and the use of security must all be considered when assigning a parent map location.

The leading practice that I employ when utilizing parent mapping is to create a location named *Source_*Mapping where Source denotes the source system for which the maps are being created. No data is ever processed through this location; it functions simply to house the maps.

Dimensions

An FDMEE dimension is used to build a relationship between the source system chart field (or fields) and the target application dimension. This concept should be familiar especially after the discussion in chapter two regarding import formats and target systems as well as chapter three where we discussed period and category mapping.

FDMEE has two classifications of dimensions – global and mappable. The global dimensions are those that are controlled by the point-of-view (i.e., Scenario, Year, Period) or by a system default or target application option (e.g., Value, View).

Every dimension associated with a registered target application that is not defined as global is considered a mappable dimension. Mappable dimensions are those fields for which a transformation needs to be defined.

FDMEE includes the following 23 mappable dimensions:

- Account
- Entity
- ICP

- Custom1 through Custom20 (also known as UD1-UD20

This does not mean that there are 23 active dimensions requiring mapping; it simply means that FDMEE can accommodate up to 23 target dimensions for which mapping can be created.

There is sometimes a point of confusion with mappable dimensions when integrating source data whose chart fields exactly match the target application's dimensionality. Even in these instances, a mapping definition is required. Each defined mappable dimension requires mapping rules that will transform the source system code into the target application's dimension members – even if that mapping rule is a simple pass through of the source system code. This pass through is often referred to as a star to star (* to *) map.

Mapping Process

The mapping process of FDMEE executes during two possible scenarios. It is a common misconception that mapping is applied during the validate workflow step; mapping is actually applied during the import workflow step.

In FDM Classic, performance intensive mappings would manifest themselves in the form of prolonged import times. In FDMEE, since the Import and Validate workflow steps are coupled, the average user may not realize that the mapping process is actually occurring as part of the import step. This order of operation is important to consider especially when designing mapping for large, frequently updated datasets. Since the data will need to be imported multiple times, the design of the maps and their impact to performance will become evident.

The second time that maps can be applied is during the validate workflow stage but only if the mapping tables are updated *after* data has already been imported for the point-of-view being processed. This reapplication of maps is automatic when the Validate workflow step is initialized.

Figure 4-1: Recalculate

The below image shows the recalculate icon in the POV bar indicating that maps have been changed since the data was imported. The new/changed maps will be automatically applied when the validate workflow step is re-executed.

Location **1000_Comma** Period **Dec-2014** Category **Actual** Rule **1000_Comma-Actual-GL** Source **File** Target **COMMA**

A key difference between FDM Classic and FDMEE is that FDM Classic forced the reapplication of maps to the dataset. FDMEE, in contrast, does not force the application of new maps unless the validate workflow step was unsuccessful. This means that a map can be changed and the user can execute the Export workflow step and not reapply the maps. This additional capability is powerful but also needs to be carefully considered especially for those organizations that previously utilized FDM Classic since the user needs to make a conscious decision to reapply the maps to an existing validated dataset.

Dimension Processing Order

When mapping is applied, the entire dataset is processed but each dimension is transformed individually and in sequence. Dimensions are processed in the following order unless specifically overridden in the sequence field of the target application registration:

- Account

- Entity

- ICP

- UD1 through UD20

Figure 4-2: Dimension Sequence

In the below image, the entity dimension is specified to process first. The remaining dimensions process in the above noted order after the entity dimension.

When a custom dimension sequence is specified then the dimensions for which a sequence order is defined are processed as per that order. Any dimensions not specifically sequenced are processed using the default order after the dimensions with a sequence have processed. Sequencing only applies to dimensions that have a corresponding Data Table Column Name.

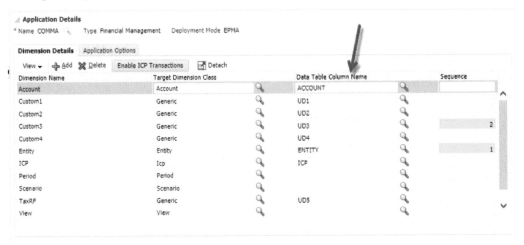

In simpler terms, account maps are applied to the data set to transform source system codes to target system account members. Next are the entity maps, then ICP, and so on until all mappable dimensions are processed. Once all mappable dimensions are processed, the Validate workflow step is executed to determine if all source system codes have been transformed.

Cross Dimensional Maps

FDMEE has the ability to map one dimension based on the source and/or mapped (target) value of another dimension. These are known as cross dimensional maps. The order in which dimensions are processed is especially important to consider when designing cross dimensional maps that are based on the mapped result of another dimension.

Let's explore a straightforward example. The import format specifies the source entity as the cost center chart field and the source account as the natural account field. The mapping requirement dictates that the target entity is *Corporate* for all records where the G/L cost centers are finance (those ending in 65), and the mapped account is interest expense (IntExp). Since the entity dimension is dependent on the account dimension's mapped result, it is imperative that the account dimension is processed before the entity dimension. This example is viable – when the default sequence is used for each of the dimensions registered for a target application – since the account dimension is processed before the entity dimension.

Figure 4-3: Cross Dimensional Map

The below image illustrates the above cross dimensional mapping example.

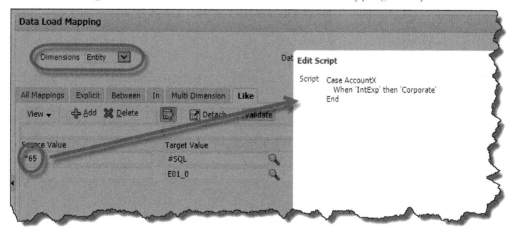

Conversely, a cross dimensional mapping requirement that dictates that the account be mapped, based on the mapped result of the entity dimension, cannot be accommodated without modifying the dimension sequence of the target application. This is because, by default, the entity dimension processes after the account dimension.

More technical information about creating cross dimensional maps will follow later in this chapter.

Lookup Dimensions

Each of the FDMEE dimensions is associated with a dimension class as defined by the target application. The dimension class controls certain behavior within the target application as well as within FDMEE. For example, the account dimension class enables the Change Sign indicator within the FDMEE data load mapping screen.

Lookup dimensions are a separate class of dimension which is not associated with the target application. Lookup dimensions can be used to aid in the mapping process without exporting the information contained in the dimension to the target application.

Lookup dimensions have been enhanced since their introduction in FDM Classic. In FDM Classic, when a dimension was flagged as a lookup dimension then the dimension was available in the mapping screen; however, you were not able to import it into the dimension from the workflow screen. This made lookup dimensions useful for scripting purposes but less so for cross dimensional mapping. With FDMEE, the restriction preventing importing data into a lookup dimension has been lifted. Now lookup dimensions can fully support cross dimensional mapping as well as scripting processes.

Figure 4-4: Lookup Dimensions

Lookup dimensions can be added to a target application registration by accessing the dimension details and clicking the Add button. Specify a dimension name. This is the text that will show on import formats, data load mapping and the data load workbench. Make sure the dimension class is LOOKUP. Select an FDM dimension to which the lookup dimension should be associated.

A good practice is to associate Lookup dimensions to an FDM data column in descending order starting at Custom20 (UD20) and working backward. This provides for future growth of the target application to eventually have additional custom dimensions become active. While this is not overly common, it has and does happen.

Mapping Types

Before we delve into the topic of designing and building maps it is important to understand the different mapping techniques (types) that are available within the application. Below, we explore each mapping type available to the user. A discussion of how these can be used in various combinations will follow in the Mapping Design section later in this chapter.

Explicit

An explicit map defines a one to one relationship between a source system code and a target system member. The below table provides some example Explicit maps.

Source Chart Field Item	Target System Member
G/L Account: 400010	HFM Account: **Revenue**
G/L Company Code: 1000	HFM Entity: **US**
G/L Cost Center: 10065	Planning Function: **Finance**

Explicit maps are often the easiest maps for a user to understand.

Between

A between map defines a continuous range of source system codes that map to a single target system member. The below table provides example Between maps.

Source Chart Field Item	Target System Member
G/L Account: 10000 through 10999	HFM Account: **Cash**
G/L Account: 40010 through 40099	HFM Entity: **Revenue**
G/L Cost Center: 10060 through 10069	Planning Function: **Finance**

The range specified in the between map is inclusive. This means that the upper and lower bounds of the mapping definition are mapped to the target system member specified. For example, in the sample mapping definition above for G/L account 10000 through 10099, both 10000 as well as 10999 are mapped to Cash as are 10001, 10002, 10003 and so on.

Between maps do **not** support wildcard characters in the source or target values. Additionally, the upper and lower bound members in the source definition must be of equivalent field lengths.

Figure 4-5A: Invalid Between Map Definition

The below image shows an invalid Between map. The use of wildcards is not supported.

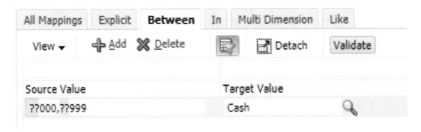

Figure 4-5B: Invalid Between Map Range

The below image shows an invalid between map. Notice that left hand side (yellow) of the source definition is four digits while the right hand side (green) is five digits.

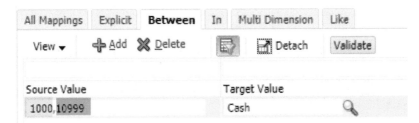

The source value of a between map is defined by specifying the upper and lower values that are separated by a comma (,).

In my experience, Between maps are used sparingly. One of the reasons for this is that in FDM Classic, Between maps would slide. This means that if there were Between mapping definitions that were overlapping, the latter mapping definition would be used by the application to transform the source value. This was completely opposite to the behavior in the other mapping types (Explicit, In Like) where the first matching definition was used to transform the source code. As such, many FDM customers shied away from heavy usage of Between maps. While the behavior in FDMEE is different, many FDMEE applications have been built using the FDM Classic application as a starting point for the upgraded application so the utilization of Between maps continues to be limited.

Between maps can be useful but in general Like maps can often accommodate most, if not all, Between mapping logic as well as offer additional opportunities for wildcarding. As a result, Like maps tend to be favored over Between maps.

In

An In map defines a non-continuous range of source system codes that map to a single target system member. The below table provides example In maps.

Source Chart Field Item	Target System Member
G/L Account: 10117, 10235, 10430	HFM Account: **ST_Investments**
G/L Account: 40050, 40055, 40060	HFM Entity: **IC_Revenue**

The source value field of an In map specifies each of the source system codes that should be mapped to a single target system member. The source system codes specified are separated by a comma (,) and unlike a Between map do not need to be of equivalent length.

Figure 4-6: In Map Example

The below image shows an example In map.

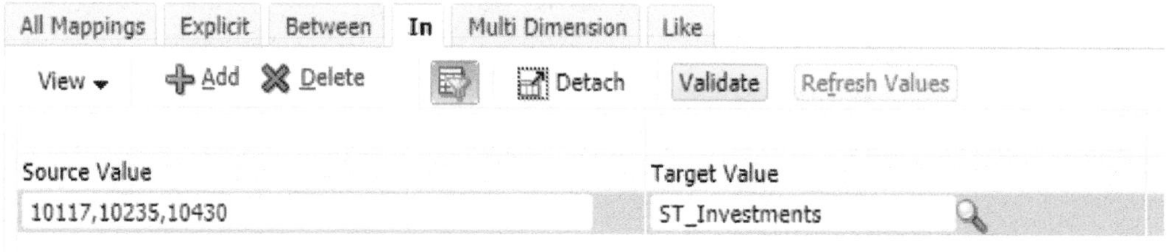

In map types are also less popular than Explicit and Like map types. This is largely attributed to the fact that In maps are less efficient than Explicit maps. FDMEE is optimized to process the Explicit map type very efficiently. While an In map can be useful if a scripting statement is necessary to derive the target system member, in general, a series of explicit maps is easier to create and performs better.

Like

Like maps, along with Explicit maps, are the most commonly used mapping types in FDMEE. Like maps are often referred to as wildcard maps since one or more characters in the source value do not need to be specified. The below table provides example Like maps.

Source Chart Field Item	Target System Member
G/L Account: 10*	HFM Account: **Cash**
G/L Cost Center: 1006?	Planning Function: **Finance**

Like maps are very powerful because a single Like map has the potential to eliminate a significant number of explicit maps. Further discussion outlining how Like maps can be used effectively in concert with overlapping Like map definitions as well as explicit maps will follow in the Map Type Processing Order Section.

Like maps support several wildcard types which are outlined below.

Single Character Wildcard (?)

The question mark is used as a single character wildcard. One or more question marks can be used in the source or target definition. The below table illustrates how a single character wildcard maps functions.

Map Source Value	Map Target Value	Source System Code	Mapped Result
1006?	Finance	10067	Finance
40050.??	IC_??	40050.10	IC_10
???30	IT	23030	IT

In the first example above, the mapping definition states that any source value that is five digits and begins with 1006, regardless of the last digit, maps to a target system member called Finance. This mapping definition eliminates up to 36 (10 numeric, 26 alpha) explicit maps. The second mapping definition employs concatenation along with a stripping technique. The last two digits of the source value are combined with the text IC_ to create the target/mapped result. This single mapping definition has the potential to eliminate 1260 (assuming standard alpha and numeric characters) permutations of explicit maps. Finally the last mapping definition states that any source value that is 5 digits and ends with 30 will map to the target system member IT. Following our previous two examples, this mapping definition can potentially eliminate 42,480 explicit maps.

Single character wildcards are most useful for source system codes that have a specific fixed length. If a source system code is variable length then multiple definitions may be needed to accommodate the varying length of the source system code. In this case, a Like map using a multiple character wildcard may be more useful.

Multiple Character Wildcard (*)

The multiple character wildcard is perhaps the most powerful and most frequently used mapping technique in FDMEE. The asterisk is used to specify a pattern where the value of one or more characters in the source value is not of consequence to the application of the mapping definition. The below table provides examples of Like maps using the asterisk.

Map Source Value	Map Target Value	Source System Code	Mapped Result
*65	Finance	13065	Finance
*	CC_*	14235	CC_14235
1000*	US	1000_10010	US
*	*	Germany	Germany

The asterisk allows the creation of very dynamic mapping definitions. In the first example above, all source system codes ending with 65 map to a target system code of Finance. In the second example, the source system value is prefixed with CC_ so the mapped result is the CC_*SourceSystemValue*. In the third example, any source system value that begins with 1000 maps to the target system code of US. The last example is a commonly used pass through (also known as star to star) map where the source system code is simply passed through as the target system member.

It should be noted that the map source value (definition) cannot contain multiple asterisks. This is an illegal definition and the application will simply not evaluate these mapping records. However, the use of single character wildcards in combination with the asterisks is supported and can be an effective mapping technique.

While multiple character wildcard maps can be very effective, one should be cautious when defining the map source value and take care to consider how an improperly scoped definition may be applied to records for which it is not intended. There is no steadfast rule to prevent this, it is simply a function of the source system chart of accounts and how the maps are designed.

Segment

Segment Like mapping is new functionality in FDMEE. Segment mapping is an effective way to parse concatenated source values. The below table provides examples of Like maps using the segment wildcard.

Map Source Value	Map Target Value	Source System Code	Mapped Result
<2>	*	1000_10065	10065
??<1>	*	DC900_1000	900
?<2>	Plant_*	1200_M100_23030	Plant_100

In the first example above, the second field from the source value is used as the target system code to which data is mapped. The second example parses the first two characters of the first segment and then passes the remaining characters of the segment as the target system code. The third example parses the first character of the second segment and then maps to a target system code of *Plant_* and the remaining characters of the second segment.

The segment wildcard only supports source system values that have been concatenated using an underscore (_) character. The segment wildcard can be combined with the single character (?) wildcard but cannot be used with the asterisks in the source value.

<BLANK>

The Blank wildcard, like the segment wildcard, is new to FDMEE. It was largely created for data write back to PeopleSoft; however, it can be leveraged for inbound data integrations as well. The blank wildcard will map any source system value that contains a single blank space to the target member specified in the mapping definition. The below table provides examples of Like maps using the <BLANK> wildcard. The apostrophe is used to denote the beginning and end of the source system value.

Map Source Value	Map Target Value	Source System Code	Mapped Result
<BLANK>	No_CC	' '	No_CC
<BLANK>	No_CC	''	
<BLANK>	[None]	'4000 '	[None]
*	<BLANK>	Prod180235	NULL

The first example maps any blank field to the target system code of No_CC. The second example has the same mapping definition, however the source system code does not contain a space and therefore the mapping definition is not applied. The third example maps any source system value with a blank to the target system code of [None]. The source system code contains a blank space after 4000 and therefore this mapping definition is applied. The fourth example illustrates how to use the <BLANK> as a target which is intended specifically for loading data to PeopleSoft. Regardless of the source system code, FDMEE will supply a null value to PeopleSoft.

From the examples above you can see that the <BLANK> mapping definition contains several nuances. First the wildcard must be specified in capital letters. Second, the source value for which the blank map is applied must contain a blank space and cannot be null. Finally, any source system value that contains a blank space will have the blank mapping definition applied.

The <BLANK> wildcard is an effective way to eliminate the need for import scripts that perform a similar action.

Multidimension

Multidimension maps are maps that use the **source** system value from one or more dimensions to determine the target system member to which the current dimension for the current record should be mapped. There are multiple ways to approach this mapping need including, but not limited to, import scripting, import formats that concatenate chart fields or multidimension maps. The below table provides examples of multidimension maps.

Map Source Value	Map Target Value	Source System Code	Mapped Result
[ACCOUNT like 23*] and [ICP = 100]	101	100	101
[Account = 87001] and [UD1 like *65]	E_Corporate	1400	E_Corporate

In the first example, above, the intercompany partner is mapped based on the source system account beginning with 23 and the source system ICP field being equal to 101. When this condition is met, the target system ICP code to which the data is mapped is 101. In the second example, the entity is mapped based on the source system account being equal to 87001 and the source system cost center ending in 65. When these conditions are met, the target system entity code to which the data is mapped is E_Corporate.

Figure 4-7A: Multidimension Mapping Example – ICP

The below image shows the mapping for example one from the table above. Note that this map is created in the ICP dimensional mapping. This map is useful since another Like map exists that simply passes through the source system ICP value. Without this map, the mapped result would be 100, not 101.

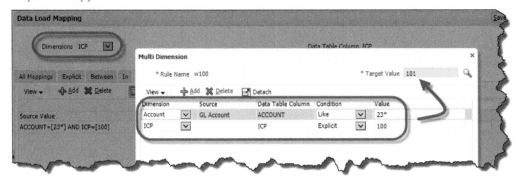

Figure 4-7B: Multidimension Mapping Example – Entity

The below image shows the mapping for example two from the table above. Note that this map is created in the Entity dimensional mapping even though the source entity is not referenced anywhere in the map. This map is useful since another Like map exists that simply passes through the source system entity value. Without this map, the mapped result would be E_SourceEntity, not E_Corporate. SourceEntity is value defined by the import format and in this example would be the company code.

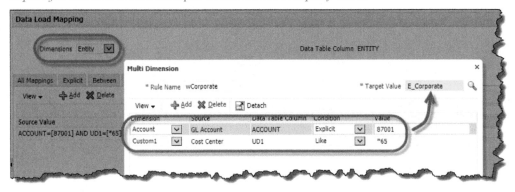

Multidimension maps are new to FDMEE in the web interface but are not new to the product in functionality. In FDM Classic, multidimension maps were possible through mapping scripts which used a function known as **varvalues**. The addition of multidimension maps to the mapping web interface has eliminated a portion of the scripting that was previously required for mapping based on one or more dimensions. This has made mapping easier to create, maintain and understand for the average end user. Multidimension maps are a powerful addition to the mapping options available in FDMEE.

The one limitation of multidimension maps is that they do not support using mapped or target system codes (across another dimension) to determine the target system code to which the current dimension should be mapped. For this function, mapping scripts are still required. More information about achieving this mapping result is detailed in the Scripting section later in this chapter.

Advanced Mapping Types

While the mapping types outlined above can be extremely powerful and effective, there are instances when additional mapping capabilities are needed to manage the transformation of source system chart fields into target system dimensionality. FDMEE includes two additional mapping techniques that further extend the transformation capabilities of the application. These advanced mapping types are available to extend the functionality of the Between, In and Like mapping types and are highlighted below.

Format Mask

The format mask mapping type is new to FDMEE. It was introduced in the 11.1.2.3.510 patch set. The format mask was specifically designed for integrations with the **Account Reconciliation Manager**. ARM has a single dimension (other than the POV) to which data is loaded called the profile. The profile often represents the combination of multiple chart fields. The format mask enables the target member to which data will be loaded to include multiple wildcards. This makes format mask maps extremely dynamic while providing the opportunity to eliminate a significant number of maps.

Format mask works by treating each segment of a concatenated source value independently. Each segment of the source value can be mapped using a combination of explicit as well as Like mapping capabilities. There are four legal format mask operators which are outlined below.

Operator	Function
Character	Text that should replace the segment value. The character operator acts like an explicit map where the text specified represents the actual value the mapped segment will contain. The character operator can be used in combination with any of the other segment operators.
?	A single character wildcard that functions in the same way as the ? wildcard of Like mapping. The ? operator can be used in combination with any of the other segment operators.
#	A single character wildcard that indicates that the character at a certain position should be ignored when a mapped result is derived. The # can be used in combination with any of the other segment operators.
*	A multi-character wildcard that functions identically to the multi-character wildcard of Like mapping. The * operator can be used in combination with any of the other segment operators; however, any characters or operators that occur after the * operator (within a given segment) are ignored.

The below table illustrates the usage of each operator within an individual segment.

Operator	Segment Map Definition	Source System Code	Mapped Result
Character	Sales	400010	Sales
Character and *	CC_*	10065	CC_10065
Character, # and ?	Plant_#??	M900	Plant_90

In the above examples, the source value of a segment (400010) is replaced by the text Sales. In the second example, the source value (10065) is passed through but prefixed with the text CC_. In the last example, the source value (M900) is prefixed with the text Plant_, the M character is dropped and the next two characters (90) are combined with the character map for a result of Plant_90. The power of the format mask becomes evident particularly in the last example where certain characters are simply truncated from the source value while other hard coded text values are appended. The true power of the format mask becomes even more pronounced when you explore its ability to map a multi-segment source value.

The below table provides examples of a complete format mask mapping across multiple segments of a single source value.

Map Source Value	Map Target Value	Source System Code	Mapped Result
400010-*	#FORMAT("Sales-*-Seg_##*-???", "-")	400010-Premium-5065-USD02453	Sales-Premium-Seg_65-USD
400010-*	#FORMAT("Sales-*-Seg_##*-???", "-")	400010-Discount-1835-USD90210	Sales-Discount-Seg_35-USD

In the above examples, the format mask is invoked from the Like maps when any source value begins with 400010-. The format mask indicates that the source field is delimited by the dash ("-") character. The mapping takes the first field (400010) and replaces it with the word Sales. The second field (Premium/Discount) is a simple pass through of the second segment of the source field. The third field (5065/1835) removes the first two characters of the third segment of the source value and adds a prefix of Seg_ to the remaining characters of the segment. The fourth segment (USD02453/USD90210) takes the first three characters of the fourth segment of the source value and ignores the rest of the field.

While format mask mapping was designed for ARM integration, it has utility beyond integrations with that application, especially when the target application has dimensionality that represents the concatenation of multiple dimensions in a single dimension. In general, Oracle Hyperion applications heavily leverage multidimensional analysis whether it is through OLAP engines like Essbase or ROLAP engines like HFM. The benefit of multidimensional applications is clearly the ability to dynamically pivot and analyse data across multiple independent but inter-related dimensions.

However, there are instances when the members of a dimension may need to represent the concatenation of multiple dimensions that would otherwise be independent. There are also instances when members are added to a dimension that otherwise represents a single chart field that are a concatenation of multiple chart fields for reporting purposes. These reporting members can often be populated through calculations but there may be instances when the target system simply does not, and should not, contain the granularity needed to support populating these members. Finally, when considering the ability to generate a data file for downstream systems that employ a more ERP-like chart of accounts (i.e., a concatenated chart field), the format mask mapping can be incredibly useful.

Let's consider an example where the target application is an Essbase ASO cube. This cube contains the following dimensions – year, period, scenario, account, entity, function and division. The primary function of this cube is to support income statement reporting by division. In addition, there is a need to support detailed sales reporting by SKU and sold to country. The product dimension does not include SKUs and there is no dimension that represents the market/sold to country. Without debating the merits of Essbase design, let's assume that the account dimension includes statistical members that represent sales and returns by SKU and by sold to country (e.g., Sales_1000586_ITA) to which FDMEE needs to load data. The format mask can be used to efficiently map and load data to these concatenated statistical account dimension members.

Another example would be a general ledger to which Hyperion Planning budget data needs to be written back. Again, let's assume that the general ledger has a single chart field that is delimited by a period character. FDMEE can combine the multiple dimensions of Hyperion Planning via the import format and then apply the format mask to strip prefixes, map or simply pass through certain values all through a series of format mask maps.

The utility of the format mask is unlimited when the target application contains a concatenated dimension. While its use outside of ARM integrations is still relatively limited, the above examples serve to provide additional use cases that should be remembered when new and challenging mapping requirements surface.

Scripting

The final mapping capability that this chapter discusses is scripting. This is not to be confused with application scripting (Import, Event and Custom scripts) which is detailed in the next chapter. Scripting, as it relates to mapping, is an out of the box function of the application that allows for more complex mapping. Map scripting provides mapping capabilities that are otherwise not supported to be leveraged to build powerful and efficient maps.

Language Options

There are two supported languages for FDMEE mapping scripts – Jython and SQL. When a Jython mapping script is invoked it performs a row by row update of the data set. A SQL mapping script, on the other hand, performs a bulk update of the entire data set for which the mapping definition applies. As a result, SQL mapping scripts are significantly more efficient, especially for large data sets, and should be used whenever possible. As such, this chapter will focus solely on SQL mapping scripts. Additional information about Jython mapping scripts can be found in the Oracle supplied Administrator's Guide.

One of the primary uses for a mapping script is to create a cross dimensional map. As noted previously, a cross dimensional map is one in which the mapped member for a given dimension is based on the source or target (mapped) member of one or more dimensions within the record. While a multi dimension map can accommodate mapping based on the source value of another dimension, when needing to interrogate the target member of another dimension – a mapping script is required.

Figure 4-8A: Activate Cross Dimensional Map

To create a cross dimensional SQL map, simply enter #SQL (all upper case) as the target. This will activate the script field. Click the pencil to open the editor and specify the mapping script.

Figure 4-8B: Cross Dimensional Map Script

The below image shows an example cross dimensional SQL script map. In this example, the entity is mapped to Corporate when the mapped account is IntExp. In other words, when interest expense is incurred, the entity under which it should be reported is Corporate.

A SQL mapping script is essentially a SQL UPDATE statement where the SQL that is executed is dynamically generated based on the source mapping value as well as the script text entered. Let's explore this for a moment by translating the script in Figure 4-8 into the SQL that the application executes. The template of the SQL that is executed is below:

```
UPDATE TDATASEG_T
SET ENTITYX =
CASE ACCOUNTX
      WHEN 'IntExp' then 'Corporate'
END
WHERE ENTITY LIKE '%65'
AND (ENTITYX IS NULL or ENTITYX = '')
```

The first two lines of the SQL are auto generated by the application. The case statement is exactly copied from the script editor window which is shown in Figure 4-8B. The first portion of the where clause is based on the mapping definition which is highlighted in yellow in Figure 4-8A. The last line of the where clause – AND (ENTITYX IS NULL or ENTITYX = '') – is also generated by the application but is critical. This portion ensures that the SQL update only applies to rows in the dataset where the mapped column (ENTITYX) does not contain a value. In layman's terms, the mapping script will only affect rows where the entity is not yet mapped. While there are other criteria that the application generates, these are the critical elements that help one understand how the update functions and how its scope is limited.

It should be noted that, when defining a SQL mapping script, one should employ good SQL coding practices. For example, Oracle databases are generally case sensitive meaning that a string comparison of *IntExp* and *INTEXP* will yield a result that says these strings are not equal to one another. To avoid case sensitivity problems, the use of simple functions like UPPER can be used.

Figure 4-9: SQL Mapping Script – Case Insensitive

The below image shows a modified SQL mapping script that maps the application of the map case insensitive through the use of the UPPER function.

Mapping scripts also have the ability to impact multiple columns on the TDATASEG_T table. Relative to FDM Classic, this is a significant new feature of FDMEE. To impact another column on the table, simply add it to the script in the form of another row.

Figure 4-10: SQL Mapping Script – Impact Multiple Columns

The below image shows a SQL mapping script which impacts multiple columns.

Mapping Rule Names

Mapping rule names are required for all non-Explicit maps. The primary function of the mapping rule name is to control the order in which the mapping rule is processed. In turn, the mapping rule can be used as a method to describe the purpose of the map.

The industry standard for mapping rule names has evolved into prefix of "w" and then a description of the mapping rule. This came to be for several reasons. First as described in the Foreword, the product from which FDMEE was born was originally named Upstream Weblink. The use of the w as a prefix was, in some small part, branding. The second, and more important, reason for the w prefix is that mapping rules are processed in alphanumeric order based on the mapping rule name. A mapping rule with a prefix of w ensured that any exceptions to mapping rule could be accommodated by simply creating another mapping rule with a prefix that would be processed (e.g., a, b, c or d) before the default w prefixed mapping rule.

Figure 4-11A: Mapping Rule Name

The below image shows two mapping rules where the source value definitions could overlap. This situation is accounted for by naming the mapping rules appropriately. The default mapping rule (w10) applies for any source account that begins with 10. The exception mapping rule (a104xx) applies for any account that begins with 104 and is five digits in length.

Figure 4-11B: Mapping Rule Name Processing Order

The below image shows in the process log that the exception map (a104xx) was applied before the default (w10) mapping rule.

```
2015-10-08 11:01:23,367 INFO  [AIF]: Data Rows Updated by Location Mapping 'a104xx' (LIKE): 0
2015-10-08 11:01:23,367 DEBUG [AIF]:
            UPDATE TDATASEG_T
            SET ACCOUNTX = 'Cash'
            ,ACCOUNTR = 481
            ,ACCOUNTF = 3

            WHERE LOADID = 11081
            AND PARTITIONKEY = 13
            AND CATKEY = 3
            AND (ACCOUNTX IS NULL OR ACCOUNTX = '')

        AND (ACCOUNT LIKE '10%')
            AND PERIODKEY = '2014-12-01'
2015-10-08 11:01:23,368 INFO  [AIF]: Data Rows Updated by Location Mapping 'w10' (LIKE): 0
2015-10-08 11:01:23,368 INFO  [AIF]:
```

While mapping rules are applied in alphanumeric order, it is important to understand that casing is part of how an alphanumeric rule name is evaluated. For example, a rule name of B104 would be evaluated before the rule name a104.

Figure 4-12: Rule Name Casing

The below image shows how casing controls the order of execution of mapping rules.

```
2015-10-08 11:17:38,466 INFO  [AIF]: Data Rows Updated by Location Mapping 'B1045x' (LIKE): 0
2015-10-08 11:17:38,467 DEBUG [AIF]:
            UPDATE TDATASEG_T
            SET ACCOUNTX = 'ST_Investments'
            ,ACCOUNTR = 482
            ,ACCOUNTF = 3

            WHERE LOADID = 11102
            AND PARTITIONKEY = 13
            AND CATKEY = 3
            AND (ACCOUNTX IS NULL OR ACCOUNTX = '')

        AND (ACCOUNT LIKE '104__')
            AND PERIODKEY = '2014-12-01'
2015-10-08 11:17:38,468 INFO  [AIF]: Data Rows Updated by Location Mapping 'a104xx' (LIKE): 0
2015-10-08 11:17:38,469 DEBUG [AIF]:
            UPDATE TDATASEG_T
            SET ACCOUNTX = 'Cash'
            ,ACCOUNTR = 481
            ,ACCOUNTF = 3

            WHERE LOADID = 11102
            AND PARTITIONKEY = 13
            AND CATKEY = 3
            AND (ACCOUNTX IS NULL OR ACCOUNTX = '')

        AND (ACCOUNT LIKE '10%')
            AND PERIODKEY = '2014-12-01'
2015-10-08 11:17:38,471 INFO  [AIF]: Data Rows Updated by Location Mapping 'w10' (LIKE): 0
```

Given the importance of the mapping rule name and how it is used to control the order in which maps are applied (and thereby data quality), it is good practice to establish a mapping rule name standard and adhere to it. Personally, I prefer camel casing – the reasons for which will become more clear after reading Chapter 5 – where the first character of the mapping rule name is lower case and then the first character of each word (if applicable) is capitalized. For example, **aCash** or **wIntIncExp**.

I also prefer for the mapping rule name to align to the source definition. I use this standard because if mapping needs to be changed to a different target member and the mapping rule name were associated with the target then the mapping rule name would need to be updated or there would be a disconnect between the rule name and the target member to which data is loaded. While this would not impact upon how the map performs the transformation, it could be confusing to users.

Finally, a mapping rule should not include any spaces, wildcards or SQL operator characters. The below table provides examples for mapping rule names based on the source mapping definition.

Map Type	Source Value	Map Rule Name
Between	10000,10399	w10000-10399
Like	10*	w10x
Like	104??	a104xx
Like	*65	wx65

In the first example, the Between map for accounts 10000 through 10399 is created with a default map rule naming convention. The comma is replaced by a dash. In the second rule, the Like map for accounts beginning with 10 is created with a default map rule naming convention. The asterisk is replaced by an x. In the third rule, the Like map for accounts that begins with 104 and which is five digits is created with an exception mapping rule name convention (**a** prefix) that dictates that it will process before the default (w10x) map rule. The question marks are each replaced by an x. In the final rule, the Like map for cost centers that end in 65 is created with a default mapping rule convention.

Lastly, multiple default (w) mapping definitions can exist within a given dimension and mapping type. For example, if all accounts that begin with 10 map to Cash and all accounts that begin with 15 map to Fixed Assets, then having mapping rules names of w10x and w15x is expected. Exceptions to the default naming convention should be utilized only when there are overlapping definitions within the same dimension and mapping type. For example, let's consider the below account mapping requirements:

- Accounts that begin with 10 map to Cash

- Accounts that begin with 104 map to ST_Investments

- Accounts between 104100 and 104199 map to Cash_Lock_Box

- Accounts that begin with 15 map to Fixed_Assets

These mapping requirements could be addressed using the below mapping rule names:

Map Type	Source Value	Map Rule Name	Target
Between	104100,104199	w104100-104199	Cash_Lock_Box
Like	104???	a104xxx	ST_Investments
Like	10*	w10x	Cash
Like	15*	w15x	Fixed_Assets

Mapping Type Processing Order

The mapping types that have been discussed throughout this chapter are powerful and can be used to accommodate a variety of mapping requirements. In addition to understanding the different mapping types available, it is important to understand the order in which the mapping type is processed. The processing order for map types is:

- Explicit
- Between
- In
- Multidimension
- Like

Explicit maps are processed first. When a source value matches the mapping definition in the Explicit map, the source value is transformed as per the mapping definition and the next record is processed. If no Explicit maps are found that apply to the source value, FDMEE then processes the Between maps. The same process applies for each of the mapping types until either all source values have been transformed or the entire data set has been evaluated.

If all values have been successfully transformed then the next workflow steps can be initiated. In the event of HFM-related integrations, this is (if enabled) the intersection validation. In all other cases, the Export workflow step follows. If each source value in the data set is not transformed then the Validate workflow fails and the unmapped items are displayed to the end user.

We will discuss more about how the processing order of the map types is important to consider when designing maps in the design section later in this chapter.

DLR Specific Mapping Rules

Data Load Rule specific mapping rules are a new feature introduced in FDMEE. DLR specific mapping rules allow for identical source value mapping definitions to map to different target dimension members depending on the data load rule being executed.

This functionality is useful when operating with multiple scenarios within a target system that have different granularlity. For example, consider an environment where the only Oracle Hyperion system is HFM. Actual trial balance data is loaded at a detailed account level from the general ledger into the Actual scenario. Notwithstanding the obvious debate about approach, assume the HFM application is also used to generate a quarterly forecast at a summarized account level. To support this activity, general ledger data is loaded to representative forecast accounts in each of the Forecast scenarios. This is a prime example of when DLR specific mapping rules can be useful.

Figure 4-13: DLR Specific Mapping Rules

In the below image, there are two mapping rules that have an identical source value (4*). The second mapping rule is applied specifically to the DLR used to load the Actual scenario and simply passes through the source system code. The other DLR maps all source system accounts that begin with 4 to the forecast member Rev_Input.

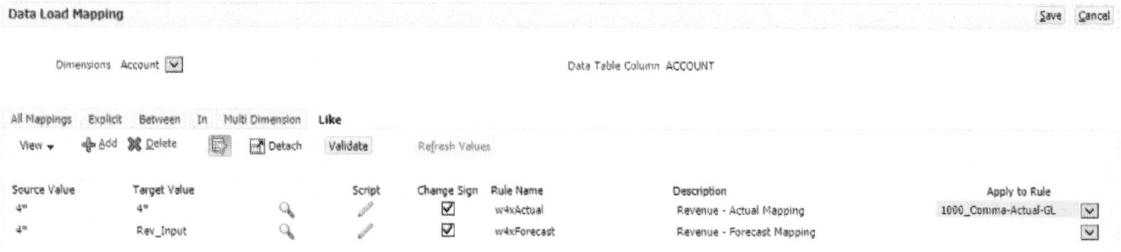

[Here is the above information as text]

Source Value	Target Value	Script	Change Sign	Rule Name	Description	Apply to Rule
4*	Rev_Input	✏	☑	W4xForecast	Revenue – Forecast Mapping	
4*	4*	✏	☑	W4xActual	Revenue – Actual Mapping	1000_Comma-Actual-GL

Data load rule specific mapping rules are optional. The DLR to which a mapping applies does not need to be assigned. When left unassigned, the mapping will apply to all data load rules. There are a couple of limitations to consider when generating mapping rules that are specific to a given data load rule.

First, DLR specific mapping rules can only be specified for a single data load rule. This impacts on how mapping rules need to be designed. When considering the example in Figure 4-13, it would have been acceptable to create five (four quarterly forecasts, one actual) mapping records; however, this is unnecessary, and inefficient when initially defining maps, and also creates a risk that there will be significant future maintenance in the event that quarterly forecasts become monthly or simply that mappings need to be changed. Instead one should create a default mapping rule that applies across the largest number of data load rules and manage the exceptions to the default with data load rule specific mapping rules. In the aforementioned example, since there are more forecast scenarios and data load rules, the exception mapping that is data load rule specific should be created for the actual data load rule.

The other limitation of data load rule specific mapping rules is that the mapping rule cannot be applied to any DLR in a location that has been assigned a parent mapping location.

Figure 4-14: Location with Parent Mapping Assigned

Notice in the below image that a parent location (1000_Comma) has been assigned. The Apply to Rule field that allows the data load rule to which the mapping should be specific is absent since this functionality does not apply to locations which have been applied a parent mapping.

Source Value	Target Value	Script	Change Sign	Rule Name	Description
4*	Rev_Input	✎	☑	W4xForecast	Revenue – Forecast Mapping
4*	4*	✎	☑	W4xActual	Revenue – Actual Mapping

This limitation may be lifted in future releases as Oracle evaluates enhancement requests submitted by partners and customers. Currently, there is no workaround other than to forgo the use of parent mapping locations. The decision as to whether this is a viable option needs to be evaluated on a case by case basis and there is no leading practice defined.

Mapping Design – The Science and The Art

Designing mapping is one of the most underappreciated activities performed in FDMEE. The primary and most important goal of mapping is to ensure data quality. Properly defined maps are critical to this goal. The secondary goals are a balance of performance and usability/maintainability. The balance of these three goals provides a system that allows a user to quickly and easily load data to a target application with confidence that the data loaded is accurate and reliable.

The Science

The science of defining maps is relatively straightforward. Determining the relationship between source system chart fields and target system dimensionality is the foundation of creating a map. Once those relationships are understood, then the transformation that needs to be applied can be defined.

In a simple example, the company code segment defines the entity dimension, the general ledger account segment defines the target system account dimension, the affiliate code segment defines the intercompany partner dimension, and the cost center segment defines the target system function dimension. In this simple example, now the maps that need to be applied to transform the source system segment codes to the target system dimensional members can be defined. Once the relationships are understood, a simple From-To table can be defined that maps the source system chart field to the target system dimension.

To better prepare for the activity of mapping, it is helpful to create a matrix to define the relationship between the source system chart fields and target system dimensionality. The below matrix is an example illustrating the simple example above.

	Target System			
Source	Entity	Account	ICP	Function (Custom1)
Company Code	X			
G/L Account		X		
Affiliate Code			X	
Department				X

This matrix helps to ensure that, as maps are being defined, each of the source system chart fields are being considered. This helps to avoid the potential for significant rework since taking the time to analyse the relationships needed to determine appropriate mapping helps to uncover complexities in the source system data. This is especially important when examining more complex relationships between source system chart fields and target system dimensionality.

In a more complex example, the company code segment defines the entity dimension and the general ledger account segment defines the target system account dimension. However, the general ledger account segment, in conjunction with the affiliate code segment, defines the intercompany partner dimension. The target system function dimension too requires the general ledger account segment in conjunction with the cost center segment.

The Art

Simple source system to target system mapping relationships offer an opportunity to apply some art to the mapping design process to find the right balance of Explicit, Between and Like maps; however, multiple segment mapping relationships generally require much more thoughtful consideration. Determining how to use each of the mapping types available will impact how efficiently the mapping will process – as well as how easy it is for the end user to understand and maintain it.

Performance

Without applying any database tuning, the more non-Explicit maps that the application includes, the longer the mapping will take to apply. Each Between, In, Multidimension and Like mapping record results in a SQL statement being executed – even if no source dimension values are impacted by the mapping record. While the timing of each SQL execution will vary by environment and be influenced by such factors as database type, database server physical location relative to the FDMEE application server, and database hard disk performance, the result is still the same – more maps result in longer mapping execution times. Any unnecessary mapping definitions should be avoided. Existing mapping tables should be periodically evaluated to purge superfluous mapping records.

Figure 4-15: Map Performance

In the below image, the performance time of each map can be determined by investigating the start (yellow) and end (green) time of each map execution.

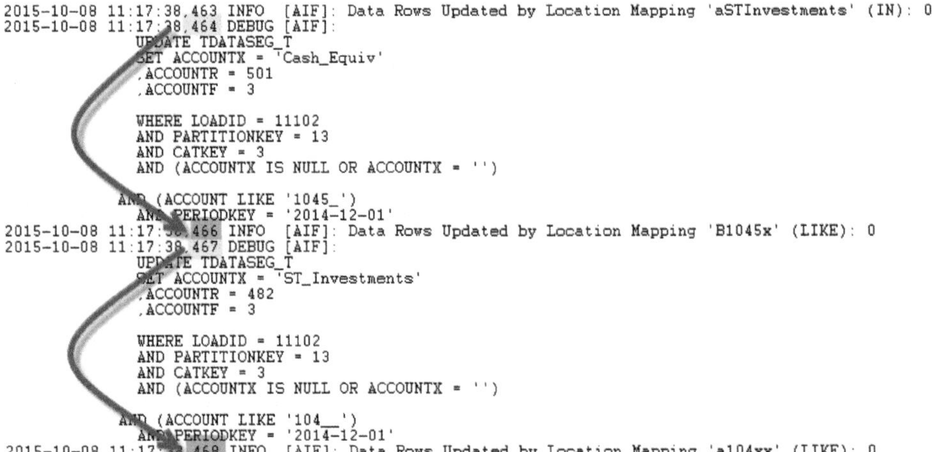

```
2015-10-08 11:17:38,463 INFO  [AIF]: Data Rows Updated by Location Mapping 'aSTInvestments' (IN): 0
2015-10-08 11:17:38,464 DEBUG [AIF]:
        UPDATE TDATASEG_T
        SET ACCOUNTX = 'Cash_Equiv'
        ,ACCOUNTR = 501
        ,ACCOUNTF = 3

        WHERE LOADID = 11102
        AND PARTITIONKEY = 13
        AND CATKEY = 3
        AND (ACCOUNTX IS NULL OR ACCOUNTX = '')

        AND (ACCOUNT LIKE '1045_')
        AND PERIODKEY = '2014-12-01'
2015-10-08 11:17:38,466 INFO  [AIF]: Data Rows Updated by Location Mapping 'B1045x' (LIKE): 0
2015-10-08 11:17:38,467 DEBUG [AIF]:
        UPDATE TDATASEG_T
        SET ACCOUNTX = 'ST_Investments'
        ,ACCOUNTR = 482
        ,ACCOUNTF = 3

        WHERE LOADID = 11102
        AND PARTITIONKEY = 13
        AND CATKEY = 3
        AND (ACCOUNTX IS NULL OR ACCOUNTX = '')

        AND (ACCOUNT LIKE '104__')
        AND PERIODKEY = '2014-12-01'
2015-10-08 11:17:38,468 INFO  [AIF]: Data Rows Updated by Location Mapping 'a104xx' (LIKE): 0
```

To account for the performance impact of non-Explicit maps, the mapping definitions that are created should be defined as broadly as possible to capture as many of the source system values for which the mapping definition would apply. For example, the source system general ledger account range 10000-10999 defines the target system account Cash. However, the range of 10200-10275 maps to ST_Investments. Three Between maps could be created to address this requirement: 10000-10199, 10200-10275, 10276-10999. But, a combination of Between and Like maps can be used to reduce the mapping records to two… a Between for 10200-10275 and a Like for 10*. Since Between maps process before Like maps, the exception to the 10* rule would be applied before the default map. While a reduction of just one mapping record may not be significant, when evaluating the reduction in terms of percentage, a 33% reduction is indeed significant.

A careful examination of the mapping requirements will usually uncover a series of ranges or patterns that can be used to create a single mapping record that replaces a much larger volume of mapping records. This becomes even more pronounced when multiple chart fields are necessary to map to the target system dimension.

Usability and Maintainability

The average end user of FDMEE is often most comfortable with simple Explicit maps. They are easy to understand and easy to create. However, Explicit maps are a constant point of maintenance. Each time a new element is added to a given chart field, the mapping table needs to be updated. This point of maintenance becomes especially burdensome when multiple source system segments need to be evaluated to determine the target system member for a single dimension. For example, in the event that general ledger account and affiliate code are used to define the intercompany partner, any time there is a new account or affiliate code, the explicit mapping table would need to be updated. The effect of this is multiplicative and can result in a large volume of Explicit maps and maintenance.

By leveraging the mapping capabilities of FDMEE, the maintenance required can be decreased significantly (or eliminated) while requiring just simple education of the end user. Returning to the previous example for intercompany mapping, the requirement to evaluate the source system general ledger account and affiliate code is needed because the data in the general ledger has affiliate codes assigned to third party transactions. This is a data quality problem at the source. Third party transactions should not have an affiliate code as this represents the intercompany trading partner. Due to this data quality issue at the source, FDMEE needs to evaluate both fields to map the intercompany partner accurately.

There are multiple ways to address the above requirement. The easiest example is to combine the general ledger account and affiliate code in the import format. The intercompany mapping table would then be created with all Explicit maps that transform the source intercompany partner (as defined by the import format) to the proper target intercompany partner. While this approach would work technically, it is not an approach I would advocate due to the constant maintenance that would be required.

Another approach would leverage the same import format but instead have a mapping table that combines Explicit maps for intercompany records and a default Like map that maps everything else to the third party dimension member code - [ICP None] when integrating to HFM. This approach would perform well, is easy for most end users to understand, and would only require maintenance when new affiliate codes or new account codes are added. The downside of this approach is that any ranges of general ledger accounts or affiliate codes cannot be leveraged due to the use of the Explicit mapping table. This is would be the most commonly deployed approach, particularly in an application where mapping maintenance is distributed to the end users.

Yet another approach would be to modify the import format to only use the affiliate code. The mapping table would be created with multidimensional maps for intercompany records and a default Like map that maps everything else to the third party dimension member code. This approach would not perform as well as the second option (since multidimension maps are not as efficient as Explicit maps), would be harder for most end users to understand and maintain, and would still likely require maintenance when new affiliate codes or new account codes are added. The benefit of this approach though is that the source data in FDMEE would be easier for the end user to understand – the affiliate code to intercompany partner relationship. Additionally, since multidimension maps can leverage Between, In, and Like mapping types, fewer mapping records would be needed. In the event that mapping is maintained centrally or by a power user, this approach may actually be preferred.

As you can see from the above example, there is not a single right answer for how to design mapping tables in FDMEE. For this relatively simple requirement, three possible solutions were outlined; however, there are others, namely scripting, that could also address this requirement. The mapping design will largely be a function of the requirements and the owner of the mapping table. My hope is that this chapter has educated you into the full capabilities of FDMEE and that you will explore how your existing maps can be enhanced and how your future mapping needs can be addressed in an elegant way.

Summary

In this chapter we explored the different mapping capabilities that are available in FDMEE. We outlined how independent dimensions are used in the mapping process. We highlighted the mapping types available including advanced features like format mask and mapping scripts. We shared how processing order across dimensions, mapping types and mapping rule names impacts which map takes precedence. Finally, we discussed how mapping design is a combination of science and art. We will continue to explore best practices for mapping design in Chapter 6 which explores best practices for integrating new data sources. Before we can delve into this topic, we have one final topic that needs to be discussed to complete the level setting required to have the discussion be meaningful.

In the next chapter, we will explore FDMEE scripting, including how the use of scripting can enhance the data integration process and how scripts can be used to address various data integration needs including data quality, automation and end user reporting.

5

FDMEE Scripts

In this chapter, we will begin to explore scripting in FDMEE. Scripting, to me, is one of the most exciting elements of an FDMEE application. Scripting is how the application comes to life, how a mundane process can be automated, how data quality can be further enhanced and how an application can do so much more than the simple workflow. Scripting is vast and can be very complex. I could dedicate an entire book to this topic and as such this chapter will only begin to scratch the surface. However, after reading this chapter, you will be empowered. You will have gained a better understanding of the scripting capabilities that exist in FDMEE. You will have learned how to configure a script editor and will be ready to begin your journal with scripting. And, hopefully, you will be as passionate about scripting as I am.

Scripting Language Options

Before we dive into the different scripting types that are available in FDMEE, let's take a moment to discuss the scripting language options that are available to generate FDMEE scripts. For core scripting – Event, Import and Custom – there are two language options available – Jython and Visual Basic Script.

Jython

Jython is a scripting language that combines JAVA and Python. It sounds far more nefarious to a nonprogrammer than it actually is. Jython is a scripting language, not a programming language. You do not need a computer science degree to understand and script in Jython. Jython does enforce certain programming best practices though. This can be difficult for those who have not previously adhered to these standards; however, it is easy to adapt and many of the scripting editors assist with this transition.

One of the reasons that Jython is a powerful scripting language is because it provides the ability to leverage JAVA classes. The next question might be: what is a class? The technical definition of a class is nothing but a blueprint or a template for creating different objects which defines its properties and behaviors[1]; I like to think of them, more practically, as prewritten code that can be used within the FDMEE scripts that you write.

---

[1] http://www.wideskills.com/Java-tutorial/Java-classes-and-objects

The use of classes allows for the efficient creation of scripts that leverage standardized coding. For example, the JAVA os class allows you to interact with the file system in a uniform way regardless of the actual operating system.

Another fundamental differentiator of Jython is the ability to be platform agnostic. This means that Jython scripts can be written to execute on a Windows deployment of FDMEE as well as a UNIX/Linux deployment. This cross platform capability is essential especially when considering Exalytics and its growth and expansion in the EPM platform.

Finally, Jython has advanced error handling and error trapping abilities through the use of try…except…finally statements. The value of this cannot be understated. Not only can a script that encounters an error exit cleanly, the error trapping can provide you with detailed information about the cause of the error as well as the line number on which the error occurred.

Visual Basic Script

Visual Basic Script – or VBScript – is a Microsoft developed programming language. VBScript is a variant of Visual Basic. Visual Basic variants includeVBScript and Visual Basic for Applications (VBA) and are familiar to many finance, accounting and information technology professionals. VBA is the language used to create Excel macros. VBScript is the scripting language of FDM Classic.

VBScript is Microsoft dependent. This means that in order to use VBScript as the scripting language for FDMEE, the application would need to be deployed on a server with a Windows operating system. Any deployment of FDMEE on an Exalytics server would preclude the use of VBScript as the scripting language since Exalytics leverages Linux or Solaris as its operating system.

The error handling abilities of VBScript are rudimentary at best. A simple On Error Resume Next is the error handling statement. To capture errors at a specific line of code, one would need to test the error level after each major statement. For example:

```
On Error Resume Next
If strLoc = "ABC" then

    Do Something

    lngErr = Err.Number

    If lngErr > 0 then

        'There was an error, exit
        Wscript.Quit

    End if

End if
```

This approach is unrealistic and, as such, error trapping and handling is virtually nonexistent in VBScript-based scripts.

Language Recommendation

VBScript may be enticing, especially for those accustomed to FDM Classic, as the language in which to develop FDMEE scripts due to the familiarity of the language. However, there are several reasons why I recommend against using VBScript as the scripting language for FDMEE.

First and foremost, as previously noted, VBScript is Microsoft dependent. While Oracle will continue to support Microsoft operating systems, they are working diligently to eliminate any *dependency* on Microsoft components. This is evident in the 11.1.2.4 release of HFM which was the first to support HFM being installed on an Exalytics server.

Oracle seems to have a strategic two-tier approach to its software delivery. The first is cloud based which eliminates the need for any locally owned and administered hardware. The Oracle cloud solutions are certainly not Microsoft operating system deployments. While it is irrelevant right now since FDMEE in the cloud does not support scripting, it likely will in the future and VBScript would not be supported. The second major initiative of Oracle is Exalytics. We've discussed Exalytics several times throughout this book. Exalytics leverages either the Linux or Solaris operating system and as such does not support VBScript.

You may not consider either of these deployment options relevant to your organization since your organization prefers on premise hardware and/or is explicitly a Microsoft shop. Even in this instance, I would strongly encourage the use of Jython over VBScript. While your organization may subscribe to the on premise Windows model today, that does not preclude a change in strategy in the future. With Jython-based scripts, the movement to Exalytics or the cloud (once scripts are supported) would have minimal disruption to the application whereas a move to either platform with VBScript-based scripts would require complete rewrites.

Another key reason I recommend Jython is again the strategic direction of Oracle and the elimination of any dependence on Microsoft. It is rare that Oracle removes support for application components – yes they sunset entire applications but generally not specific functionality – so I will not employ fear, uncertainty and doubt (FUD) to say that Oracle will eventually stop supporting VBScript. However, one could question if Oracle will continue to enrich the VB API as much as they would the Jython API. Jython clearly fits the strategic direction of Oracle so it is reasonable to assume continued growth and enhancement to the Jython API.

Finally, the robust error handling capabilities of Jython scripting should eliminate any lingering doubt as to the benefit of learning a new scripting language. The ability to cleanly capture the error as well as the offending line of code while allowing the script to exit cleanly is a significant differentiator relative to VBScript.

For the reasons noted above, Jython is the language I recommend for all FDMEE import, custom and event scripts. As such, this chapter will focus entirely on Jython. For more information about VBScript and the VB API for FDMEE, please refer to the Oracle provided Administrator's Guide.

Script Types

In FDMEE there are four script types – **Import**, **Event**, **Custom** and **Mapping**. Since we discussed mapping scripts in the previous chapter, this chapter will not include any additional information about mapping scripts. For more information about mapping scripts, please refer to the previous chapter.

Import Scripts

Import scripts are used to manipulate data during the import workflow process. An import script executes when assigned to the import format associated with the location and/or data load rule that is being processed.

Import Script Syntax

An import script has a defined format that must be followed in order for FDMEE to properly leverage the script.

```
def ScriptName(FieldParameter, RecordParameter):
    #Do Some Actions
    return Some_Value
```

Below is a line by line analysis of the above script.

Line 1 – `def FunctionName(FieldParameter, RecordParameter):`

Text	Explanation
`def`	Defines the function through the use of the keyword `def`
`FunctionName`	Defines the function name; this should match the name of the import script
`FieldParameter, RecordParameter`	Parameters that are passed to the function by the FDMEE application. `FieldParameter` represents the field value as defined by the import format for the dimension to which the import script is assigned. `RecordParameter` represents the entire record from the data file as parsed by the application. The first parameter is often designated as `strField` and the second parameter is often `strRecord`.
`:`	Colon represents the end of the declaration of the function. This is required.

Line 2 - `#Do Some Actions` – is a simply a comment as indicated by the hashtag (`#`). Any text following the hashtag will not be executed. This is the portion of the script that performs the actions needed. Notice the indentation of this line.

Line 3 – `return Some_Value`

Text	Explanation
`return`	Keyword that instructs the function to set the source dimension field to the text in the `Some_Value` variable. This keyword is required. Also notice the indentation of this line.
`Some_Value`	The value resulting from the script operation on line 2. This will be the actual text displayed in the source dimension field.

Import Script Considerations

An import script will execute multiple times during a single import process – once for each row in the data file being processed. In addition, if multiple dimensions within the import format are assigned an import script, then each script will execute multiple times.

Let's consider an example. We have a data file that is 10,000 data rows and has no headers or footers. The import format has import scripts assigned to the account and entity dimensions. When the import workflow step for the location to which the import format is assigned is executed, 20,000 script executions are performed.

Prior to the 11.1.2.3.530 release of FDMEE, large files that leveraged import scripts experienced significant performance degradation. While this has been addressed, there is still a performance cost to utilizing import scripts that should be considered when determining if and how an import script will be used.

If you are at all familiar with any of my previous writings, you likely have heard my discourse on import scripts. For those of you who are not familiar, I'll summarize; the use of import scripts is often unnecessary and I discourage their usage unless absolutely required. To further clarify my position, the usage of import scripts is not necessarily a bad practice; it is the usage of import scripts for performing mapping operations to which I am opposed.

Unfortunately I have often seen import scripts that are essentially performing transformation (i.e., mapping) within the script. Unequivocally, this is a terrible approach for the below reasons.

Figure 5-1: Import Script "Mapping"

The below is an example of an import script used to map the ICP dimension based on the source account.

```
aICPAccts = [26000,26100,26200,36000,36500]

if strAcct not in aICPAccts:
    return '[ICP None]'
elif strICP == '10':
    return 'CO_' + strICP
elif strICP == '5':
    return 'CO_05'
elif len(strICP) < 2:
    return '[ICP None]'
elif strICP == '99':
    return '[ICP None]'
else:
    return 'CO_' + strICP
```

The overarching reason that I discourage the use of import scripts is that there is limited visibility and auditability surrounding the actions that the script is performing. A feature that is new to FDMEE is that the application logs the import script syntax to the process log. However, this logging does not provide, on a row by row basis, the impact that the script has on the data. By contrast, a user is able to investigate the data in Workbench and see the mapping that way applied to each dimension.

Figure 5-2: Transformation Detail

The below image is the display of the mapping rules that were applied to a data record. This view is available for each record so the user can better understand the transformation applied. This detail is not available for transformations performed by import scripts.

Mapping Details   ×

Dimension Name	Type	Source	Target	Script	Rule Name	Description
TaxRF	Like	*	[None]	✎	wC5	
Custom4	Like	"	[None]	✎	wC4	
Custom3	Like	"	[None]	✎	wC3	
Custom2	Like	"	[None]	✎	wC2	
Custom1	Like	"	[None]	✎	wC1	
ICP	Like	"	"	✎	wICP	
Account	Explicit	400010	411300	✎	400010	411100
Entity	Like	"	E01_0	✎	wEntity	

The ability for any user to investigate and understand the mapping applied to each record is one of the core value-add features of FDMEE. This lack of transparency into the transformation applied to the data is a fundamental deficiency of import scripts.

Moreover, the ability to audit any transformations performed by an import script is impractical. Consider the average audit (internal or external) request – prove that the data from the source system was loaded to the reporting application accurately and completely. When leveraging the mapping capabilities of FDMEE, this is an easy request to accommodate by simply running a trial balance report (more information on reporting in Chapter 7) showing the source and target members for each record. By contrast, to prove the transformation performed by an import script you would need to provide the auditor with the original source data file, the process log for the last execution of the POV showing the import script executed for each dimension and then explain to the auditor the script logic and how it applied to a given record. As I said, this is highly impractical.

Lastly, import scripts do not offer any native version control. Certainly this can be achieved through a robust software development lifecycle process; however, it is subject to failure by a user or administrator who simply fails to follow the process. Mapping, by contrast, natively includes versioning. A user has the ability through the Restore Mapping (more in Chapter 7) feature to roll back to a previously defined map. In addition, the application will eventually include the ability to run a report to determine when a map was changed and by whom. These features are simply unavailable for import scripts.

Another reason to avoid the use of import scripts is that scripting is generally an administrative function. Scripting can be complex. The average end user of FDMEE will not be able to write import scripts and even if they are, an administrator would be remiss to grant security access for an end user to modify scripts since modify rights to FDMEE scripts through the user interface cannot be specified at the individual script level. Once a user is granted modify access to one script, they have modify access to *all* scripts. The security implications mean that scripts are generally maintained by the administrator. As a result, any changes required to the script would need to be performed by the administrator. This is problematic on several fronts.

First, it places an unnecessary burden on the administrator to maintain mapping for potentially multiple business units. Second, particularly in a global deployment, this is wholly inefficient. Consider this scenario. The administrator is based in North America and a business unit in Asia has an import script that needs to be updated for a new mapping requirement. The workflow process stops until the user in Asia submits a request to the administrator in North America. One to two business days could be lost simply as a result of the time zone differences between the two regions.

Finally, another limitation of import scripts is that they require data to be reimported in the event of a change to the logic in the import script. One of the differentiators of FDMEE relative to other ETL or data transformation solutions is that the application stores the data which affords a high level of auditability. A tangential benefit of this data storage is that anytime a change to the transformation logic is required, the data simply needs to be revalidated and then exported to the target system in order to effect the change. By contrast, when transformation logic is incorporated in an import script, the entire workflow needs to be executed.

At first blush this may not seem significant but when you consider a scenario where historical data needs to be restated to account for organizational or accounting realignments (i.e., not changes in the data but changes in where the data is reported) the need to reimport the data becomes daunting. In general, when restating history, the reported results at the total company level cannot change. If the usage of an import script results in data needing to be reimported, there is a risk that the data file used during the reimport could have data that differs from the originally processed data file and thereby impacts the target system's total results.

One may argue that this is a scenario that can be mitigated and I don't fully disagree. Yes, through a solid business process, prior period adjustments should not be booked in a source system. And yes, the Open Source Document (more in Chapter 7) functionality of FDMEE can restore the original data file. However, neither of these is a guarantee. A simple departure from the process could result in a prior period adjustment. The deletion of files from the FDMEE share as part of a quarter or annual purge (more in Chapter 11) could prevent the use of Open Source Document functionality. Conversely, if transformations are maintained entirely within the mapping, then the new transformations would be able to be applied to the historically imported data with a simple execution of the validate workflow step. This ensures that the data being loaded to the target application is exactly the same dataset previously loaded.

Leveraging Import Scripts

While the use of import scripts to perform transformation is not a leading practice, there certainly are instances where an import script is necessary and useful. Below are examples of data integration requirements for which an import script is valuable.

Leveraging the FDMEE Context

It is common for multiple business units to utilize the same source system. There are instances when the data extract does not explicitly include information that can be used to identify the entity for each of the data records. Instead, the entity is determined when the extract is run meaning that individual files are created for each entity/business unit. In FDMEE, this can be handled in a variety of ways.

One method to handle this situation is to create multiple versions of the import format and simply hard code the business unit name in the expression field for the entity dimension. A more elegant and dynamic solution would be to create an import script that utilizes the location name as the source entity. An example script is below.

```
#This script is used to set the source entity based on the
#location where the data is being imported

def GetEntityFromLocation(strField,strRecord):

  #Get the full location name
  strLoc = fdmContext["LOCNAME"]
```

```
#Split the location name apart and get the first field
strEntity = strLoc.split("_")[0]

return strEntity
```

The above example utilizes an import script to set the source entity equal to the FDMEE location name. This import script would be assigned to the entity dimension within the import format.

Figure 5-3A: Import Format Script

In the below image, the import script is GetEntityFromLocation and is assigned to the Entity dimension. The source entity will be determined by the result of the import script operation.

Source Column	Field Number	Expression	Add Expression	Target
GL Account	2		✎	Account
	1		✎	Amount
Cost Center	1		✎	Custom1
	1	[NONE]	✎	Custom2
	1	[NONE]	✎	Custom3
	1	[NONE]	✎	Custom4
	1	Script=GetEntityFromLocation.py	✎	Entity
	1	[ICP None]	✎	ICP
	1	[NONE]	✎	TaxRF

Figure 5-3B: Import Script Results

When assigned to the import format that is assigned to the location 1000_Comma, the source entity for all records when the data is imported will be 1000.

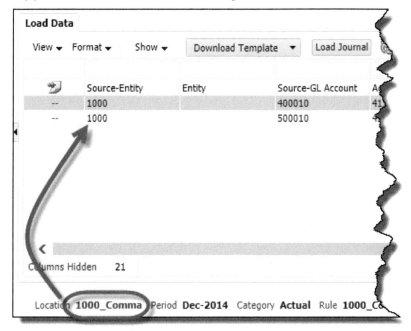

This example illustrates how the FDMEE context can be utilized in an import script to enable an import format to be used across different locations.

Chart Field Parsing

Another potential use for an import script is to parse a single chart field that represents multiple segments. This is common in smaller general ledger systems where the "account" represents multiple segments like legal entity, natural account, cost center or product.

Figure 5-4: Multisegment Chart Field

In the below image, the source system account represents multiple segments ranging from one to four segments.

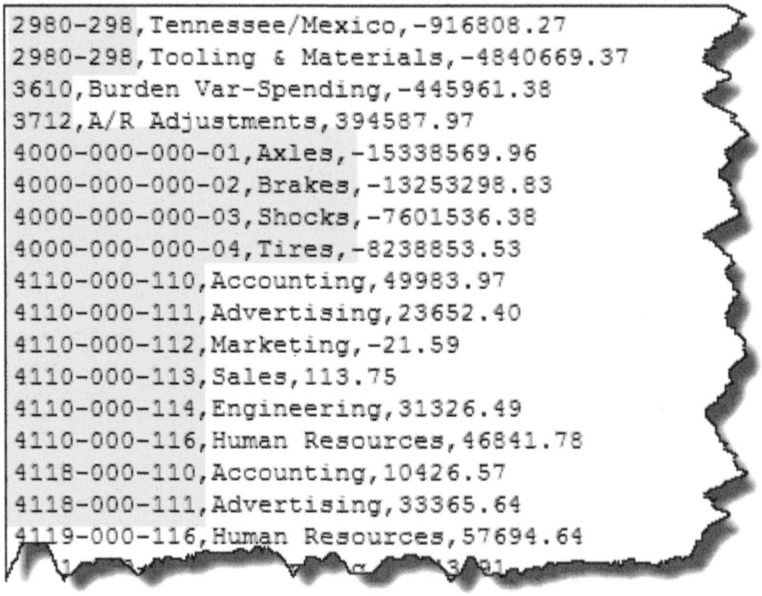

```
2980-298,Tennessee/Mexico,-916808.27
2980-298,Tooling & Materials,-4840669.37
3610,Burden Var-Spending,-445961.38
3712,A/R Adjustments,394587.97
4000-000-000-01,Axles,-15338569.96
4000-000-000-02,Brakes,-13253298.83
4000-000-000-03,Shocks,-7601536.38
4000-000-000-04,Tires,-8238853.53
4110-000-110,Accounting,49983.97
4110-000-111,Advertising,23652.40
4110-000-112,Marketing,-21.59
4110-000-113,Sales,113.75
4110-000-114,Engineering,31326.49
4110-000-116,Human Resources,46841.78
4118-000-110,Accounting,10426.57
4118-000-111,Advertising,33365.64
4119-000-116,Human Resources,57694.64
```

When encountering this type of concatenated chart field, especially in a delimited file, a simple import script can be leveraged to parse the required segment from the chart field. An example script is below:

```
#This script is used to parse the cost center - field 3 - from
#the source system account

def ParseCostCenter(strField,strRecord):

strResult = "000"
aField = strField.split("-")

#Make sure field has at least 3 segments
if len(aField) >= 2:
```

```
    strResult = aField[2]

    return strResult
```

This script will separate the field into multiple segments based on a dash (-) delimiter. If the number of segments is three or more then the third segment is returned, otherwise the default value of `000` is returned.

One may review the script and compare it to the description and believe that there is a mistake, particularly since the third field is returned using the following: `strResult = aField[2]`. Rest assured, this is correct. Jython lists – created in the above by `aField = strField.split("-")` – are zero based. The position of each element in a list is referenced based on counting from zero, not from one.

This simple import script is an effective way to parse information from a chart field that includes multiple segments.

Leveraging Temporary Variables

Temporary variables are a powerful component of FDMEE scripting. There are instances when a data file may not contain all the information in each data record to properly define the source values for each of the dimensions that require mapping. Instead, certain dimensional information may be contained in the header of the data file.

Figure 5-5: Header Containing Dimensional Information

In the below image, the information to define the source entity – 8500 – is contained in the header of the source system report to be processed through FDMEE.

FDMEE temporary variables are designed to accommodate this exact situation. A combination of two import scripts is needed. The first script retrieves the value from the header and populates the temporary variable. This script is often referred to as the **Get** script. This script should be assigned to the amount field of the import format since the scripts associated with the amount field execute for every line in the data file. By contrast, scripts assigned to dimensions are only executed when a valid numeric value is detected for the Amount field.

```
#Initialize the temporary variable
#This is required before the function declaration
strEntity = ""
```

```
#Get the entity from the header row that starts with "Period:"
def GetEntity(strField,strRecord):

  if strRecord[:8] == " Period:":

  #Define the temporary variable
  global strEntity

  #Populate the temporary variable
  strEntity = strRecord[53:57]

  return strField
```

The second script assigns the value from the temporary variable as the source value for the dimension to which the script is assigned in the import format. This script is often referred to as the **Put** script.

```
#This script is used to populate the entity from
#the temporary variable 'strEntity'

def PutEntity(strField,strRecord):
  return strEntity
```

Figure 5-6A: Import Format Using Get and Put Scripts

In the below image, the import format leverages the Get and Put import scripts to populate the entity dimension from the header of the data file.

Figure 5-6B: Import Script Results

The below image shows the result of the import format using the Get and Put import scripts to populate the source entity.

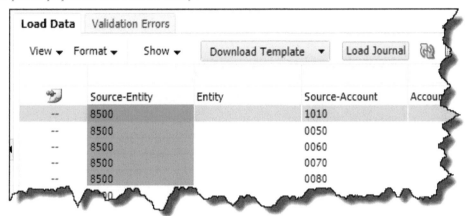

The use of temporary variables extends the ability of FDMEE to handle a variety of source system formats including those that do not contain dimensional data within each data record.

Event Scripts

FDMEE event scripts run when defined actions are executed in the application. Event scripts are akin to Excel workbook/worksheet macros that execute when a certain action occurs such as a workbook being opened. The actions/events around which scripting can be created are predefined and are currently associated with the different stages of the workflow process. Additional events cannot be added.

Event scripts can be extremely useful for extending the capabilities of the application. They can be leveraged with the open interface adaptor to populate data in the `AIF_OPEN_BALANCES` table, email users in the event of an error during the workflow process, or enrich the data integration process with custom solutions like Smart Replace and Essbase Enhanced Validation.

I'll briefly describe the Smart Replace and Essbase Enhanced validation solutions to help you understand how event scripts can be leveraged. This is not intended to be an outline of the scripting required to create these solutions but, instead, a sharing of the thought process and logic required to create event scripts that enhance your data integration process.

Smart Replace

Smart Replace is a custom solution I developed years ago – 2009 if memory serves. Smart Replace is not to be confused with Smart Merge. Smart Merge is a custom solution that is a scripting-based alternative to out of the box data protection functionality. Smart Merge is useful when a target application does not have a data type dimension or when data is being loaded to multiple members within the data type dimension.

Smart Replace is a solution that is used to address the issue of orphaned data. One of the key benefits of FDMEE is that a user can execute multiple data loads to a target application. As data is refreshed in the source system, data can be processed through FDMEE and loaded to the target Oracle Hyperion application. The one risk that arises from this process is orphaned data.

When loading data to HFM using the replace method, FDMEE will clear all account, ICP and custom dimension intersections for each entity contained in the data set. Orphaned data occurs when data that was previously loaded to one entity is completely reclassed in the source system or mapped in FDMEE – to another entity. The new data file that is processed by FDMEE no longer contains that entity. When the load to HFM is performed, the previously loaded entity is not cleared. This is by design since HFM will only clear data for the entities contained in the data file being loaded. This allows individual entities to load data without impacting the data for other entities in the application. While this description focused on HFM, a similar challenge could surface with Essbase integrations depending on how the data integration is designed.

Smart Replace can be used to eliminate the risk of orphaned data. The solution works by maintaining a list of entities to which data was loaded for a given point-of-view. The solution will then interrogate the current data set being loaded and determine if there are any entities that were previously loaded and no longer present in the data. In the event that orphaned entities are detected, the solution will take action to clear the data from the target application.

Smart Replace can be accomplished by utilizing the **AftLoad** event script.

Essbase Enhanced Validate

Essbase Enhanced Validate is a solution that I developed in conjunction with Oracle ACE, Mike Killeen. Essbase Enhanced Validate is a custom solution that extends the HFM Invalid Intersection report methodology to Essbase integrations. HFM metadata is used to create valid intersections to prevent input to nonsensical intersections. The HFM intersection validation report of FDMEE (discussed in Chapter 2) alerts a user when data has been mapped to an invalid intersection as defined by the HFM metadata.

Essbase does not have the concept of a valid intersection. Data can be loaded to literally any intersection. Since Essbase lacks the concept of a valid intersection there is no out of the box intersection validation report. One of referential integrity checks that the HFM intersection validation report performs is ensuring that the mapped member on the data record is a valid base or level zero member in the application to which data will be loaded. This prevents errors during the data load cycle since anything mapped to a non-existent member would not be able to be loaded.

For Essbase integrations, mapping to a member that does not exist in the outline has the potential to not only cause failures during the data load but also in the actions that occur before the actual data load (most notably the clearing of the Essbase intersections to be loaded). In the event that a calc script is created that clears data based on mapped members, the calc script will fail to execute since the calc is trying to perform an Essbase operation on a member that does not exist.

The Essbase Enhanced Validate feature is very simply a comparison of the mapped data set to metadata data in Essbase. In the event that any record contains a mapped member that is not found to be a level zero member in the Essbase outline, then the workflow process stops and a list of the unique invalid mapped members is displayed to the user.

Essbase Enhanced Validate can be accomplished by utilizing the **AftValidate** event script.

Available Event Scripts

There are a number of event scripts available in the application. The below summarizes each of the events available.

Event	Summary	Workflow Step
BefImport	This script executes before any actions of the import workflow step begin. This script can be used to populate the AIF_OPEN_INTERFACE table that is used by the Open Interface Adaptor. This script can also be used to dynamically change the import format associated with a location or data load rule.	Import
AftImport	This script executes after data has been imported to the TDATASEG_T staging table. This script can be used to perform manipulation of the data.	Import
BefProcLogicGrp	This script executes before the logic account is executed. Be aware, this script runs even if a logic account is not assigned to the location.	Import Validate (if executed standalone)
AftProcLogicGrp	This script executes after the logic account is executed. As with the BefProcLogicGrp event, this script will run even when a location is not assigned a Logic Account.	Import Validate (if executed standalone)
BefProcMap	This script executes before the mapping process. Any modification to the data to support mapping should be included in this script instead of the BefImport or	Import Validate (if executed standalone)

Event	Summary	Workflow Step
	[cont…] AftImport events to remove the dependency on reexecution of the import process. For example, to ensure the <BLANK> mapping wildcard works, any NULL fields can be changed to include a single space.	
AftProcMap	This script executes after the mapping process executes. There is no dependency on the result of the mapping process. For example, if there are unmapped members this script will still execute.	Import Validate (if executed standalone)
BefValidate	This script executes before the validate workflow process.	Validate
AftValidate	This script executes after the validate workflow process. Like the AftProcMap script, this script runs regardless of the result of the Validate workflow process.	Validate
BefCalculate	This script runs during an execution of just the validation workflow process. This is similar to the BefValidate event script but does not execute during a workflow process that was initiated by the Import workflow step. Use this script *with caution* since it will only execute when the Validate workflow process is explicitly executed as opposed to executed as part of the joint Import-Validate workflow process.	Validate (if executed standalone)
AftCalculate	This script runs after an execution of just the validation workflow process. As with the BefCalculate, use this script *with caution*.	Validate (if executed standalone)
BefExportToDat	This script executes before data is exported to a flat file for FDMEE to load to a target application. This script will not execute when loading to Essbase and leveraging the SQL load method.	Export
AftExportToDat	This script executes after FDMEE generates the flat file that will be loaded	Export

Event	Summary	Workflow Step
	[cont...] to the target application. This script will not execute when loading to Essbase and leveraging the SQL load method.	
BefLoad	This script executes before FDMEE loads data from its repository to a target application.	Export
AftLoad	This script executes after FDMEE completes a data load to a target application. This script will execute regardless of the result of the data load.	Export
BefConsolidate	This script executes before FDMEE runs a post load calculation in the target application. This script only executes if the data load completed successfully. For HFM integrations, this script only executes if the target application option Enable Consolidation is set to Yes.	Export
AftConsolidate	This script executes after FDMEE runs a post load calculate in the target application. This script only executes if the data load completed successfully. For HFM integrations, this script only executes if the target application option Enable Consolidation is set to Yes.	Export
BefCheck	This script executes before the Check workflow step. This script will execute regardless if a check rule group is assigned to a location. The script will run only if the data load process completes successfully.	Export Check
AftCheck	This script executes after the Check workflow step. This script will execute regardless if a check rule group is assigned to a location. The script will run only if the data load process completes successfully.	Export Check

Any of the event scripts associated with the Export and Check workflow steps are unavailable for Account Reconciliation Manager integrations.

Event Script Syntax

Event script syntax varies from import scripts only in the fact that the script does not need to be defined. An example BefImport event script is below that highlights the syntax.

BefImport Example

The below represents a sample BefImport event script to populate the AIF_OPEN_INTERFACE table for use by the open interface adaptor.

```
##############################################################
#FDMEE Event Script
#
#Created By: Tony Scalese
#
#Creation Date: 12 October 2015
#
#Purpose: This script is an example of how to populate the
# Open Interface table
#
##############################################################

#Import needed JAVA classes
import Java.text.SimpleDateFormat as SimpleDateFormat

strmsg = "Populating data using the below:\n"

try:

 params = None

 #Get POV Information
 strPOVPer = fdmContext["PERIODKEY"]
 strYear = SimpleDateFormat("yyyy").format(strPOVPer)
 lngMonth = SimpleDateFormat("MM").format(strPOVPer).upper()
 strMonth = SimpleDateFormat("MMM").format(strPOVPer)

 strmsg += "FDMEE POV Period: " + str(strPOVPer) + "\n\n"

 #Build SQL to import data
 strSQL = "Insert in AIF_OPEN_INTERFACE(BATCH_NAME, YEAR,
            PERIOD, PERIOD_NUM, CURRENCY, COL01, COL02, COL03,
            COL04, AMOUNT) \n"
 strSQL += "Select \n"
 strSQL += "'BATCH_" + fdmContext["RULENAME"] + "' \n"
 strSQL += ",'" + str(strYear) + "' \n"
 strSQL += ",'" + str(strMonth) + "' \n"
 strSQL += ",'" + str(lngMonth) + "' \n"
 strSQL += ",'USD' \n"
 strSQL += ",GL_Account \n"
 strSQL += ",Company \n"
```

```
strSQL += ",Cost_Center \n"
strSQL += ",'FINAL' \n"
strSQL += ",Value \n"
strSQL += "from Table_Name@Database_Link \n"
strSQL += "Where 1=1 \n"
strSQL += "And Period_Num = " + str(lngMonth) + " \n"
strSQL += "And Year = " + str(strYear) + " \n"

strmsg += "Insert SQL: \n"
strmsg += "\t" + str(strSQL) + "\n\n"

fdmAPI.executeDML(strSQL, params, True)


except:

strmsg += "Error encounter during import. \n\n"

fdmAPI.logDebug(strMsg)
```

This script is a very simplistic example but provides several useful features. First is the use of a JAVA `SimpleDataFormat` class which is used to extract the year and period information from the current point of view. The use of the PeriodKey from the POV assumes that the global period keys align to the source system. In the event that they do not then the FDMEE API method `getPeriodDetail` could be used to retrieve the source system period mapping.

Next the script utilizes an `INSERT` with `SELECT` subquery that makes use of a database link. This allows the connection information to be maintained at the database tier. This is often preferred so that database credentials can be maintained centrally. The `SELECT` subquery makes use of the FDMEE Context to retrieve the name of the data load rule for the current execution. The FDMEE Context is an invaluable component of the FDMEE JAVA API.

Finally, the script leverages the `fdmAPI.logDebug` method. This method allows information about script execution to be added to the process log. This approach is a leading practice. The use of logging allows a developer as well as potentially an end user to debug a failed process.

Custom Scripts

Custom scripts in FDMEE are used to further extend the application. Custom scripts do not necessarily need to be tied to any specific event in the application in the way that import and event scripts are. There is no limit on the number of custom scripts that can be created in an application and an administrator can create new custom scripts whenever needed.

Custom scripts can be used for a variety of needs including running processes before and after batch execution, extracting data and/or maps from the application, or publishing reports on a scheduled basis. These are but a few of the use cases for custom scripts. When you face a situation where out of the box functionality does not provide a mechanism to address the requirement, custom scripts can often be utilized to meet the need.

Custom scripts are extremely powerful. To get the most out of custom scripts, it is imperative to learn and understand the FDMEE API as well as the database model for FDMEE. The FDMEE JAVA API and its associated methods and properties are noted in the Oracle supplied FDMEE administrator guide. The database can be explored using any RDBMS client such as SQL Developer in the case of an Oracle RDBMS or Microsoft SQL Server Management Studio Express in the case of a SQL Server RDBMS. Both clients are available as freeware downloads from the Oracle and Microsoft websites respectively. It should be noted that when connecting to the database through an RDBMS client, one should take extreme care not to modify any database objects or data within tables as this could impact the stability and integrity of the application.

Custom scripts, like Event scripts, do not require a script declaration.

Executing Custom Scripts

Since custom script execution is not tied to an application event like importing a data file or executing the Validate workflow step, the application includes a mechanism for administrators and end users to execute a custom script. This mechanism is a link on the Workflow tab called Script Execution. This feature is the FDMEE equivalent of FDM Classic Task Flows.

Script Execution has been significantly enhanced in FDMEE allowing security to be assigned to individual scripts or even groups of scripts. The following sections outline how to register a Custom script and execute it from the web interface as well as from the command line.

Registration

Once a custom script has been written, it needs to be registered so it can be executed from the web interface. Registration is not only the mechanism to execute a script but also the means by which to apply security.

Custom Script Group

Each registered script needs to be assigned a Custom Script group. Groups can be defined as required to limit execution of individual scripts. A good practice is to create security groups which align to the security user type design of the application; however, it is a good practice to create an ALL group which can be used to grant all users access to the script regardless of their user type. More information about designing user type security roles is contained in Chapter 8.

Figure 5-7: Custom Script Groups

In the below image, four script groups have been created that align to the security model for user profiles.

Custom Script Registration	**Custom Script Group**

View ▾   ➕ Add   ✖ Delete   🗒   🔳 Detach

Name	Sequence
Data_Mappers_Loaders	1
Data_Loaders	2
Data_Mappers	3
ALL	999

Once the Script Groups have been defined, individual custom scripts can be registered.

When registering a script you must define a name. The name field is the text that will display on the web interface when a user is selecting which custom script to execute. It is generally a good practice to avoid SQL reserved characters like the percent sign (%) or ampersand (&) in these fields as it can often cause the application to behave inconsistently. The script is then assigned a Custom Script Group based on the security filtering that is required.

Prior to the 11.1.2.4.100 release, the target application to which the script is associated is a required field. If the script is not performing actions that are specific to a specific target application and an application-specific root folder has not been specified, then the application specified is inconsequential. However, if application specific root folders have been specified, the application specified in this field will dictate the script file that is able to be selected in the Script File field as it will read from the `data\scripts\custom` folder location of the target application.

Figure 5-8: Custom Script Registration

The below image illustrates an example script registration. The name field in green is the hyperlinked text that is displayed to an end user when executing the registered script. The script to be executed is highlighted in yellow.

Script Parameters

An optional portion of a custom script and its registration is the Script Parameters section. Script parameters allow for a run time prompt to the end user. These are similar to FDMEE reports which allow an end user to specify the point of view for which a report executes. Script parameters are not limited to POV items. They can be leveraged to gather any information needed in order for the script to execute. For example, the script registered in Figure 5-8A exports maps for one or all locations. The script will also email the output results to a user.

Figure 5-9A: Registering Script Parameters

In the below image, script parameters for the Location and Email address have been assigned. When a user executes the script, he/she will be prompted to specify values for these parameters.

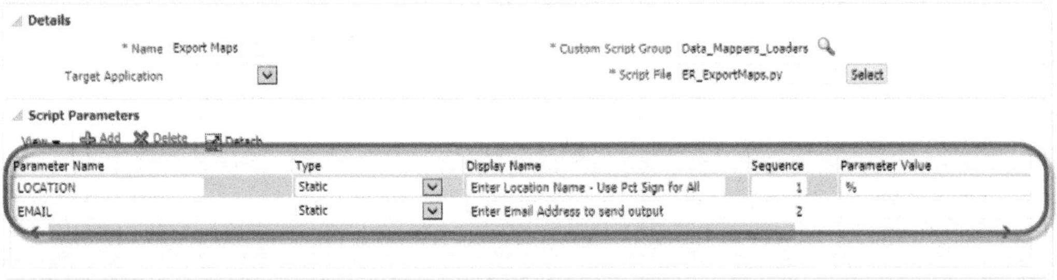

Figure 5-9B: Script Parameter Retrieval

In the below image, the script parameters that were created when the script was registered are retrieved by the script through the use of the API method getCustomScriptParameterValue. Notice that the parameter name (in yellow) is in the same case as the parameter name specified in the script registration.

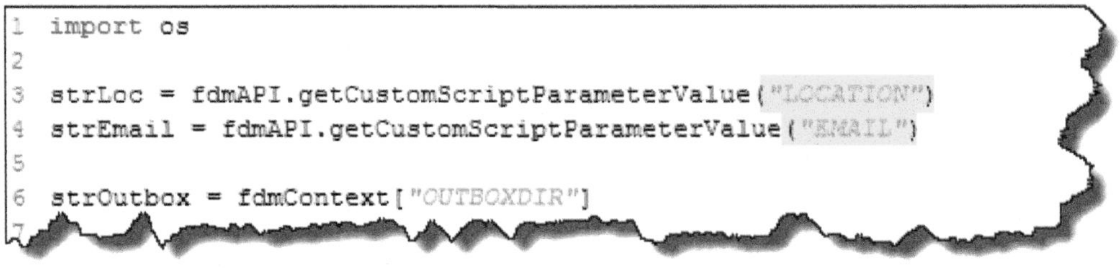

```
1  import os
2
3  strLoc = fdmAPI.getCustomScriptParameterValue("LOCATION")
4  strEmail = fdmAPI.getCustomScriptParameterValue("EMAIL")
5
6  strOutbox = fdmContext["OUTBOXDIR"]
```

End User Execution

Executing a custom script is a straightforward process. On the Workflow tab, click the Script Execution link. Then, select the custom script group to which the script has been assigned. The custom script groups which are visible to an end user will be controlled by the security assigned to the group. Select the script to run and click Execute. When script parameters are assigned, a dialogue box will open for the end user to provide the parameter values that will be used when the script executes. The result of the script execution can be reviewed in the Process Details.

Figure 5-10: Custom Script Execution

In the below image, when the script to export maps is executed, the user is prompted for the location name for which the maps should be exported as well as the email address to which the output should be sent.

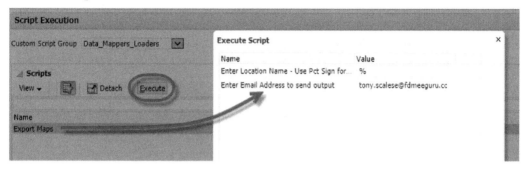

Command Line Execution

Technically, there is no stand-alone command line utility for the execution of custom scripts. However, by exercising a bit of creativity, a custom script can be executed from a command line. FDMEE includes several command line utilities including those to run reports, import maps and execute batches. An FDMEE batch can be assigned a custom script to execute before and after the batch runs.

Figure 5-11: Leveraging Dummy Batches to Execute Custom Scripts

The below image shows a dummy batch of type Batch. The batch definition has the ER_ExportMaps custom script assigned which will execute whenever the batch is called either from the web interface or from the command line.

An FDMEE batch can be executed from the command line using the RunBatch (.bat or .sh depending on operating system) command line utility in the bin directory of the FinancialDataQuality product installation folder.

Figure 5-11: Batch Command Line Execution

The below image shows an example Windows command line execution of the RunBatch utility. The three parameters passed to the utility are the user name, password and the name of the FDMEE batch to execute.

Bear in mind that when executing a custom script from the command line, there is no ability to pass script parameter values. Due to this restriction, scripts that need to be executed from the command line should be created to not have a dependency on end user input.

Script Development

As we discussed at the beginning of this chapter, Jython scripts are extremely powerful but also require an adherence to certain coding standards – one of the more notable being the need to indent in a consistent manner. While the script editor within the FDMEE web interface allows for a script to be viewed and modified, any development or significant changes to the code of a script should be managed from a script editor.

A script editor is preferred for several reasons. The first being that script editors when configured offer color coding which is a powerful visual indicator for syntactical errors like a simple failure to include a close double quote. In this case, the remaining text of the code line would appear in a different color than expected and alert the developer of a problem.

Another critically valuable feature of a script editor is the ability to use the tab key to indent. While this may sound like an overstatement, consider an instance where you have two or three nested conditional statements. Each line of code in the third conditional statement requires at least six spaces of indentation when assuming a minimum of two spaces per indent. The use of the tab key is far easier than the space bar and most integrated development environment (IDE) editors automatically respect the indentation associated with the previous line of code. The use of the tab key on the web interface will simply move the cursor focus to another portion of the web page.

Finally, an IDE offers autocomplete on many JAVA and registered API objects. When typing something as simple as `os.`, a dialogue box will display the available methods and properties for the object being utilized.

Figure 5-13: Eclipse Autocomplete

The below image shows how Eclipse provides a dialogue box of the available methods and properties for a given object.

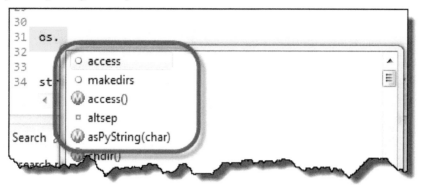

The web interface does not offer any of these features and for that reason the use of a script editor is highly preferred.

Configuring a Script Editor

There are a number of editors that are available for script development. My preference is Eclipse. Eclipse is a JAVA-based open source platform and has a powerful and user friendly IDE. The decision of where Eclipse (or another editor) is installed and configured will vary for each implementation. This will often be dictated by the security policies and procedures of an organization which can limit one's ability to remotely connect to a server.

An additional consideration is the operating system of the FDMEE application server. This is important since FDMEE supports Windows as well as UNIX and Linux. While FDMEE may be hosted on an application server running Linux, an administrator may not be as familiar with that operating system and may wish to install and configure Eclipse in a Windows environment. In this scenario, Eclipse can be installed locally as long as the PC is part of the same domain as the FDMEE application server and the user has administrative rights to install software on the PC.

The below outlines how to configure Eclipse for FDMEE script development in a Windows environment and assumes that the developer has administrative access to the FDMEE application server.

Install Java Runtime Environment (JRE)

The Java Runtime Environment (JRE) is a required component to develop Jython scripts. This is a one-time installation for each machine to which Eclipse will be deployed. As of the writing of this book, Java SE Runtime Environment 8 is the latest release. To ensure that the latest version of the JRE is being installed, I recommend a google search for **Java Runtime Environment**. Accept the license agreement and then select the JRE that corresponds to the operating system on which the Eclipse install is going to be completed – in this instance, Windows x64.

Figure 5-14: JRE Download

In the below image, the Windows x64 install package is highlighted. This package will be downloaded to install the JRE.

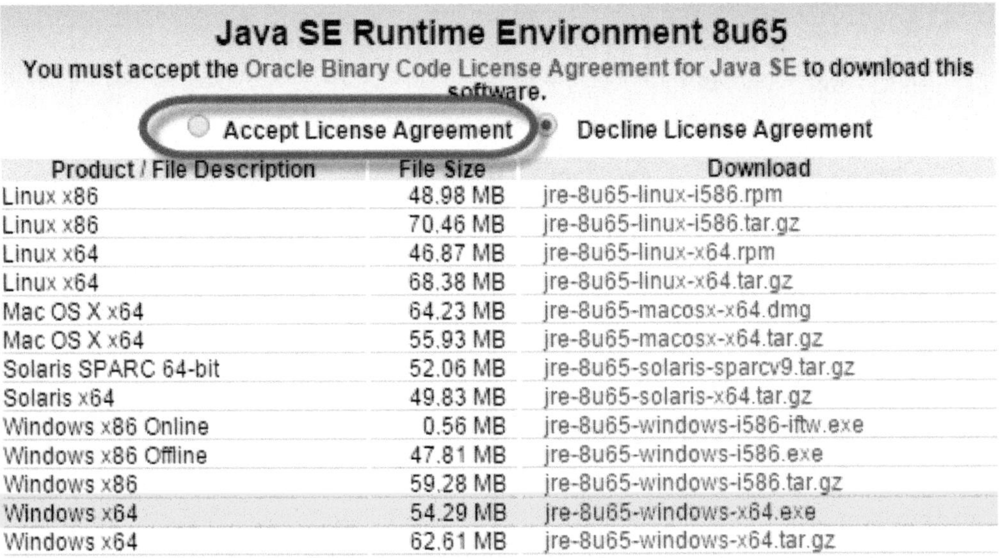

Java SE Runtime Environment 8u65

You must accept the Oracle Binary Code License Agreement for Java SE to download this software.

Accept License Agreement   Decline License Agreement

Product / File Description	File Size	Download
Linux x86	48.98 MB	jre-8u65-linux-i586.rpm
Linux x86	70.46 MB	jre-8u65-linux-i586.tar.gz
Linux x64	46.87 MB	jre-8u65-linux-x64.rpm
Linux x64	68.38 MB	jre-8u65-linux-x64.tar.gz
Mac OS X x64	64.23 MB	jre-8u65-macosx-x64.dmg
Mac OS X x64	55.93 MB	jre-8u65-macosx-x64.tar.gz
Solaris SPARC 64-bit	52.06 MB	jre-8u65-solaris-sparcv9.tar.gz
Solaris x64	49.83 MB	jre-8u65-solaris-x64.tar.gz
Windows x86 Online	0.56 MB	jre-8u65-windows-i586-iftw.exe
Windows x86 Offline	47.81 MB	jre-8u65-windows-i586.exe
Windows x86	59.28 MB	jre-8u65-windows-i586.tar.gz
Windows x64	54.29 MB	jre-8u65-windows-x64.exe
Windows x64	62.61 MB	jre-8u65-windows-x64.tar.gz

Once the JRE installer is downloaded, run the installation package. When installing, you can choose to change the default install directory if needed. Once the installation completes, a confirmation dialogue box will be displayed.

Figure 5-15: JRE Installation Confirmation

Install Jython

Jython needs to be installed in order to develop and test scripts using Eclipse. As with the JRE installation, this is a one-time activity for each machine where Eclipse will be deployed.

According to Jython.org – Jython is freely available for both commercial and non-commercial use. To download Jython navigate to http://www.jython.org/downloads.html. Select the link to download version 2.5.1 – do not install a more recent version as it may not be compatible with FDMEE.

Once the package (jython_installer-2.5.1.jar) is downloaded, launch the installer. You will be prompted to select your language. Click Next, accept the license agreement and then click Next again. Select the default Standard installation and click Next.

Figure 5-16: Jython Installation Type

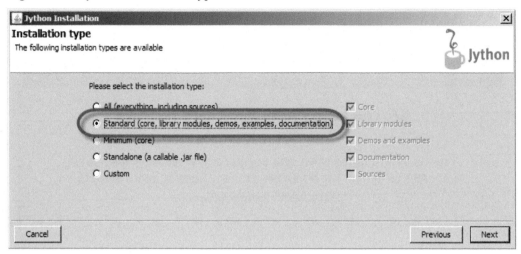

The next screen prompts for the installation directory. When installing on the FDMEE application server, I recommend utilizing the same drive where the FDMEE application is installed. This can be determined by reviewing the HYPERION_HOME environment variable. Once a directory is selected/specified, click Next. If prompted that the directory was created, click OK and click Next again.

Figure 5-17: Jython Install Directory

The below image shows a common practice which is to create a Software folder on the root of the Hyperion installation drive.

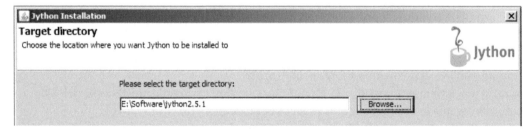

The next screen asks for confirmation of the Java home directory. Assuming the JRE was installed as per the above, then select Current and click Next. Otherwise, select the Java home directory and click Next.

Figure 5-18: Jython Java Home

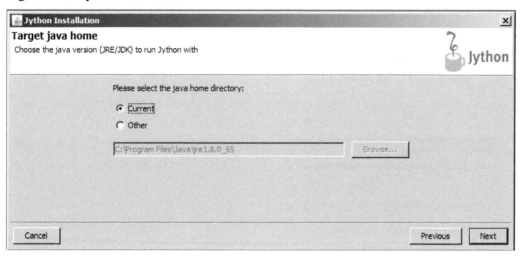

The next script will display the installation parameters. Click Next to begin the installation.

Figure 5-19: Jython Installation Confirmation

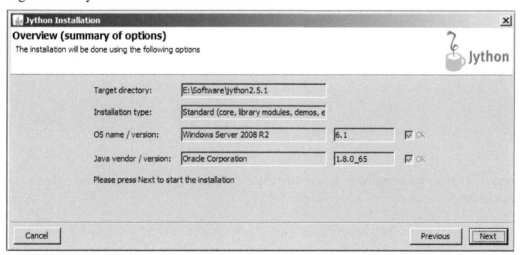

Once Jython is installed, a confirmation screen will appear. Click Next and Finish to complete the installation.

Install Eclipse

The installation of Eclipse is extraordinarily straightforward and, in reality, there is no installation. To download Eclipse, navigate to http://www.eclipse.org/downloads. Select the download link for the Eclipse IDE for Java EE Developers that corresponds to the operating system on which Eclipse will be run. The package is downloaded as a zipped archive. Extract the contents of the zipped archive to a location.

Figure 5-20: Eclipse Extraction

In the below image, the Software folder on the root Hyperion installation drive is selected as the target for the zipped archive extraction.

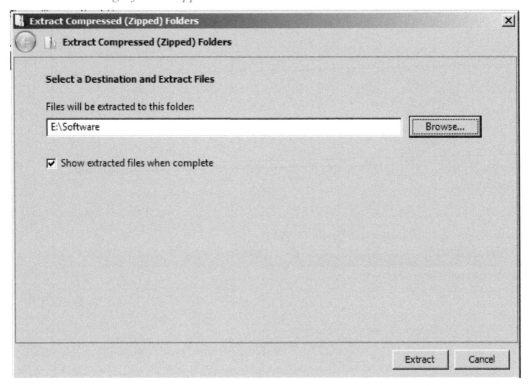

Once the extraction completes, Eclipse can be executed simply by running the eclipse executable (`eclipse.exe`) in the eclipse folder.

Figure 5-21: Executing Eclipse

While there are additional one-time configurations that need to occur in Eclipse, this is the executable that is used to run Eclipse for any script maintenance and/or development.

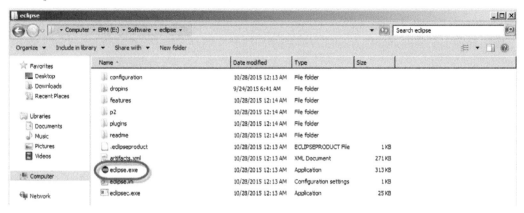

Configuring Eclipse

There are a number of one-time steps that need to occur to configure Eclipse for the development and testing of FDMEE scripts. These steps need to occur for each machine upon which Eclipse is deployed.

Specify Workspace

The workspace is the directory where configuration settings for Eclipse are stored. My recommendation is to specify the scripts directory of the application root folder. Once a directory is specified, you can check the tickbox option so you are not prompted for the workspace location again. This is useful as otherwise, each time Eclipse is opened, the dialogue will display.

Figure 5-22: Eclipse Workspace

In the below image, the workspace is specified in the scripts directory of the system application share.

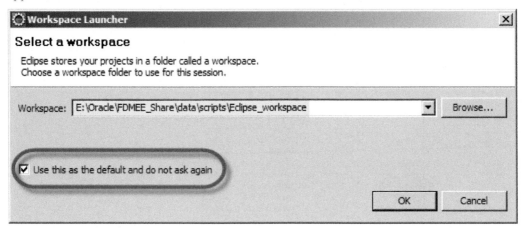

Install PyDev

PyDev is a plugin for Eclipse that enables it to be used to create Python modules. While FDMEE scripts are Jython based, the modules and their development are Python based so it is important to configure Eclipse to leverage Python.

Eclipse needs to be configured to install PyDev which means adding the installation site to the configuration. Select Help → Install New Software. Click the Add button in upper right corner. Specify PyDev for the Name and http://pydev.org/updates/ for the Location.

Figure 5-23: Add PyDev

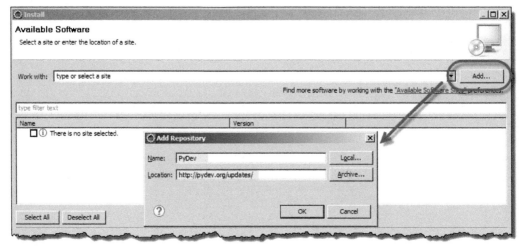

Once PyDev is added as a software repository, select PyDev and click Next.

Figure 5-24: Install PyDev

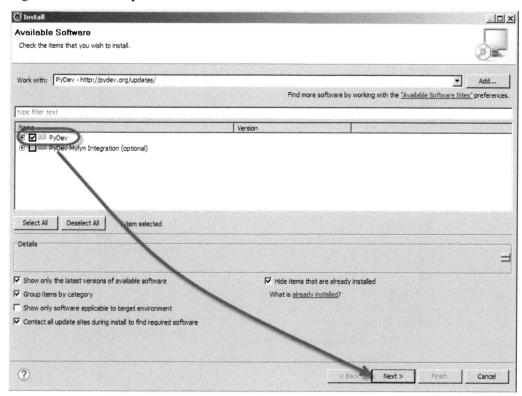

You may be asked to confirm the installation of Pydev. Click Next to continue. Accept the licensing agreement and click Finish. The installation of PyDev will begin. Do not close the installation progress window. You will be prompted to confirm that the certificate is trusted. Select the Brainwy Software certificate and click OK.

Figure 5-25: PyDev Certificate

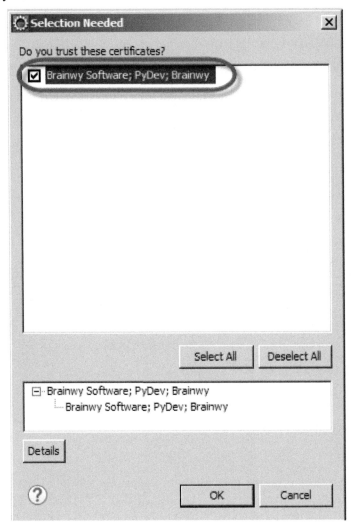

Once the installation of PyDev completes, you will be prompted to restart Eclipse. Restart Eclipse before continuing to the next configuration step.

Configure Editor Options

Both PyDev as well as Eclipse general options need to be configured. Both options are accessed by selecting Window → Preferences within Eclipse. Expand the General section and then expand the Editors. Click on the Text Editors group. Change the Displayed tab width to two (2) and check the box for Insert Spaces for Tabs. Click Apply.

Figure 5-27: General Options

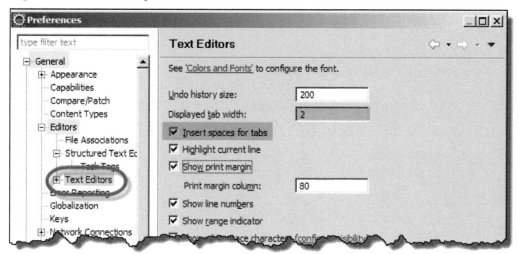

Next, the PyDev specific options need to be specified. Collapse the General group and expand the PyDev group. Expand the Editor group and click on Tabs. Change the Tab length to two (2) and click Apply.

Figure 5-28: PyDev Text Options

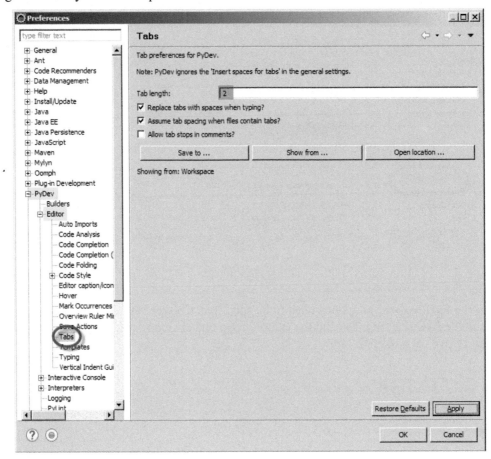

Next expand the Interpreters group. Click on Jython Interpreter. Click New. Browse for the Jython jar that was installed in the earlier step. In the Name field, replace the path with the text Jython2.5.1. Click OK.

Figure 5-18: Jython Interpreter

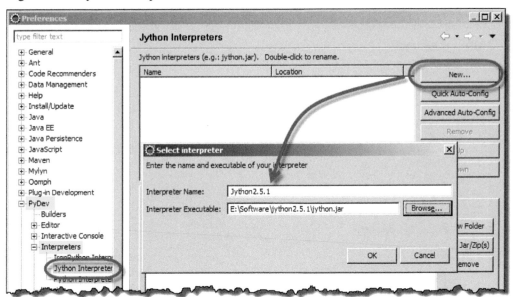

When prompted to update the python path, click OK. Click Apply and click OK to close the Preferences window.

Create Development Project

Once PyDev has been configured, a project needs to be created to enable the development of scripts. Select File → New → Project. A dialogue box will open. Expand the PyDev group and click PyDev Project and click Next.

Figure 5-29: Select PyDev Project

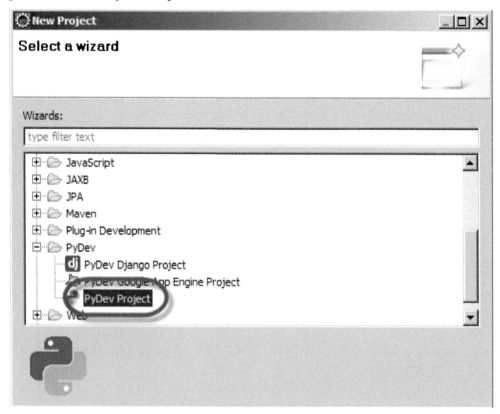

On the next screen, specify the project name. `FDMEE_Development` is a common project name. Change the project type to Jython and click Finish.

Figure 5-30: Name PyDev Project

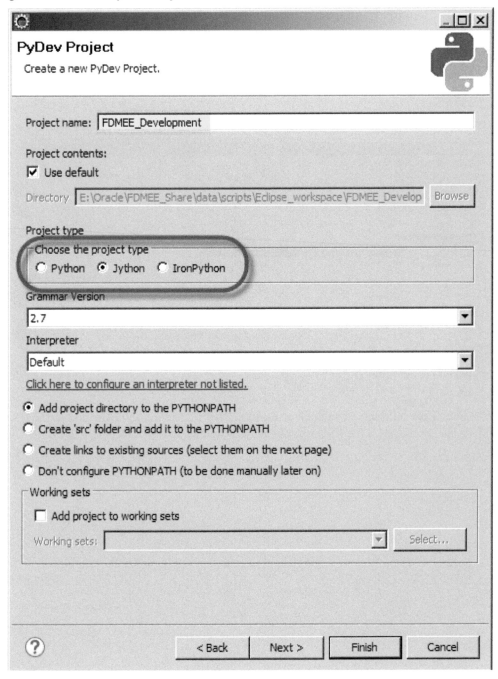

When prompted to associate the new project with the PyDev perspective, choose Remember my decision and click Yes.

Link To Script Folders

Once the development project is created, each of the script types in the folder – Event, Import and Custom – can be added to the project. This allows each of these script types to be directly created and/or edited from Eclipse.

Right click the project and select New → Link to Existing Source.

Figure 5-31: Link to Source

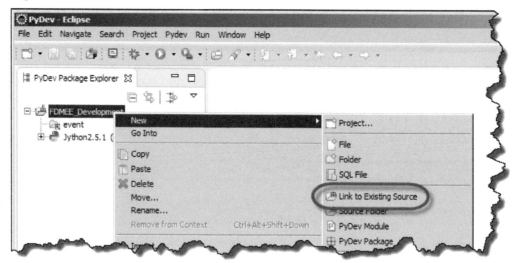

Click the Browse button next to the Location of existing source field. Browse to the FDMEE share and select the Event folder within the data\scripts folder. Click Finish.

Figure 5-32: Select Source

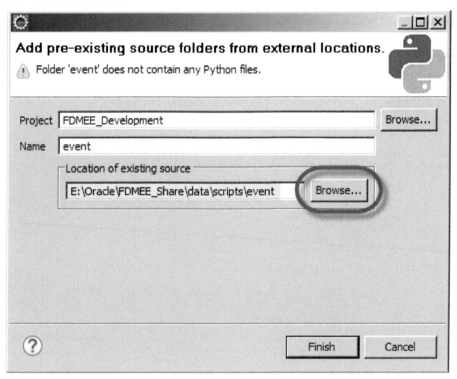

Repeat the above for the Import and Custom folders.

Maintain Python Path

The Python path needs to be maintained for any jar file whose classes are utilized in FDMEE scripts. By default, the FDMEE API needs to be added to the Python path. This would also apply for the SQL Server jar file if the RDBMS for FDMEE is SQL Server.

To maintain the python path, right click the project and select Properties. Click on PyDev – PYTHONPATH. Click the External Libraries tab. Click Add zip/jar/egg. Browse to %hyperion_home%\products\FinancialDataQuality\lib and select the aif-apis.jar file. Click OK and the python path is updated.

Figure 5-33: Update Python Path

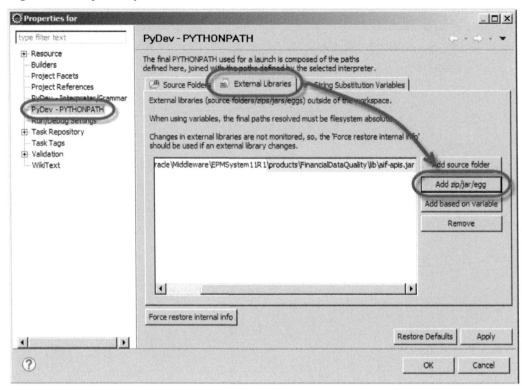

Test Eclipse Configuration

The configuration of Eclipse can be tested with a simple script. This procedure ensures that PyDev is properly configured and can leverage the FDMEE API.

In order to test Eclipse, click the custom folder. Click File → New → PyDev Module. Specify a name for the script – for this purpose, zTemp is a commonly used script name. When prompted for the template to apply, select <Empty>.

Once the new script is created, add the following import statement

```
import com.hyperion.aif.scripting.API as fdmAPI
```

Type fdmAPI. If a dialogue box displays showing the available FDMEE API objects, properties and methods, the update of the python path for the FDMEE API was successful.

Figure 5-34: FDMEE API Test

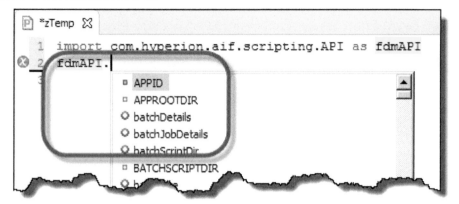

To test the configuration of PyDev, replace the text in the test script and add the following:

```
import com.hyperion.aif.scripting.API as fdmAPI

print "hello"
```

Save the script file. Execute the script by selecting Run → Run As → Jython Run.

Figure 5-35: Execute Script

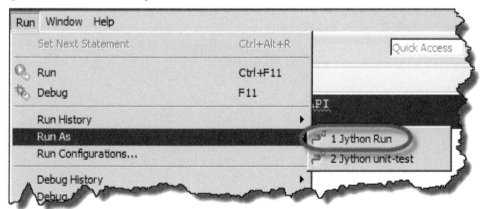

If the script runs successfully, the console window of Eclipse will display the text hello.

Figure 5-36: Successful Execution

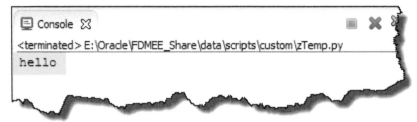

Once the script executes successfully, the configuration of Eclipse is complete and is ready for script development.

Summary

In this chapter we scratched the surface of FDMEE scripting. We learned why Jython is the preferred language for FDMEE script development. We discussed the different scripting types – Import, Event and Custom – and their syntax. We explored how custom scripts can be executed by end users in a similar way to FDM Classic Task Flows. And finally, we outlined the steps to configure Eclipse as a script editor for FDMEE script development and maintenance.

The next chapter represents a shift point in the book – from education about the FDMEE application and its core capabilities – to a focus on administration. The subsequent chapter will discuss best practices for integrating new data sources. We will explore practical methods and techniques to efficiently and accurately build new integrations. We will discuss best practices for metadata creation and empower you to take ownership of the process. This chapter is critical for any administrator that faces the prospect of having to build an integration for a new data source.

6

Leading Practices for Integrating New Data Sources

This chapter is a pivot point in the book. The first half of the book was spent level setting on application components. This was done to ensure that all of the core metadata and functionality is fully understood. This second section of the book transitions into more real world usage of the product... such as "a day in the life of an FDMEE administrator." Having a deep understanding of the application helps an administrator better understand not only what can be done with the application but also ensures that future design decisions and product usage are optimal.

In this chapter, we explore a common situation that almost every FDMEE administrator will face – the need to integrate a new data source. This chapter will provide you with the knowledge needed to properly scope and build a new integration. We will also share leading practices for metadata naming conventions to leverage when developing application components.

This chapter assumes that the target applications already exist and that new data sources are simply being integrated to a system which, for all intents and purposes, is a live production application. This assumption was made to eliminate the lengthy discussion that could result regarding how and why target application metadata is designed and deployed. This discussion is relevant to new EPM deployments and as such is beyond the scope of this book. That's not to suggest that this book cannot be leveraged to support a deployment of FDMEE in a net new EPM implementation. However, there are far too many variables – which applications are being deployed, what is the timeline, what is the budget, to name but a few – for which this book is simply not written to address.

Data Discovery

When a new data source is identified for which an FDMEE integration needs to be developed, it is important to spend time better understanding the source – in short, data discovery. This exercise allows you to better understand the source system, its chart fields and how they may relate to the target application to which data needs to be loaded.

It is important during this exercise to be cognizant of the target application to which data will be loaded but avoid the inclination to begin designing an FDMEE integration. This means that while knowing the dimensionality of the target application is important during data discovery, one should try to avoid creating import formats and maps needed to process data from the source. Instead, one should spend time unraveling the source system to gain a better understanding of how the source system is used and how conceptually it can be integrated using FDMEE.

Business Units

When integrating a new data source, determine if there is a logical business unit grouping. Determine if data is identified by legal entity, company code, business unit or some other measure. There are several benefits to this analysis.

First, data in the target application will often need to be secured by the entity dimension, particularly in applications that are utilized for financial statement reporting purposes. By identifying how the source system segregates its data, an integration can be designed that respects the need for data security. More information on how FDMEE security is impacted by source and target system data security needs is detailed in Chapter 8.

There is still a benefit to performing the business unit analysis even when the target application requires a more granular security model. Identifying multiple business units which represent subsets of the complete data set can be invaluable when designing for performance.

The analysis and identification of business units enables you to begin to envision the locations that will be needed to support the integration of the new source system. While this is an important component to integrating a new source, there is additional analysis that is required before embarking on the actual build.

Charts of Accounts and CoA Utilization

Each source system has at least one chart of accounts. Larger source systems may have multiple charts of accounts. When integrating a new source system, it is important to inventory the charts of accounts in use. Having a proper inventory of the charts of accounts is imperative to scoping the level of effort required to map the data from the source system into the target system.

Another vital analysis that needs to be performed, in addition to determining the number of charts of accounts, is assessing if each of the charts of accounts are used uniformly across all of the business units to which the charts are assigned.

Initially this may sound like an impossible scenario and at a technical level it is. One might question how a G/L account (e.g., 10050) could be utilized differently across business units. The answer is that while technically the account (or any other segment) is the same; the functional or accounting definition of what balances are stored in that source system segment member may not be consistent across the various business units.

Consider these examples. The corporate standard for G/L account 10050 is to track cash balances. All business units conform to this functional definition except one which treats balances in this account as short term investments. In another example, any cost center that ends with 60 through 69 is considered a finance cost center. However, one business unit uses a cost center ending in 66 to track IT expenses. Depending on the master data governance and accounting policies and procedures, these situations can be more common than one might anticipate.

Uncovering discrepancies like the above, before beginning the FDMEE component build, will help to eliminate any reworking as well as drive data quality since the appropriate steps can be taken to eliminate (or account for) this inconsistency. This activity is key to properly scoping the volume of import formats and mapping tables that need to be considered for the new integration. However, additional understanding of the components (segments) of the chart will further refine and/or validate this analysis.

Segments

Some charts of accounts are extraordinarily simplistic, containing just a single segment. Others are very complex with multiple segments that represent various business functions. For example, legal entity, natural account, cost center, profit center, trading partner and the always interesting 'future use' segment which never actually seems to be used.

Gaining a proper understanding of each segment is vital to determining the relationship that each segment, or combination of segments, will have to the target system dimensionality. The process of unraveling the segments is not dissimilar to the process of a global chart of account redesign. During this activity, you should be developing an understanding of the business function of each segment, the structure of each segment as well as any interdependencies that may exist between the segments. This is critical to developing mapping and is an activity that often requires a partnership with the source system owner or power users.

A word of caution related to CoA segment analysis (especially with large, complex source systems contain multiple segments). Often the first pass analysis to define the relationship will result in a one for one relationship between the source system segment and the target system dimensionality. While there are instances where this holds, it is a rarity. I have found that after additional discovery and probing, you will often find a multisegment relationship is needed to properly transform source system data to the appropriate target system dimensionality. The lesson is to challenge the source system owner with whom you have partnered to gain a better understanding of the chance for those situations.

The time invested in this activity provides the groundwork for the development of import formats and mapping tables. Having a deeper knowledge and understanding of the source system will minimize the need for any reworking and repetitive data load and validation exercises.

Data Quality Concerns

An often overlooked area when integrating a new data source is data quality within the source system. This is not to suggest that the source system data is inaccurate. More so there can be a concern with the segment values on individual transactions, especially those generated as a result of human data entry.

As an example, consider intercompany and third party transactions. Assume that the source system has a trading partner segment. In an ideal world, third party transactions would not have a trading partner while intercompany transactions would have a trading partner. In practice, this is often violated. Consider another example where the cost center segment is populated when it is not applicable to a transaction like revenue or possibly the balance sheet.

Acknowledging that situations like the above can arise and having a better understanding of the different segments is valuable to uncovering data quality issues around which the integration can be designed. As with the analysis of the segments, this is a partnership with the source system owner. Do not be afraid to challenge, since the design and use of the import formats, maps or even the Check report to capture data quality issues is far more efficient if a proactive approach is taken.

Leverage Data Discovery

The next step once data discovery is complete is to translate the learnings from that analysis into the technical elements of the application. While locations, check rule and check entity groups are important, this activity will focus largely on defining the import formats and maps.

At this stage, the focus should be on the map definition. By defining the maps needed to transform the source system segments to the target system dimensionality, the import format will naturally follow. Generally it is a good practice to prepare a grid that can be used to track the relationship between the source system segments and the target system dimensionality.

Figure 6-1: Source to Target Relationship

The below image shows an example grid that defines the relationship between the source segments and the target system dimensions. This can be used to begin the mapping and import format definition process.

Sample Chart String:	1000.600010.10065.0000.000.000	
	Company Code.Natural Account.Cost Center.Trading Partner.Profit Center.Future Use	

Target Dimension	Source Segment	Notes
Entity	Company Code (1)	
Account	Natural Account (2)	
ICP	Trading Partner (4)	Only for I/C Accounts; [ICP None] for all others
Custom1 (Cost Center)	Cost Center (3)	Not applicable for Revenue & COGS accounts (4x,5x)
Custom2 (Product)	Profit Center (5)	Not applicable for balance sheet accounts (1x-3x)
Custom3 (Cash Flow)	N/A	Fixed Value - [None]
Custom4 (Data Type)	N/A	Fixed value - GL

Once the relationship is documented, the process of defining maps can begin. Let's walk through the above grid as an example of how to move from the data discovery portion to the process of defining the mapping and import format.

The information in the notes section is critical. Starting with the intercompany partner, we have multiple options of how to handle this requirement. We can concatenate the natural account and trading partner fields together in the import format. We can use an import script to set the source ICP to [ICP None] when the natural account on the record is a third party account. And finally, we can use the trading partner field as the source intercompany and leverage multidimension or SQL mapping scripts to map-based on the account type – third party or intercompany.

Let's start by eliminating an option. In Chapter 5, we discussed the pitfalls of using import scripts to essentially perform mapping. While a valid technical possibility, this functionality is suboptimal for the reasons previously discussed so we can eliminate this approach. Now we have two remaining options.

The remaining options – concatenated natural account and trading partner or trading partner with multidimensional and/or SQL mapping scripts – need to be evaluated in relation to the mapping goals as outlined in Chapter 4. In the interest of keeping this analysis as straightforward as possible, assume that the trading partner segment code is simply a pass through to the target system dimension member and that the natural account segment is not replicated in the HFM but instead requires mapping to a target EPM specific account. Assuming data quality and accuracy for either approach, finding the right blend of performance, usability and maintainability will be determined largely by the eventual owner of the integration.

Let's delve into each option a bit further, starting with the concatenated natural account and trading partner. When concatenating multiple source system segments, the result is a multiplicative effect on the potential source "members" that need to be mapped. For example, if we have 100 trading partners and 2,000 natural accounts then there are 200,000 potential combinations that could need to be mapped. This combination explosion can be handled through a combination of Explicit and Like maps. In its simplest form, the Explicit maps would list each intercompany account-trading partner combination and map to a valid intercompany partner in HFM. All other combinations would be mapped to [ICP None] utilizing a catch all Like map.

It is important to explore the advantages and disadvantages of any design decision. For this option, the advantages are that the mapping tables are easy to understand. Nearly any end user could interpret the natural account-trading partner combination and understand how that defines the target application intercompany partner member. This solution would also be very performant since there is only a single Like map.

Conversely, the disadvantage to this approach is that the explicit maps need to be maintained any time a new intercompany account and/or trading partner is added to the source system. Depending on the frequency of additions, this could become a consistent point of maintenance which introduces a risk pertaining to data quality. Since the Like map defaults any unmapped combination to the [ICP None] member, any new intercompany accounts or trading partners that are not added to the mapping table would be mapped to the incorrect intercompany partner.

Now let's explore the options for utilizing multidimensional mapping or SQL mapping scripts. In either mapping approach, the import format would specify that the trading partner segment defines the source ICP. The natural account also defines the source account. A single multidimension map could be created where each of the intercompany natural accounts is listed using the In criteria. A second criteria, while not needed, would be all trading partners. The target value would be a simple pass through the trading partner segment value. As with the concatenation approach, all other combinations would be mapped to [ICP None] utilizing a catch all Like map.

Figure 6-2A: Multidimension Sample for Intercompany

The below image shows an example multidimension map that leverages the source account. This is used in conjunction with the map in Figure 6-2B.

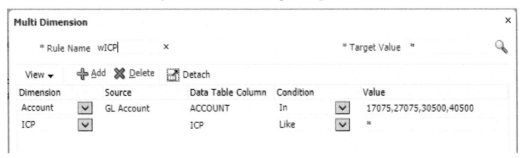

Figure 6-2B: Catch All Map

The below image shows the catch all Like map that forces any combination not handled by the Multidimension map to the [ICP None] target system member.

The advantages of a multidimension map are that they are easy for an end user to maintain, the source intercompany partner field is more logical (trading partner as opposed to natural account and trading partner combination), and the performance will be fairly good as long as the assumption that the trading partner is a pass through holds.

The disadvantages are similar to the concatenated source intercompany approach above. Each time an intercompany natural account is added to the source system, the mapping rule would need to be maintained. Since the Like map defaults any unmapped combination to the [ICP None] member, any new intercompany account that is not added to the multidimension mapping definition would be mapped to the incorrect intercompany partner.

We also have the option to leverage SQL Mapping scripts. Mapping could be achieved with a single mapping definition. The SQL statement would evaluate the mapped account. When the mapped account is one of the target system (HFM) intercompany accounts, then the source trading partner is passed through as the target intercompany partner. For all other mapped (HFM) accounts, the intercompany partner is mapped to the [ICP None] member.

Figure 6-3: SQL Map Example

The below image shows a map that passes through the trading partner when the mapped account is an intercompany member and maps to the [ICP None] member for all other accounts.

```
Edit Script                                                          ×

Script  Case
          When Upper(AccountX) in ('ICAR','ICAP','ICREV','ICCOS','ICINTINCEXP') then ICP
          Else '[ICP None]'
        End
```

There are four key benefits to using a SQL map for this requirement. The intercompany dimension is fully mapped for all rows in the dataset with this one line SQL map. The result is excellent performance. The other benefit is that this script likely requires less maintenance as new intercompany accounts will probably be added to the target system less frequently than to the source system. As long as the source system's natural accounts continue to map to the existing target system's intercompany accounts then no maintenance to the script is required for any new source system intercompany accounts or trading partners. An ancillary benefit of this approach is that the risk of data quality issues is reduced since inadvertently mapping to [ICP None] would only occur if a new target system intercompany account is added and the SQL map was not updated. As previously noted, adding target system accounts is less common. Finally, as with the multidimension map approach, the source intercompany partner field is more logical as the pure trading partner.

The only significant drawback to the use of a SQL map is that it requires the eventual owner of the map to understand the construct of a SQL UPDATE statement. While they are not responsible for writing the entire update statement, they do need to understand

and be able to maintain the script. For some end users this may be a nonstarter while for others they could easily maintain and/or create it.

Below is a summary of the pros and cons of the two approaches:

Approach	Pros	Cons
Concatenated Segments	• Easy to understand • Good performance assuming a single catch all map	• Maintenance required with every new I/C account or trading partner added to the source • Possible data quality concerns
Multidimension Map	• Easy to understand • More logical source members • Good performance	• Maintenance required for every new I/C account or trading partner added to the source • Possible data quality concerns
SQL Map	• Excellent performance • Maintenance needed only if new I/C accounts added to target (HFM) • More logical source members • Reduced data quality risk	• Difficult for average end user to maintain or understand

The decision upon which mapping approach to utilize should be driven by determining the right balance of performance and ability for the eventual owner of the FDMEE process to maintain and understand the maps. There is no one right answer but given the knowledge that has been shared throughout this chapter (and book), you are now empowered to make an educated decision as to which best fits the needs of your application and your organization.

Metadata Leading Practices

As important as it is to be able to deconstruct a new source system, it is equally important to have a methodical approach to building the FDMEE components of a new integration. This section focuses on the core components that define an integration.

Source Period Mapping

We briefly discussed source period mapping in Chapter 3. Source period mapping is used to establish a relationship between the time period in the FDMEE point of view and the source system period key. Source period mapping is used to ensure that the correct period and year of data is being retrieved from the source system when the Import workflow process is executed.

Source period mapping is only necessary when directly integrating to a source using Oracle prebuilt functionality for Oracle eBusiness Suite or PeopleSoft, leveraging source adaptors for systems like J.D Edwards or SAP ECC and Business Warehouse (BW) or utilizing the open interface adaptor. Technically, source period mapping is not required if the FDMEE time periods exactly align to the source system, However, it is rare that they would and even if the time periods align today, that does not guarantee that future integrations of additional source systems would. As such, it is a leading practice to define source period mapping for any of the above source system integrations.

Figure 6-4: Source Period Mapping Example

The below image shows a source period mapping example for the EBS registered source system. Notice that the period key of FDMEE (MM-DD-YYY) is associated with the source system calendar (Fiscal), the GL Year, and the GL Period. The GL Period number is derived from the source system calendar information. In this example, G/L period Apr-10 is the first period of the G/L year.

It is important to note that when integrating with a single source system that has multiple calendars from which data must be sourced, the source system should be registered multiple times and a source period mapping should be created for each registered source system for the calendar associated with that source system.

Figure 6-5A: Multiple Source System Registrations

The below image shows how registering the same source system with a distinct name enables period mapping as per registration of the source system. EBS and EBS-Accounting are both linked to the same EBS instance.

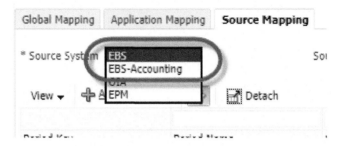

Figure 6-5B: Source Period Mapping for Additional Calendar

The below image shows how the secondarily registered source system can be used to link to a different calendar (Accounting) and map to different source system periods. In the below example, fiscal period one (P01) is mapped to EBS period Jan (1).

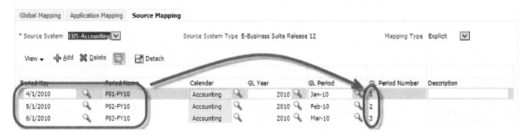

While FDMEE will allow a global period key to be mapped to multiple source calendars for a single source system, the execution of the data integration process will fail as FDMEE does not perform a lookup of the calendar to the source accounting entity when the workflow is executed. If multiple period maps are established for a single global period then this can result in data being associated to multiple source system periods and the process will fail or return inaccurate data – so it is a leading practice to map each active calendar individually.

Import Formats

Import formats were detailed in Chapter 2. At a glance, an import format defines a relationship between a source and a target. Given this, it is a good practice to name import formats using a *Source_Target* (e.g., `EBS_Comma`) convention. The import format name field is limited to 20 characters so there might be instances when abbreviation is necessary.

Direct Connection and Adaptor Based

When creating an import format with a direct connection to either Oracle EBS or PeopleSoft, it is important to consider the concatenation character specified. It is a good practice to avoid the use of the underscore (_) since underscore is a SQL wildcard operator.

Figure 6-6: Impact of Underscore Concatenation Character to Like Maps

The below image shows how the Like map using the wildcard characters is interpreted when executed by the application.

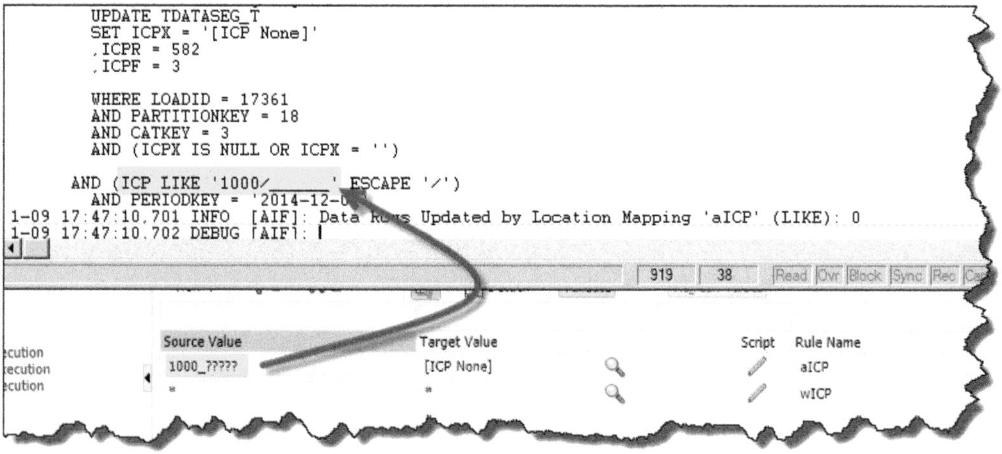

While the underscore character is handled by the mapping engine for native Like mapping, any SQL mapping scripts developed by an end user would need to include the same logic. Failure of an end user to properly escape the underscore character could surface an issue when segment values are variable lengths.

If we examine the example in Figure 6-6, it assumes that the first segment is four digits and the second segment is five digits. However this logic, if specified in a SQL mapping script, would apply to any source value that is 10 digits and begins with 1000. Depending on the segment lengths, the expected result could vary. This potential variability can be easily eliminated by using a different concatenation character. I prefer the dash (-) or period (.) characters.

Flat File Based

File-based import formats – delimited or fixed width – have several considerations. First, when specifying an expression for a given dimensional row, do not enter a zero-based field number or field length. Second, when applicable, specify a field name for the source column. This is not required but is a powerful way to indicate to the end user the source system segment that defines the source dimensional value to be mapped.

Figure 6-7A: File Based Import Format Example

The below image highlights an incorrect entry in the field number (red highlight) as well as a correct entry (green highlight) when leveraging the expression field to hard code a source value. The Source Column field is also populated when associated to a source system segment.

Figure 6-7B: Source Column Headers

The below image shows how the source column headers display the text from the Source Column field of the import format from Figure 6-7A.

A final consideration with flat file import formats for delimited files is the delimiter. If given a choice, I prefer and recommend the pipe delimiter. The pipe delimiter is preferred for a couple of reasons. First, the pipe character is exceedingly rare in text fields like a description and virtually non-existent in segment values. This eliminates the risk that an errant character in the description or segment values results in an improper parsing of the record containing the superfluous character. Second, a pipe delimiter increases the likelihood that a flat file is generated systematically. Files that utilize tab or comma as the field delimiter are notorious examples of flat files that are manually generated – usually by an end user manually converting an Excel file to a CSV or Tab Delimited format.

Locations

As with Import Formats, we discussed Locations in Chapter 2. To summarize, the location is a container of data. A location is created to support integrating data from different source systems, to allow a different set of maps, to optimize data load performance (especially when utilizing batch processing), and to address data security requirements.

Each location is associated with a single target application by virtue of being assigned an import format. While the import format can be overridden at the data load rule and (by extension) change the association of the target system to the location, this would deviate from leading practices and is something I would caution against. Given this one-to-one relationship between the location and the target application, it is a leading practice to include the target application name in the location name. This can be in the form of a suffix or prefix and is driven by organizational preference.

Additionally, as we discussed in Chapter 2, multiple locations are often created even when a single one would suffice based on the source system (import format) and mapping requirements. In this instance, multiple locations are created to address security requirements and can often be associated with a business unit or legal entity. In these instances, including the business unit name or code in the location name is a leading practice.

Consider this example. In Oracle eBusiness Suite R12, data is grouped by Ledgers. The ledger represents the three C's – Chart of Accounts, Calendar and Currency. Each Ledger is stored in the ERP with a numeric key and a textual field called `Accounting Entity`. In one implementation, the client was more familiar with their Ledgers based on the numeric key and, as such, each location name included the Ledger code - `10000_ABCHFM` – where `10000` is the ledger key and `ABCHFM` is the target application name.

One may question why the target application name should be included in the location name. The reason for this practice is that a single source system, or the business units associated with the source system, may leverage FDMEE to load to multiple target applications. By including the name of the target application, multiple locations can be created that support integrating the same business unit to multiple targets. It should be noted that the location name field supports a maximum of 20 characters so abbreviation of the business unit and/or the target application names may be necessary. In this instance, I strongly recommend to apply this abbreviation consistently.

Location Details

The majority of the fields on the location details tab are optional.

Figure 6-8: Location Details

The below image shows the fields that are available for each location in FDMEE.

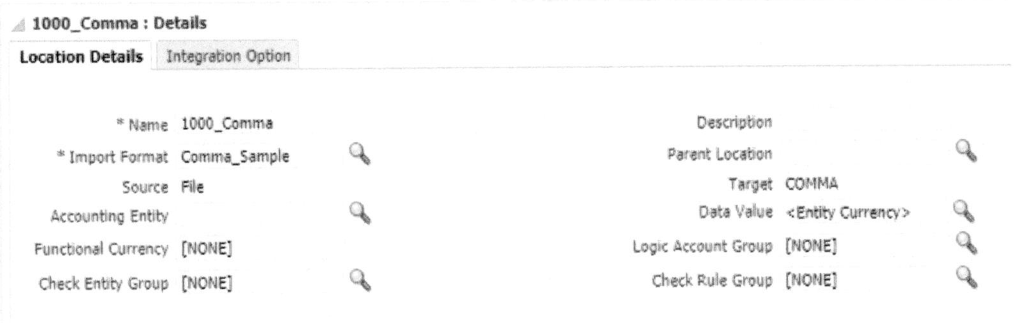

The Description and Functional Currency fields are only used in FDMEE reports. This description field can be used to specify a more detailed name of the location that will be displayed on reports. The currency field is only used to display the currency associated with the data contained in the location. This field has no impact on the data natively. The application does not perform currency transformation nor will it filter records from a data set based on the functional currency assigned to the location.

The parent location field is used to specify the location from which the location will inherit its mapping tables. This setting is very useful when multiple locations are created for a single source system. More information on Parent Mapping is contained in Chapter 4.

The source and target fields are auto-populated based on the import format assigned to the location and cannot be changed. The accounting entity field is only applicable to Oracle EBS and PeopleSoft direct integrations. See Chapter 2 for more information about Source Accounting Entities.

The Data Value field is only applicable when integrating with HFM. The value must be at a minimum <Entity Currency>. The data value field is used to specify the value dimension member to which FDMEE will load data. For those of you familiar with HFM, you will remember that data can only be loaded to the <Entity Currency> value dimension member. However, HFM journals can be posted to any of four different adjustments – <Entity Curr Adjs>, <Parent Curr Adjs>, [Parent Adjs], [Contribution Adjs] – value dimension members. The Data Value field is used to specify the adjustment value dimension member to which the journal should be loaded. When leveraging FDMEE's ability to create HFM journals, this field value should contain two values that are delimited by a semi-colon. The first value is always <Entity Currency> and the second value is the value dimension member to which FDMEE will load the HFM journal. A valid example is: <Entity Currency>;<Entity Curr Adjs>.

The remaining fields – Logic Account Group, Check Entity Group and Check Rule Group – should be assigned when needed. Information on each of these application components is contained in Chapter 3. I strongly recommend the use of the Check workflow step so the assignment of a Check Entity Group and Check Rule Group would be required.

Location Design for Essbase Integrations

The use of FDMEE to integrate with Planning or Essbase often requires a fundamental shift in data integration philosophy. Using legacy integration methods which leveraged tools like Essbase load rules, ODI, Essbase Integration Service (EIS) or Essbase Studio, a single data file containing all business units and often a full year of data is loaded to Essbase.

With FDMEE, this approach should be reconsidered. These legacy methods were far less suited to partial data clears and loads. Dynamically, clearing data from Essbase based on the data file contents was burdensome and so it became easier to simply clear data for all entities and reload the entire dataset. These methods are also hyper-efficient. This can be attributed to the fact that these methods can perform ETL functions without storing the data.

FDMEE, by contrast, stores the data which enriches the ETL process by providing very granular auditability of the ETL process, and end user ownership of the process, as well as drill through. This additional functionality comes at a price… and that is performance. FDMEE will almost always be slower than a legacy integration method; however, the additional value add of the application may lead an organization to accept that trade off.

FDMEE can be tuned significantly. Much of the tuning, as with any application, is based in design. A simple reenvisioning of the integration process can produce significant results. One key area is the ability to break the data set into multiple smaller data sets. Leveraging additional locations allows FDMEE to load individual business units concurrently. When paired with batch processing, this approach can result in greatly improved data integration cycle times.

Data Load Rules

Also discussed in Chapter 2 was Data Load Rules. A DLR extends on the concept of a location being a container of data. Within the Location container, a Data Load Rule organizes the data further. Each location requires at least one data load rule but multiple data load rules can be created within a single location. A good naming convention for data load rules is *LocationName-CategoryName*. If multiple data load rules exist for a single location then a third field should be added to the DLR name. The data load rule name supports up to 80 characters so limited abbreviation (if at all) should be needed.

Figure 6-9: Data Load Rule Name Examples

The below image shows example data load rule names using the Location Name (blue underline), Category (red underline) and additional descriptive field indicating the data type (green underline).

The use of the dash between the location name, category and optional data type fields of the data load rule name enables the DLR name to be easily parsed in any scripting that leverages the DLR name.

The data load rule options for non-flat file-based integrations are detailed well in the Oracle provided FDMEE Administrator Guide in the section **Defining Data Load Rule Details**. Below is additional information to enrich the information provided in the administrator guide related to data load rules for flat file data sources.

File Based Data Load Rules

There are several options to consider for a file-based data load rule. First is the import format. This field is optional and should only be populated if the import format assigned to the location does not align to the file layout for which the data load rule is being created. However, as a matter of leading practice, if a source file requires an import format that differs from the import format assigned to the location then another location should be created. The exception to this practice would be multi-period data files which leverage one of the multi-period file types and a revised import format.

Figure 6-10: Data Load Rule Import Format Override

The below image show how the import format override for the data load rule should be blank for Single Period Load file types. A multi-period text file would leverage an import format override assuming an additional data load rule for a single period was defined for the location.

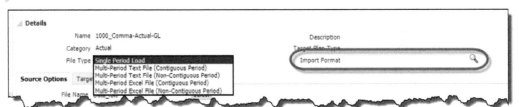

The import format assigned to a location should generally default to the single period load file format when a location will have data load rules for single and multi-period loads.

The second option for file-based DLRs to consider is the source file information. This information is optional but allows for additional control over the source file that is processed by the data load rule.

Figure 6-11: Source File Options

The below image shows a DLR that has specified the file name that the application will process during the Import workflow step. The application will automatically import the data file from the 1000_Comma subdirectory of the inbox. The file name is associated to the period being processed. For example, when executing the import workflow for Jan-2015, the file name would be Data_201501.txt.

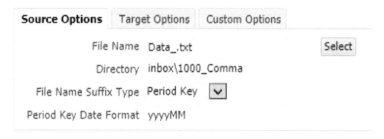

Specifying the file name is useful when a system-controlled process to generate the flat file exists. In this instance, the source system would generate a data file in a specific directory *within* the FDMEE network share, utilizing a file naming convention. Often this file naming convention includes some text and a date stamp.

In this event, the file name should exclude the date stamp and the file name suffix should be used. The file name and the file name suffix type are concatenated together. If using the Period Key as the suffix type, the Period Key Date Format should be specified in JAVA SimpleDateFormat. More information on SimpleDateFormat can be found on the Oracle website[1] or by performing a simple Google search. Remember that JAVA is case sensitive so pay particular attention to casing when using this option.

Summary

In this chapter, we explored how data discovery is critical to the process of integrating a new data source. We walked through a real life example of how to leverage the information gained from data discovery and begin to translate that into the design of a new integration. Finally, we explored the foundational components of a new integration

---

[1] http://docs.oracle.com/javase/6/docs/api/java/text/SimpleDateFormat.html

– outlining leading practices for naming conventions as well as component design. This final section is key to creating and maintaining an FDMEE application that can grow as the organization grows.

In the next chapter, we will explore the power of the FDMEE web interface. This chapter is fundamental to understanding how to more fully utilize the application to ensure data quality, investigate data, and provide value not only to users of the application but also to consumers of information housed in the application.

7

Getting the Most Out of the User Interface

In this chapter, we will explore the power of the FDMEE web interface. We will discuss how to leverage the often overlooked but very powerful features of the workbench. We will also highlight the reporting capabilities of the application. Understanding these features and their capabilities will greatly enhance one's ability to use the application to more effectively manage the data integration process.

Data Load Workbench

The data load workbench is the main information delivery vehicle by which an FDMEE user can consume data. While the workbench is useful for executing the workflow process, its larger value is its ability to investigate data in an interactive fashion.

Query By Example

One of the most powerful additions to FDMEE is **Query By Example** (QBE) functionality. This feature allows data in the Workbench to be filtered based on one or more criteria. This is extremely useful when investigating variances, confirming mapping or simply when trying to limit the amount of data in a data set for analysis.

Figure 7-1: Query By Example

The below image shows an example usage of Query By Example. The target entity is filtered to find records for CT. The source department column is filtered to find any records beginning with 1. The Source account is filtered to find any accounts that begin with 61, end with zero, and which are four digits.

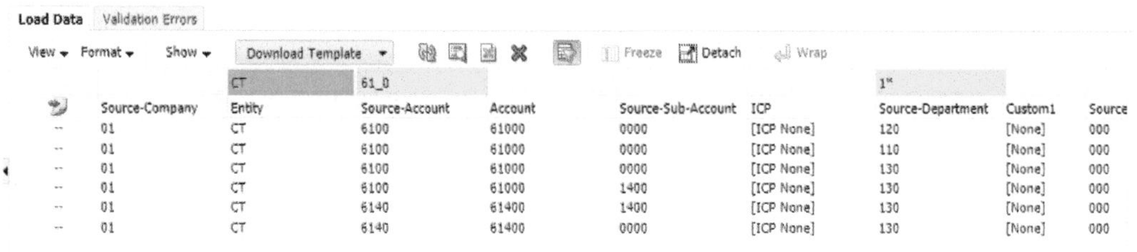

Load Data | Validation Errors

View ▾   Format ▾   Show ▾   Download Template ▾   🔀 🔀 🔀 ✖   🔀   ⫴ Freeze 🔀 Detach   ⤶ Wrap

	Source-Company	Entity	Source-Account	Account	Source-Sub-Account	ICP	Source-Department	Custom1	Source
		CT		61_0			1*		
--	01	CT	6100	61000	0000	[ICP None]	120	[None]	000
--	01	CT	6100	61000	0000	[ICP None]	110	[None]	000
--	01	CT	6100	61000	0000	[ICP None]	130	[None]	000
--	01	CT	6100	61000	1400	[ICP None]	130	[None]	000
--	01	CT	6140	61400	1400	[ICP None]	130	[None]	000
--	01	CT	6140	61400	0000	[ICP None]	130	[None]	000

Query by example supports not only explicit query criteria – CT highlighted in green in figure 7-1 – but also wildcards. The supported wildcards are asterisks (*) and underscore (_). The asterisk functions identically to the asterisk character in Like data load mapping meaning that it is a multiple wildcard character. The underscore character functions similar to the question mark character in Like data load mapping. The underscore represents a single character wildcard.

It is important to understand that Query By Example automatically treats each filter criteria like an asterisk's wildcard query. This means that (technically) an asterisk is not needed on any filtering criteria. However, it is important to understand that explicit and single character wildcard filtering criteria are treated as those suffixed with an asterisk. For example, in Figure 7-1, the Entity column is filtered to find entities equal to CT. Obviously, any entity equal to CT will be displayed in the results but any Entity *beginning* with CT will also be displayed.

Figure 7-2: QBE Explicit Filtering

The below image shows how the CT filter criteria returns not only records where the entity is CT but also CT_STAMFORD.

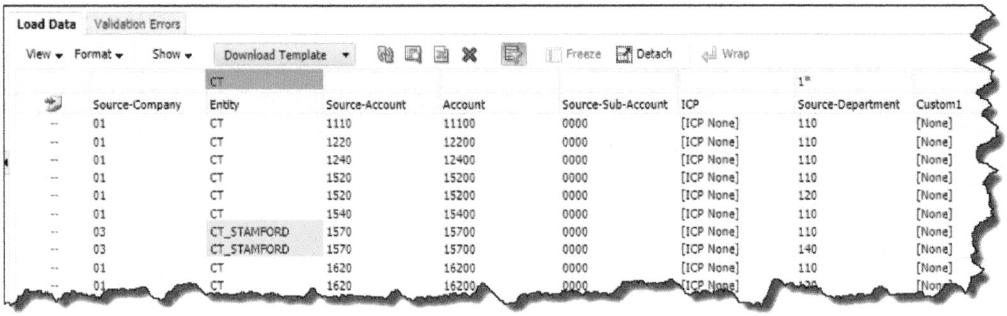

Figure 7-3: QBE Single Character Wildcard

The below image shows how the appending of an asterisk also applies to filter a criterion that leverages the single character wildcard.

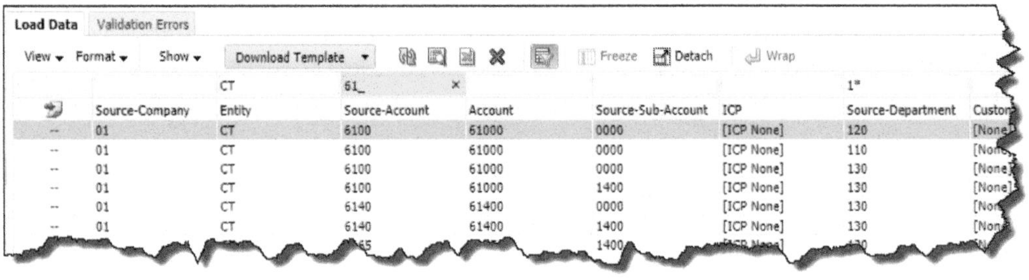

The expected result of the filter criterion of 61_ for the source account in Figure 7-3 would be any account that is three digits since the asterisk is automatically appended when the query returns all accounts that begin with 61. As a result, the single character wildcard is useful when trying to wildcard one or more characters in the middle of a string but not useful for filtering based on string length.

It is important to understand this behavior and therefore the limitations of Query By Example. Even with this shortcoming, QBE is a powerful tool for filtering results in order to perform additional data analysis.

Export To Excel

Export To Excel has been greatly enhanced in FDMEE. While this functionality existed in FDM Classic, it did not respect any grid filtering that had been applied. When exporting data, it simply dumped data for all columns in the TDATASEG table. The result was often a need to unhide and delete rows and/or columns. In FDMEE, the Export to Excel feature respects not only any filtering that has been applied to the grid – any grid, not just workbench – but also any column layout changes.

Figure 7-4A: Export To Excel

The below image has the Export To Excel icon circled in red. Notice the column layout highlighted in green and the row count highlighted in yellow in the lower right of the image.

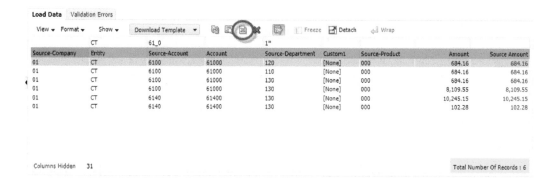

Figure 7-4B: Export to Excel Results

The below image shows the FDMEE generated Excel workbook. Notice the columns match the column layout in Figure 7-4A. Also notice that the number of records matches the number of filtered records.

	A	B	C	D	E	F	G	H	I	J
1	Source-Company	Entity	Source-Account	Account	Source-Department	Custom1	Source-Product	Amount	Source Amount	
2		1 CT	6100	61000	120	[None]	0	684.16	684.16	
3		1 CT	6100	61000	110	[None]	0	684.16	684.16	
4		1 CT	6100	61000	130	[None]	0	684.16	684.16	
5		1 CT	6100	61000	130	[None]	0	8,109.55	8,109.55	
6		1 CT	6140	61400	130	[None]	0	10,245.15	10,245.15	
7		1 CT	6140	61400	130	[None]	0	102.28	102.28	
8										
9										

The one item to consider with Export to Excel is that any field that begins with a zero (0) will drop the leading zero. While it exports properly from FDMEE, when Excel opens the document it suppresses the leading zeros. A possible work around for this is to create a custom script that will export data to a flat file format that can be imported into Excel utilizing Excel functions that allow fields to be imported as text and therefore maintain leading zeros.

Unmapped Records

The FDMEE interface allows for the quick and easy filtering of data that includes unmapped dimensions. This is especially useful when a large number of unmapped source system members exist.

Figure 7-5: Display Unmapped Records

The below image shows how unmapped records can be easily filtered. Click the Show menu drop down and select Invalid Data. The records which have one or more source system segments which are unmapped are displayed in the resulting record set. Note that the record count is the number of rows with unmapped source system segment values, not the count of how many source system segment values need to be mapped.

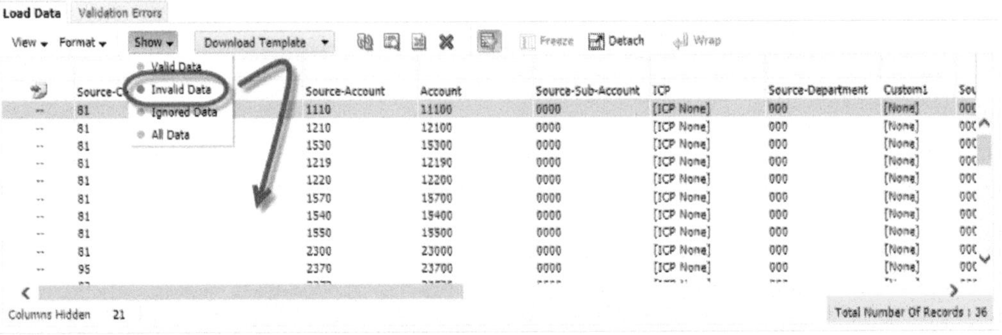

The ability to filter and output unmapped records is particularly useful in the 11.1.2.3.530 release, and higher. There is an Oracle-recognized bug where the Validation Error tab does not populate with unmapped members for all dimensions. All the unmapped members for a *single* dimension will display. Once all of those mapping errors are corrected then the unmapped source system values for the next dimension will display once the Validation workflow process is re-executed. This cycle repeats until all source system values are mapped. This is highly iterative and inefficient.

Leveraging the Show Invalid Data feature allows any unmapped records to be exported to Excel. The export can then leverage a simple pivot table to identify the unique list of unmapped source system members.

Figure 7-6: Unmapped List Pivot Table

The below image shows how a simple pivot table can be used to identify the list of unmapped members for a given dimension. In this example, source system values 2, 81, 95 and 99 for Entity (Source Company) need to be mapped.

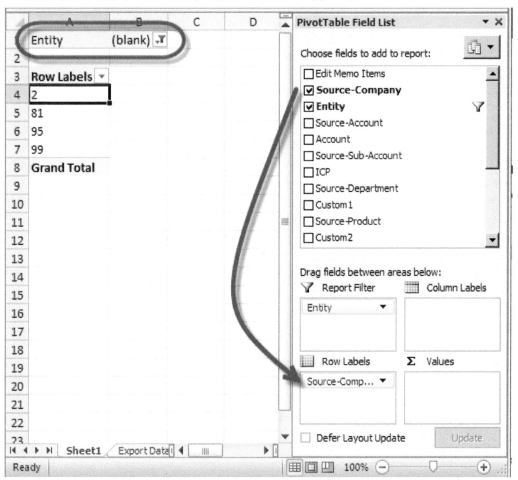

The filter criteria of the pivot table should always be set as (blank) since the Show Invalid Data feature will export records where *any* unmapped source system exists across any dimension. This means that there may be mapped members in the target dimension; so by applying the filter, one is able to isolate just the source system values which are unmapped for that particular dimension.

Mapped Data View

In FDM Classic, the Import and Validate data screens were separate. The Import screen displayed the source system data while the Validate screen showed the mapped results. The validate screen also displayed the accumulated balance for a mapped record meaning that if five source records each with a balance of $1,000 mapped to a single intersection, the validate screen would show a single record with a balance of $5,000.

FDMEE, by contrast, does not employ this same data view by default, instead displaying source and target data on the same record on the same screen. However, this legacy view is available and is particularly useful when trying to understand the source records that make up a balance.

Figure 7-7: Show Target View

The below image shows how to navigate to the option that allows data to be displayed in the legacy Validate view.

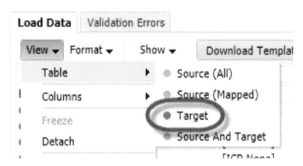

The Target view of data has been enhanced in FDMEE. When invoking this view, the user is presented with two data grids. The upper data grid displays the target (mapped) data. When selecting a record in the upper grid, the lower grid populates with the source records that contribute to the mapped data record balance.

Figure 7-8: Mapped Record Investigation

The below image shows the two grid views associated with the Target data view. Notice the source records that make up the balance as well as the departments (110, 120, 130, 810) that were mapped to the Custom1 member of [None].

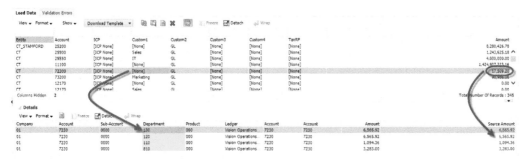

This data view is incredibly useful for quickly identifying the source data records and/or mapping which contribute to a data intersection loaded to a target application.

Customized Data Layout

Another enhancement to the FDMEE interface is the ability to customize the Workbench layout. The user has the ability to change which columns are displayed as well as the order in which they are shown. There are several methods to achieve this including drag and drop within the interface, the Reorder Columns menu item, as well as the Manage Columns feature both of which are under the View menu. I prefer the latter since I find it easier to manage and make changes not only to order but to which columns are displayed.

Chapter 7

Figure 7-9:

The below image shows how to invoke the Manage Column dialogue box by selecting
View → Columns → Managed Columns.

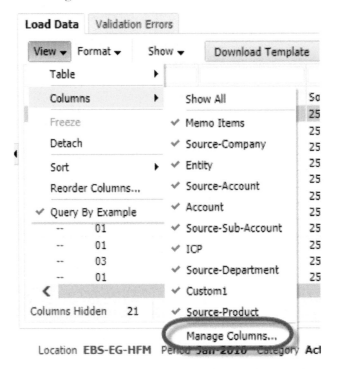

Selecting the Manage Columns option opens a dialogue box that enables columns to be
added or removed from the current display as well as change the order of the display.

Figure 7-10: Manage Columns Dialogue

The below image shows the Manage Columns dialogue box. All of the fields associated with the data table are available to be added or removed from the display. The buttons in the middle (in red) control the addition or deletion of fields. The buttons on the right (in yellow) control the order that fields are displayed.

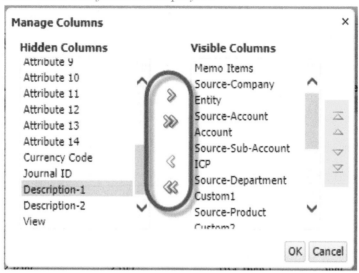

The selected layout is displayed in the Workbench after clicking the OK button on the Manage Columns dialogue box.

Figure 7-11: Custom Data Layout

The below image shows a modified data layout where the Description 1 field was added between the target Account and the Source Sub Account fields.

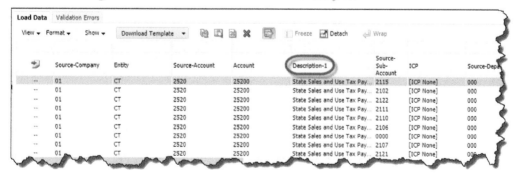

Any changes to the layout will be respected when utilizing Export to Excel. One should be aware that any layout modification including the target view and column order will revert to the default column and display when a user navigates off the Workbench and then navigates back to it. The ability to create a "sticky" custom view has been logged as an enhancement request but at the time of writing of this book, the enhancement has not been made to the web interface.

View Mappings

Another useful feature of the Data Load Workbench is the ability to view the mapping that has been applied to a specific intersection. This is useful when trying to troubleshoot unexpected transformation results. The ability to view the maps applied to a specific record can uncover instances of overlapping mapping definitions where rule types (Explicit, Between, In, MultiDimension, Like) and/or rule name processing orders, result in an inaccurate transformation.

Figure 7-12A: Show Mapping

The below image shows how clicking on a data value in the Source Amount column will open the submenu where the View Mappings option can be selected.

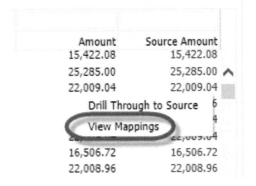

Figure 7-12B: Mapping View

The below image shows the mapping rule that was applied for each dimension. Any dimension on the record for which a mapping was not found will be excluded from this view.

Mapping Details ×

Dimension Name	Type	Source	Target	Script	Rule Name	Description
Account	Like	*	*0	🖉	wAcct	
Entity	Explicit	01	CT	🖉	01	
ICP	Like	*	[ICP None]	🖉	wICP	
Custom1	Like	5*	Finance	🖉	a5x	
Custom2	Like	*	GL	🖉	wC2	
Custom3	Like	*	[None]	🖉	wC3	
Custom4	Like	*	[None]	🖉	wC4	
TaxRF	Like	*	[None]	🖉	wC5	

OK

Reports

FDMEE reports are another feature of the FDMEE application interface that is sometimes overlooked. Reports provide a mechanism to investigate data, maps and even settings without needing to access those individual components. This is especially useful for end users who may not have access to all of the components of the application that would allow them to view this information. Moreover, reports provide an auditable mechanism to verify information within the FDMEE application.

Reports can be generated in Adobe Acrobat (PDF), Excel (XLS or XLSX) or web page (HTML) format. Adobe Acrobat is particularly useful for audit purposes since PDF files are not easily manipulated so there is a high degree of confidence in the information contained within the report.

Admittedly, there are far fewer reports in FDMEE than there were in FDM Classic. Some of this is due to the fact that certain application elements have changed while others have been sunset. For example, security that used to be native to FDM Classic has been transitioned to Hyperion Shared Services (HSS). FDM Classic security reports can now utilize Shared Service reports. Batch reports that were useful for monitoring active and past batch processes can be addressed through the use of Process Details which is covered in more detail in Chapter 9. Finally, the certification reports of FDM Classic have not been ported to FDMEE since the application does not and will not provide this functionality.

A key report that was missing before the release of 11.1.2.4.100 was the map monitor report. This report provides critical information about the mapping table including who changed a map, when it was changed, what the map was before it was changed, and how the map was changed. The lack of this report in earlier releases was a significant problem for customers who utilized FDMEE to support the month end close process. The collection of this information is vital to ensuring data quality and supporting common audit requests. If your organization currently has deployed an earlier release of FDMEE, I strongly encourage you to consider an upgrade (in the event of 11.1.2.3.XXX) or application of the patch (in the event of 11.1.2.4.000) to enable this functionality.

While FDMEE includes 25 reports prewritten by Oracle, new reports can easily be created. Creating and modifying reports requires developing SQL queries, understanding the FDMEE database structure, and a working knowledge of the BI Publisher Add-In for Word. While this book does not outline the steps needed to create and modify reports, detailed information about this task will be offered in a short supplementary title in due course. Stay tuned to the P8 website [www.p8tech.com] for more details here.

Useful Reports

A list of each of the report groups, and the reports contained in said groups, is contained in the Oracle provided FDMEE Administrator Guide. Rather than list each report group and the reports it contains, instead this section will highlight the reports that have the most utility.

Account Chase – FreeForm

This Audit report can be leveraged to support questions, particularly those asking to prove a balance in a given account. This report includes run time prompts for the user to specify the Location, Time Period, Category and Target (Mapped) Account. The Target account must exactly match the mapped/target account in the data – including the casing.

This report does not include a prompt for the data load rule so it will run for all data load rules assigned to the location.

Figure 7-13: Account Chase Report Example

The below image shows an example report for target system account member 25200 for Jan-2010 Actual data. The GL Account and GL Center fields are the source system segments. The Convert field indicates if the sign was flipped on the record and the Amount field shows the balance for the given record. The total for the account – loaded to the target application – is at the bottom of the report.

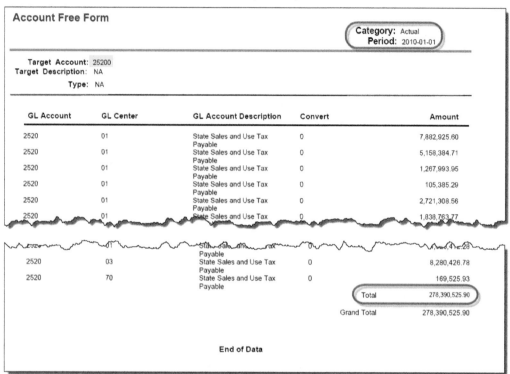

TB Current Location, With Targets

This Base Trial Balance report is useful for investigating mapped data across multiple target application entities. This report includes run time prompts for the user to specify the Location, Time Period, Category and Data Load Rule Name.

Figure 7-14: TB Current Location, With Targets Report Example

The below image shows a sample report. The source system segment values are to the left of the Amount column and the target system (mapped) members are to the right. Notice that the report is sorted by Target Account and Target Entity. All of the source records across the different target entities (yellow) are displayed for a single target account before data related to the next target account (green) is displayed.

Base Trial Balance (With Targets)

Location: EBS-EG-HFM
Category: Actual
Period: 2010-01-01
Currency: [NONE]

GL Account	GL Center	GL Account Description		Amount	Target Account	Target Entity
1110	81	Cash		14,449,980.40	11100	
			Total	14,449,980.40		
1110	01	Cash		687.37	11100	CT
1110	01	Cash		1,424,906,168.05	11100	CT
1110	01	Cash		1,055.11	11100	CT
			Total	1,424,907,910.53		
1110	70	Cash		5,120,132.85	11100	MA
			Total	5,120,132.85		
1110	03	Cash		195,681,134.62	11100	NY
1110	03	Cash		-100.00	11100	NY
			Total	195,681,034.62		
1130	01	Short Term Investments		7,010,144.30	11300	CT
			Total	7,010,144.30		

Dimension Map for POV

This Location Analysis report is incredibly useful for confirming the mapping that was applied to a specific point-of-view. This report does not retrieve data from the mapping table (tdatamap) but instead from the table (tdatamapseg) that stores the mapping applied to a data set for a specific POV.

This report is powerful because the maps and the reports that query from the mapping table always represent the most recent maps in the system. This report leverages the application functionality that stores the maps that we applied to the data set and can be useful in investigating and auditing data transformation.

This report includes run time prompts for the user to specify the Location, Time Period, Category and Dimension Name. This report does not include a prompt for the data load rule so it will run for all data load rules assigned to the location. This would only be an issue if leveraging data load rule specific mapping.

Figure 7-15: Dimension Map for POV Report Example

The below image shows a sample report. The point of view for which the report was run is in the upper right corner – highlighted in yellow.

Dimension Map for POV

Location: EBS-EG-HFM
Dimension: ENTITY
Category: Actual
Period: 2010-01-01

Source	Description	Convert	Target	Wild Card Type	Wild Card Value
01		0	CT		
03		0	NY		
70		0	MA		
80		0	NY		

Process Monitor All Categories

This Process Monitor report is a powerful and easy way for administrators as well as users who have responsibility for data across multiple locations to determine the status of the workflow process. This report includes a run time prompt for the user to specify the Time Period for which the report will be run.

Figure 7-16: Process Monitor All Categories Report Example

The below image shows a sample report. The time period (yellow highlight) for which the report was run is in the upper right corner. The report is grouped by Category which is highlighted in green. The workflow status for each Location-Data Load Rule combination is noted by the status column as well as the fish symbol. Any Status ending in an "X" indicates that the workflow status has failed. Finally, the time column (circled in red) indicates the date of the last workflow update for the point-of-view.

Process Monitor - All Categories

Period: 2014-12-01

Location and Rule	Status	Import	Validate	Export	Load	Check	Time
Actual							
1000_Comma - 1000_Comma-Actual-Stats	NA						1900-01-01 12:00:00
1000_Comma - 1000_Comma-Actual-GL	IMPx						2015-12-08 09:43:35
1000_Comma - DW-Forecast	NA						1900-01-01 12:00:00
1000_Vision - 1000_Vision_Actual	LOADx						2016-01-17 03:32:43
ABC_Comma - ABC_COMMA-ACTUAL	CHKx						2016-01-18 10:23:01
EBS-EG-HFM - EG-EBS	NA						1900-01-01 12:00:00
FB - FB_Actual	VALx						2015-09-23 11:26:10
FDMEE_Comma - FDMEE_Comma-Actual	NA						1900-01-01 12:00:00
GetPut - GetPut-Actual	VALx						2015-10-22 06:58:15
VisionUSA_Comma - VisionUSA_RanzalHFM-Actual	NA						1900-01-01 12:00:00
Vision_Ops_Comma - Vision_Ops_HFM-Actual	NA						1900-01-01 12:00:00

Map Monitor

These reports are only available in the 11.1.2.4.100 or later releases of FDMEE. These reports display any modifications to the mapping table. They track additions, changes and deletions that have been performed through the web user interface as well as Excel, text or LCM imports.

Figure 7-17: Map Monitor Report by User Example

The below image shows a sample report. The user for who the report tracked mapping updates is circled in black in the upper right hand corner. This is not necessarily the person that ran the report. The location for which the map modifications have been logged is circled in green. The dimensions impacted are highlighted in purple. The modification type is highlighted in yellow and the method for the modification is circled in blue. The details of each modification are noted in the center of the report. In the event of a change, the value of the mapping before the modification is on the left hand side of the arrow while the updated value is on the right hand side.

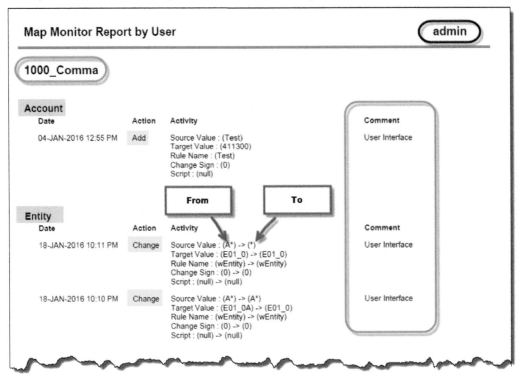

The above reports highlight those that have the most value across various deployments of FDMEE. You should explore the other reports to determine if there is utility in your organization. It should also be noted that existing reports can be modified to meet individual needs or leveraged to create new reports that more fully address the needs of your organization.

Summary

In this chapter, we explored the power of the FDMEE web interface, specifically the Data Load Workbench and FDMEE reports. We gained valuable insight about how to more fully utilize these components to enable more efficient data, mapping and process analysis. This knowledge is critical to more effectively investigating data and any potential discrepancies. An in depth knowledge of the features and functions of the application empowers an administrator and helps to ensure data quality and integrity.

In the next chapter we will explore FDMEE security. This chapter is vital for administrators to understand not only the technical application of security but also the process by which security is designed.

8
Security

In this chapter, we will explore FDMEE security. We will discuss not only the technical components of shared services and FDMEE security roles, but also unravel how to design FDMEE security. This chapter will provide a foundation that empowers an administrator to not only maintain existing security but to also respond to the changing needs of an organization by designing and implementing a revised security model.

FDMEE Security Overview

Before we delve into FDMEE security, let's take a high level overview of the security components and how they control the end user experience. We will explore each of these further but this high level overview helps to set the stage to understand the concepts that will be discussed individually.

FDMEE security is comprised of two functional components – role and location security. Security roles are essentially a profile that controls to which application features, and functions, a user has access. Location security controls the locations – and thereby the data – to which a user has view or modify rights.

An end user is assigned access to an FDMEE security role in Hyperion Shared Services. Once the role is assigned, the locations are allocated through the use of Shared Service groups. When the end user logs into the FDMEE application, the objects and locations to which he/she can gain access are controlled by the role and location group assignment in Shared Services.

FDMEE Security Design

Before implementing or changing the technical components of FDMEE security, it is important to understand the needs of the security model. FDMEE security is comprised of two foundational components – functional and data. Obviously users and authentication are an important component of any EPM application but in the context of this chapter, those items do not necessarily have a material impact on the design of FDMEE security.

Functional security controls which activities a user is able to perform in the application. For example, can a user execute the workflow process, update maps or maintain the period mapping? Data security controls access to the data within the application. We have discussed several times throughout this book, including in Chapters 2 and 6, how the design of locations is influenced by security needs. Since data is only secured at the location level, an effective design of the Locations is critical to ensuring that security requirements are fully addressed.

Security Roles

Before creating or updating security in FDMEE, it is vital to define the security roles that need to be accommodated. A security role is simply a collection of functional security rights. This should not be designed in the context of FDMEE technical components but more so in the context of business needs.

To add context to the concept of a security role, consider these example security role definitions:

Security Role	Description
Application Administrator	This user has access to all FDMEE components except the ability to modify security definitions and user assignment to the application.
Data Owner	This user has access to the required components to process data through the application including the ability to maintain the mapping tables needed to transform data.
Data Processer	This user has access to the required components to process data through the application but has no ability to modify the mapping tables.
Data Reviewer	This user has view only access to the data in FDMEE for drill through, reporting and investigation purposes.

The above security roles are examples of the type of functional requirements that have presented themselves in various implementations. This is not an exhaustive list but instead a sample to help illustrate how security roles can be defined. The exercise of creating and defining security roles is critical to effectively managing security in FDMEE. Once security roles are conceptually defined, the application components can be utilized to create technical roles that meet the functional needs.

One should exercise caution when defining security roles to avoid creating too many definitions that are unnecessarily granular. On average, most implementations utilize three or four security roles. A high count may result in a security model that is unwieldy and likely difficult to maintain especially for new user assignment. Additionally, there are a limited number (12) of technical security roles that can be created so too granular a security definition could result in a functional model that cannot be technically implemented.

Once the conceptual security roles are defined, FDMEE security roles can be configured. The following section contains information on the technical components to create functional security roles and effectively manage user assignment to roles as well as data.

FDMEE Technical Components

FDMEE security is not dissimilar to other Oracle Hyperion applications. User authentication and application access is controlled by Hyperion Shared Services (HSS) while access to application functional components is defined in the application. The intersection of the functional security roles and the user assignment to those roles in HSS controls the end user experience.

FDMEE Role Security

FDMEE Role Security is the technical deployment of functional security roles. Individual application components are assigned to a given FDMEE security role to provide a user access to that functionality.

Application components can be assigned to one or more security roles. For example, the Data Load Workbench would be provided to each of the example security roles given in the previous example. Likewise, there is no requirement to assign every application component to a security role in the application. For example, if the application is not being used to manage metadata integration, the metadata application components would not be assigned to any role that would be leveraged on the application.

There are 12 security roles contained within FDMEE:

Security Role
Create Integration
Run Integration
Drill Through
HR Integration
Intermediate 2 through 9

The first four roles are preconfigured with common components assigned based on the functional need while the Intermediate roles are a blank slate to be defined based on a business's functional requirements. *All* of these roles can be modified as per business needs.

As with the assignment of application components to security roles, the use of all security roles is not required. The use of security roles should align with the functional requirements and as previously noted, avoid over-engineering and creating too many functional security roles.

FDMEE role security is fundamentally different when compared to FDM Classic. In FDM Classic, security roles were cascading. This meant that if a user was assigned the security role of Intermediate 4, he/she would have access to all of the application functionality assigned to the Intermediate 4 role but also to the application functionality assigned to Intermediate 5, 6, 7, 8 and 9. FDMEE security roles, by contrast, do not employ a cascading functionality assignment. If a user is assigned to the Intermediate 4 security role, he/she only has access to the application functionality that has been assigned to the Intermediate 4 security role.

Securable Application Components

The application components that can be assigned are grouped into four categories – User Interface, Reports, Batches and Custom Scripts.

User Interface

Various elements of the user interface can be assigned to security roles to control the end user experience and limit the functions that can be executed by users assigned to said security role. Below is a list of the User Interface items that can be assigned to a security role:

Component	Notes
System Setting	Should be limited to Administrators only
Application Setting	Should be limited to Administrators or power users. Provides access to application settings for all target applications
Query Definition	Should be limited to Administrators or power users that create reports. Requires strong knowledge of SQL.
Source Adaptor	Should be limited to Administrators only
Source System	Should be limited to Administrators or power users that will build new integrations directly against a source system like Oracle PeopleSoft
Target Application	Should be limited to Administrators or power users. Provides access to integration options for all target applications.
Source Accounting Entity	Should be limited to Administrators or power users that have ownership for source system integrations like Oracle PeopleSoft.
Import Format	Should be limited to Administrators or power users responsible for creating new integrations.

Component	Notes
Location	Should be limited to Administrators or power users responsible for creating new integrations.
Period Mapping	Should be limited to Administrators
Category Mapping	Should be limited to Administrators
Script Editor	Should be limited to Administrators
Batch Definition	Should be limited to Administrators or power users.
Report Definition	Should be limited to Administrators or power users that create reports. Would usually require **Query Definition** as well.
Script Registration	Should be limited to Administrators or power users
Data Load Workbench	Should be assigned to any user that needs to interactively view data – all users generally require this component
Data Load Rule	Should be assigned to any user that needs to execute multi period loads
Data Load Rule Execution	Should be assigned to any security role that requires the ability to process data through the workflow
Logic Group	Should be limited to Administrators or power users
Check Group	Should be limited to Administrators or power users
Check Entity	Should be limited to Administrators or power users
Metadata	Should only be assigned if FDMEE is utilized for metadata integration. Should be assigned only to administrators or power users if applicable.
Metadata Rule Execution	Should only be assigned if FDMEE is utilized for metadata integration. Should be assigned only to administrators or power users that need to run the metadata integration process.
HR Data Load	Should only be assigned if FDMEE is utilized for HR data integration
Batch Execution	Should be assigned to any role that enables data processing
Report Execution	Should be assigned to all roles
Script Execution	Should be assigned per functional security
Process Details	Should be assigned to most security roles. Often not

Component	Notes
	[cont…] assigned to view only/reporting roles
User Settings	Should be assigned to all roles
Load From Excel	Should be assigned as per functional security
Lock POV by Location	Should be assigned as per functional security
Unlock POV by Location	Should be assigned as per functional security
Refresh Members Execution	Should be assigned for any role that requires mapping table maintenance

The components that have been identified for assignment to administrators or power users only are generally leveraged to manage the application. By granting access to any of these components, the user would be granted access to all of the items within that given component. For example, if the Import Format component is assigned to a role, then any user provisioned to that role would have access to all import formats, not just the import format of the location to which he/she was assigned.

Reports

FDMEE provides the ability to apply security to the report groups but not the reports themselves. In general, nearly all reports can be assigned to any security role. However, an organization may choose to limit certain report groups since the reports may not be applicable to the application deployment or the organization does not find value in these reports. One instance of the latter is with variance reports. While a variance (e.g., Actual vs Budget) report is a critical component of any financial analysis, this type of report is better suited to Oracle Hyperion Financial Reports that retrieve data from the target applications and include the ability to report on data that has been subjected to hierarchical consolidation as well as calculations.

Figure 8-1: Report Group Security

The below image shows the report groups (checked – Audit, Base Trial Balance, Process Monitor) that have been assigned to the Intermediate 2 Security Role.

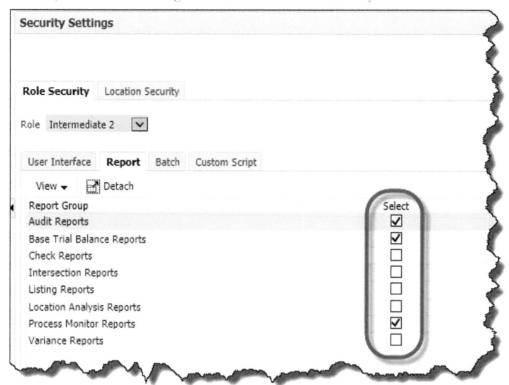

The other report group that should not be assigned to any functional end user (even power users) role is Intersection reports. These reports can only be executed by the application during the Validate workflow step. The data for these reports is generated at the application tier and as such is not stored in the application's relational database. Attempting to run these reports outside of the workflow process will result in an error and probably create end user confusion. By not provisioning access to these reports to any security role, this will eliminate the potential for end user confusion.

Finally, if there are individual reports contained in a report group that should be secured/limited, then a new group can be created and the reports can be reassigned to the new group. Groups are a more efficient way to manage access to reports as opposed to individual report level security.

Batches and Custom Scripts

Batch and custom script execution can both be secured. The security of a batch or custom script is managed by assigning a batch or custom script group to a security role. This requires planning when creating a new batch or custom script group. The groups should align to the functional security roles that we previously discussed.

Figure 8-2A: Batch Groups Example

The below image shows example batch groups based on functional security. Notice that there is no batch group for data reviewers since batch execution is associated with the workflow. Since a reviewer does not have access to process data through the workflow process, an end user assigned to the Data Reviewer role would never need access to execute a batch.

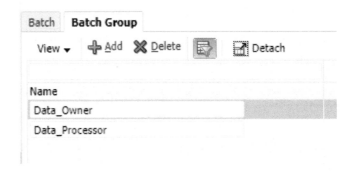

Figure 8-2B: Custom Script Groups Example

The below image shows example custom script groups based on functional security. Notice that a custom script group was created for each functional security role. Likewise, an ALL group was created since some custom scripts may need to be executed by any end user.

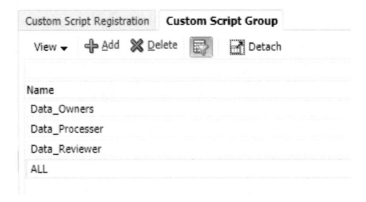

The individual batch and custom scripts are assigned a group. The security role to which the end user is assigned controls if the user is able to execute the batch or custom script.

Figure 8-3: Group to Role Assignment

In the below image, the Intermediate 2 security role is associated to the Data Owner functional security role. The Data_Owners and ALL script groups are provisioned to the Intermediate 2 security role. This means that any custom script assigned the Data_Owners or ALL Custom Script group will be accessible by the user provisioned to the Intermediate 2 security role.

FDMEE Location Security

FDMEE location security controls the locations to which an end user has access. Location security works in concert with Role Security and is therefore tightly aligned to functional security. Let's explore this further.

We previously outlined several types of functional users – data owners, data processors and data reviewers. For each of those functional roles, we then defined an FDMEE security role that would have provided access to the features of the application needed to execute that role. Location security is the next step in defining a technical security model that addresses functional definitions.

Within FDMEE, Location Security is actually the process of defining the Shared Services security group template. Within Location Security, the functional groups that are needed for each location are defined. The application then generates Shared Services native groups to which users can be provisioned.

Figure 8-4A: Location Security

The below image shows the location security defined in FDMEE. The upper grid lists each of the location security group templates defined in the application. In this example, since there are three location security group templates, clicking the Maintain User Group button will generate three Shared Services native groups for each location in the application (See Figure 8-4B).

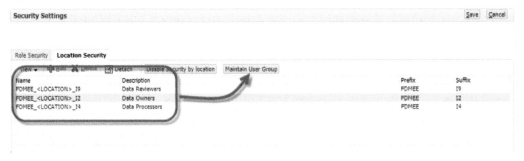

Figure 8-4B: Shared Services Location Groups

The below image shows the Shared Services native groups that were created by FDMEE. Notice the locations (varying green and yellow highlights) as part of the group name.

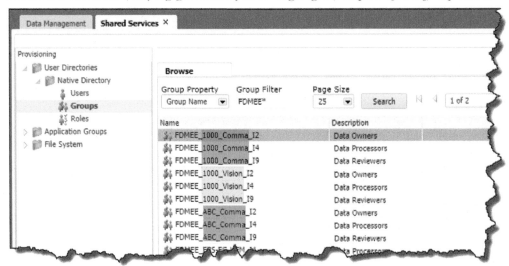

When defining a FDMEE location security template, there are several leading practices. The prefix should be FDMEE. This allows easy filtering within Shared Services to identify all FDMEE-related security groups. The suffix should align to the security role to which the functional security definition is associated. For example, if Intermediate 2 is the security role associated with the Data Owner functional security role, then the suffix for the location security template should be Intermediate 2 – or an abbreviation like **Int2** or I2. The description field is useful for associating the functional security role with technical role security. Continuing with the previous example, Data Owners would be a useful description. This description field is also pushed into Shared Services (as seen in Figure 8-4B) so a meaningful description can be leveraged when assigning users to security groups in Shared Services.

Figure 8-5: Example Location Security Template

The below image shows an example Location security template that aligns to the leading practices noted above.

Hyperion Shared Services

Hyperion Shared Services (HSS) is the mechanism for managing security across the Oracle Hyperion stack of products including FDMEE. Shared Services control authentication as well as managing the security roles and location groups to which a user has been assigned.

Figure 8-6A: User Role Provisioning

The below image shows that the Drill Through and Intermediate 2 security roles have been provisioned for user tony.scalese.

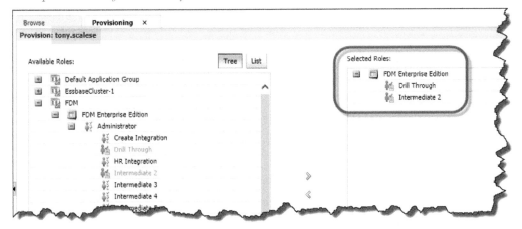

Chapter 8

Figure 8-6B: Location Group Provisioning

The below image shows how the user is provisioned to four Data Owners (I2) groups for HFM locations in the FDMEE application. Notice the use of the FDMEE prefix (yellow highlight) in the group filtering.

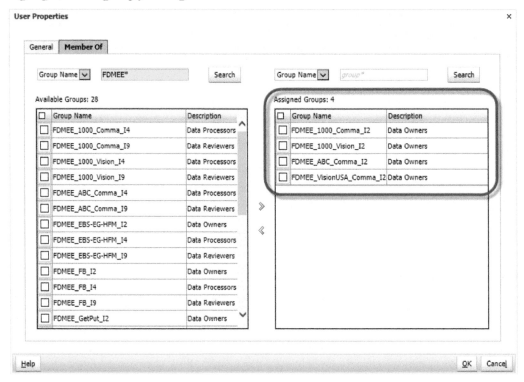

Figure 8-6C: Shared Services Provisioning Result

The below image shows the end user experience in FDMEE. Notice the Setup tab is not displayed and the Workflow tab does not include all of the functions (e.g., Metadata Rule) that an administrator user would have. Also notice how the location listing when attempting to change the point-of-view only includes the locations corresponding to the groups to which the user was assigned.

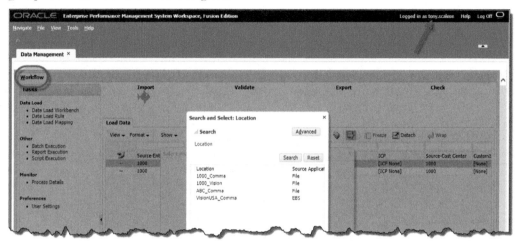

Shared Service Groups

One of the key security enhancements of FDMEE is the ability to leverage groups within Shared Services to streamline the maintenance and administration of security. FDMEE supports the use of Microsoft Active Directory (MSAD) as well as Lightweight Directory Access Protocol (LDAP) groups for user authentication, role security and location group assignment. This enables multiple end users to be provisioned with a single assignment. The other benefit of leveraging MSAD or LDAP groups is that as individuals move in and out of roles or even the organization, their access will be added or revoked automatically by the maintenance of the security provider group.

Additionally, since FDMEE leverages Shared Services native groups for location security, additional native groups can be created and leveraged to further streamline location access. Let's explore an example. Consider an FDMEE application that supports a worldwide deployment. Assume that there is an EMEA region and that multiple locations exist for this region. Assume that one or more users would need to have reviewer rights to all of the locations of EMEA. To address this requirement, a user or group could be provisioned to each location security group. However, this would require maintenance any time a new location was added.

Instead, an additional security group could be created manually and each of the EMEA location security groups could be added. The benefit of this approach is that as new locations are added, the assignment of the FDMEE generated location security groups only needs to be added to a single group as opposed to each user that needs access to the EMEA locations.

Figure 8-7A: HSS Native Group

The below image shows a new group being created. The group name is prefixed with FDMEE as with the location security template groups and is suffixed with the security role (I9) that corresponds to the functional security requirement of the group.

Figure 8-7B: Location Groups Assigned to New Group

The below image shows how FDMEE generated location security groups have been assigned to the new Shared Services native group for EMEA Data Reviewers.

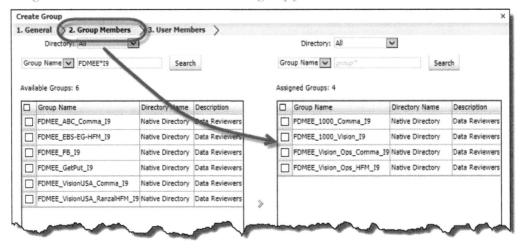

The enhancement of the integration with Shared Services to support MSAD and/or LDAP groups as well as the ability to leverage Shared Services native groups to more effectively manage location access are significant improvements to the security model of FDMEE. Properly leveraging Shared Services, Role Security and Location Security templates ensures that an administrator can effectively and efficiently control access to FDMEE.

Summary

In this chapter, we explored FDMEE security. We examined how defining a functional security model is critical to the tactical build and assignment of security. We highlighted the various components of Role security within the application. We discussed how FDMEE location security templates are used to control access to the locations and the data contained within them. Finally, we explored how Hyperion Shared Services can be leveraged to further streamline an FDMEE security model.

In the next chapter, we will explore FDMEE log analysis and troubleshooting. This chapter provides critical information that will empower an administrator during the troubleshooting process.

9

Troubleshooting and Log Analysis

In this chapter, we will explore the various troubleshooting techniques that are available to an administrator. We will begin with the process logs and learn how to effectively and efficiently identify the valuable debugging information that they contain. Next we will learn how to leverage the ODI Operator to gather additional information that may not be contained in the process logs. After the ODI Operator overview, we will explore the web application log. Finally, in the event that all of these steps are unable to identify and resolve the issue, we will explore how to leverage Oracle support to search the knowledge base and effectively log service requests.

What Is Troubleshooting?

The word troubleshooting didn't appear in books until 1910 but experienced rapid growth beginning around 1980. This should not be all that surprising given that troubleshooting is defined as a process to trace and correct faults in a mechanical or *electronic system*. In FDMEE, we need to troubleshoot any time we experience an error or encounter unexpected results. Let's define an expected result a little further. An unexpected result in FDMEE could be something as simple as data being mapped to the wrong target intersection or something more complex such as when an event script executes without error but fails to perform the task that it is expected to complete. The former can usually be addressed by leveraging the techniques introduced in Chapter 7 while the latter is the focus of this chapter.

Troubleshooting a failed FDMEE process is very much like designing FDMEE maps – it's a combination of art and science. The science is the focus of this chapter; learning how to read process and services logs as well as leverage the ODI Operator. The art of troubleshooting is the idea that software is, by its very nature, imperfect. Contrary to the opinion of some people, FDMEE is not simple or easy. If it were, you likely would not have sought out this book. Like all complicated software, learning how to find the error is the easy part. Interpretation of that error is more complicated. It is this process that is more of an art form. It takes time to cultivate this skill and become proficient at it. This chapter will not make you an artist but it will give you the proverbial paintbrush that you need to begin your journey.

Process Logs

The FDMEE process log is the first step to troubleshooting a failed process. The process log captures, in a text-based file, information about an execution of application functionality. The process log can contain an extraordinary amount of information. As highlighted in Chapter 1, the level of detail contained in the process log is determined by the Log Level setting at the System, Application or User Setting. Log level 5 is the most verbose and will result in the process log containing the greatest level of information.

The process logs can be accessed from the Workflow tab by clicking on Process Details. Each execution in the application for which a process ID is generated is displayed. The Show hyperlink in the Log column allows the process log for a given Process ID to be downloaded locally. This is extremely valuable since not all users, including administrators, will always have access to the FDMEE network share directory where the process log is generated and saved. The process logs are stored in the Logs directory of the application Outbox.

Figure 9-1: Process Details

The below image displays the process details. Clicking on the Show text in the Log column for a given process ID allows the log file to be downloaded for viewing.

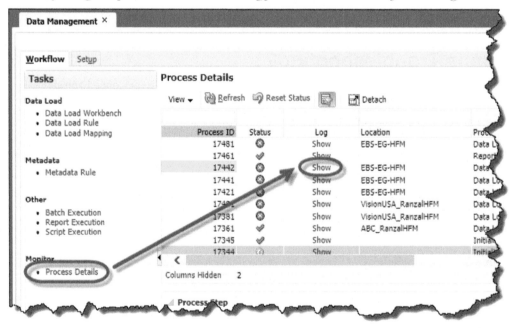

A unique process ID, and therefore process log, is generated for each execution of the workflow, batches, custom scripts, reports, initializing of a source system and purging of application elements. Importantly, there is no process ID associated with any mapping table maintenance performed within the web interface. This means that there is no ability to investigate – using the process log – any mapping changes made in the application.

Figure 9-2: Process Logs Directory

The process log file name always contains the process ID. For any execution of the workflow, the process log is named TargetApp_ProcessID.log where TargetApp is the name of the Target Application for which the POV processed and ProcessID is the numeric process ID displayed on the Process Details.

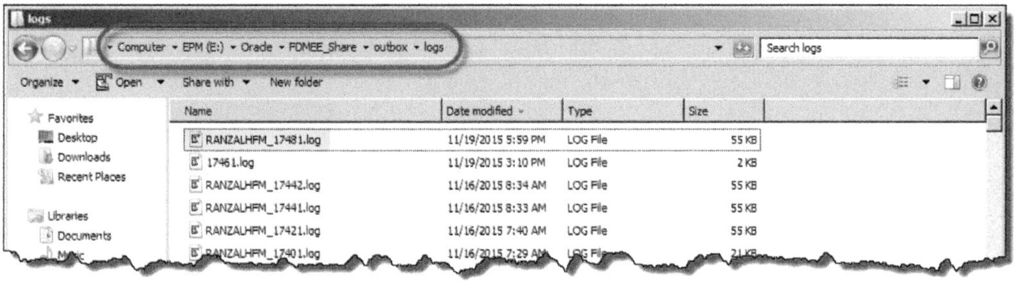

Process Log Header

The header section of every process log contains valuable information about the execution including the Log level, the user executing the process, and if applicable, the location, category, period and data load rule name processed. This is useful when needing to investigate an error associated with the workflow.

Figure 9-3: Process Log Header

The below image shows the header from a sample process log. Notice on the second line of the log file that the process log level is set to five (5) meaning the log will contain the most detailed information available.

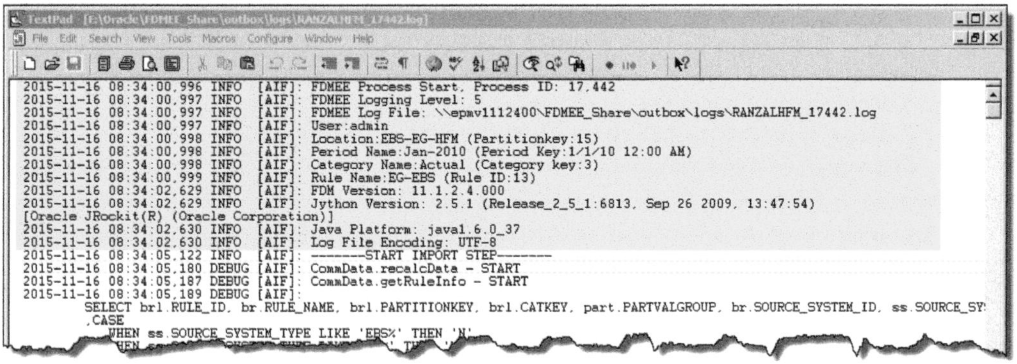

Before beginning the process of analysing the log, confirm the logging level in the header of the process log associated with the failed process. If the logging level is not set to five (5), update the log level settings, recreate the problem by executing the process again and then utilize the log file from the subsequent execution.

Process Log Analysis

As previously noted, the process log can contain very detailed information ranging from the SQL statements executed by the application to detailed Jython errors encountered during a script execution. This can be daunting to not only new users of the application but also for experienced users. When analysing a log file for a failed process, first open the log in a more powerful text editor like Notepad++ or Textpad as they better respect carriage return and line feed characters than Notepad.

Figure 9-4: Side by Side Text Editor Comparison

The below image shows a side by side comparison of Textpad (left) and Notepad (right) of the same process log. The Textpad view is far easier to visually interpret.

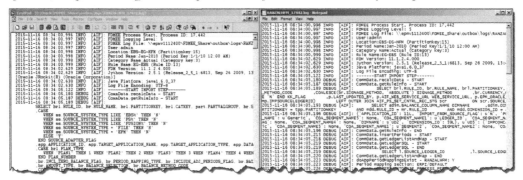

When trying to identify the source of a failed process, perform a text search for the term FATAL or ERROR. This will often bring you to the section of the log that can be used to identify the source of the problem.

Figure 9-5: FATAL Keyword

The below image displays an error in the validateData (green) process. The error highlighted in yellow indicates that the process failed due to unmapped members. This error can be resolved by checking the Validation Errors tab in the Data Load Workbench.

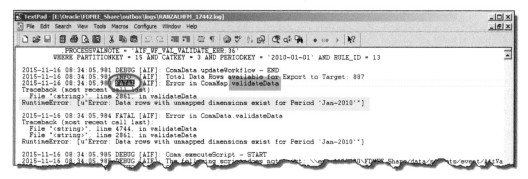

Certain errors will be easily identifiable and remedied based on the error information contained in the process log. In the event of Jython script errors, the script and the line of the script that is failing to execute is noted. This is incredibly useful even if the error information provided is not easily understood.

Figure 9-6: Script Error

The below image shows an error generated by the ER_ExportMaps script. The error was encountered when executing line 14 of the script. The error message circled in red may not have a lot of meaning at first blush but to an experienced FDMEE administrator this means that the variable strLoc was not properly populated since you cannot apply the Jython method upper() to a None variable type.

There are instances where the `FATAL` or `ERROR` keywords are not found in the process log. It can be more challenging to determine the root cause when the process log lacks explicit information about the error. In these cases there are several systematic options –

more detailed process log analysis, FDMEE services log analysis, and leveraging the ODI Studio.

Detailed Process Log Analysis

A more detailed analysis of the process log is a time consuming process but the reward of identifying and correcting an issue makes the effort worthwhile. To enable oneself to perform this analysis, a SQL client is required – SQL Developer when FDMEE is run on an Oracle RDBMS or SQL Server Management Studio in the case of Microsoft SQL Server. As noted above, the process log will contain a number of SQL statements that are executed by the application. A SQL client will allow the SQL statements contained in the process log to be executed. The resulting data set can be used to determine if there is incorrect or missing information somewhere in the application that is causing the error.

When establishing a connection to the FDMEE RDBMS repository, all of the connection information – except the password – is available in the System Settings under the ODI Profile Type.

Figure 9-7: SQL Connection Information

The below image shows how the ODI Profile Type can be used to gather database connection information. The URL specifies the database server name (yellow), the port (green), the SID for Oracle (brown) or the database name for SQL Server (not shown). The user login (pink) to the database is specified in the ODI Master Repository User field. The password can usually be supplied by IT or by the database administrator.

SQL Execution

A word of caution – when using the ODI Master Repository user credentials bear in mind that this login has full access to the database and therefore the data contained in the FDMEE application. An alternative safer approach would be to create a view only database user for troubleshooting purposes.

When executing SQL statements written to the process log, be sure not to execute any DML – INSERT or UPDATE – statements as these would impact the data contained in the database of the application. When encountering a DML statement, you can transform to a simple SELECT statement (or execute only the SELECT subquery) by removing the portion of the query that controls the update of data within the application.

Figure 9-8A: Process Log DML Statement

The below image shows a DML statement generated by the application and logged in the process log. The portion in yellow represents a portion of the SQL query that would modify data in the database. The portion in green represents the SELECT subquery which, when executed independently of the INSERT statement, would return a record set.

```
2015-11-16 08:34:05.519 DEBUG [AIF]:
          INSERT INTO TDATAMAP_T (
            LOADID
            ,DATAKEY
            ,PARTITIONKEY
            ,DIMNAME
            ,SRCKEY
            ,SRCDESC
            ,TARGKEY
            ,WHERECLAUSETYPE
            ,WHERECLAUSEVALUE
            ,CHANGESIGN
            ,SEQUENCE
            ,VBSCRIPT
            ,TDATAMAPTYPE
            ,SYSTEM_GENERATED_FLAG
            ,RULE_ID
          )
          SELECT 17442
          ,DATAKEY
          ,15 PARTITIONKEY
          ,DIMNAME
          ,SRCKEY
          ,SRCDESC
          ,CASE WHEN TARGKEY = '<BLANK>' THEN ' ' ELSE TARGKEY END
          ,WHERECLAUSETYPE
          ,CASE WHEN WHERECLAUSEVALUE = '<BLANK>' THEN ' ' ELSE WHERECLAUSEVALUE END
          ,CHANGESIGN
          ,SEQUENCE
          ,VBSCRIPT
          ,TDATAMAPTYPE
          ,SYSTEM_GENERATED_FLAG
          ,RULE_ID
```

Figure 9-8B: Modified SQL Statement for Debugging

The below image shows the result of executing the SELECT statement from the DML statement in Figure 9-8A. The records circled in red shows the result of the query.

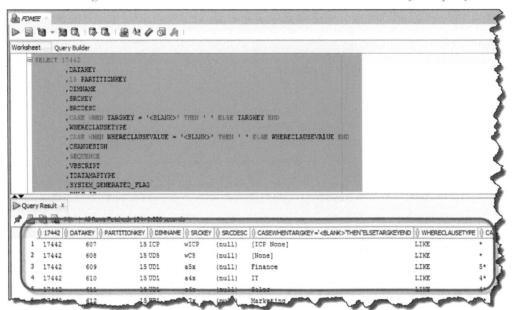

The resulting record set can be evaluated to ensure that the information contained in the record set is accurate or represents data that should be leveraged by the application. Having a deep understanding of the application, its tables and the data are critical to being able to determine if the records returned by a query execution are accurate. This level of understanding comes with experience and exploration. Taking the time to understand the database structure and how each table relates to different web components is critical to developing a strong set of troubleshooting skills.

ODI Studio

Oracle Data Integrator (ODI) Studio is a critical administrator tool. While a web front end to the ODI Console is available, it lacks much of the functionality that is key for an administrator to effectively troubleshoot errors. It is strongly recommended that an administrator gain access to ODI Studio. Please note, this chapter is not intended to provide an in depth education about ODI and as such assumes a working knowledge of the tool.

Whenever a process ID is generated by an FDMEE execution, a corresponding ODI session is generated. An ODI session tracks the various steps of an ODI scenario execution. The ODI session number associated with an FDMEE process ID can be determined in the FDMEE Process Details.

Figure 9-9: ODI Session Number

The below image shows the FDMEE process details where the ODI Session number associated with a given process ID can be found. Clicking on the session number allows the ODI information to be downloaded to an XML file that can be attached to service requests submitted to Oracle.

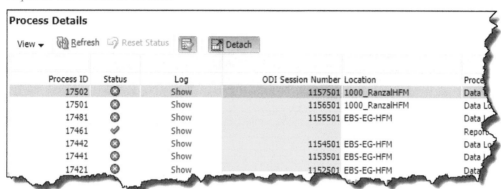

Determining the ODI session number is critical to investigating a failed process in ODI Studio. Within ODI Studio, session details are viewed on the Operator tab. There are multiple ways to locate the ODI session within the Operator as the sessions are grouped in multiple ways. If troubleshooting an error within the same day has occurred, then the Date grouping in the ODI Operator is an efficient method since only the ODI sessions for the current day are displayed in the grouping. When troubleshooting an error that is more than a week old, the All Executions list is generally the fastest way to find the session number for which the analysis needs to be performed.

Figure 9-10: ODI Session Filtering

The below image shows the session filtering that is available in Operator of ODI Studio. The Today, Yesterday and This Week groupings are useful for locating sessions related to recent errors. The All Executions grouping is useful for locating older sessions.

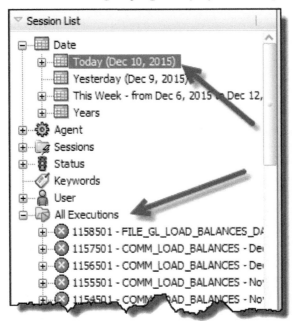

Many ODI scenarios actually spawn child sessions in which another ODI scenario is executed. It is critical to understand this behavior as using the ODI session details to troubleshoot failed FDMEE processes often requires investigating a child session.

Figure 9-11A: ODI Operator Sessions

The below image shows the Parent Session (1157501) launching a child process (1158501) during step 42 which is highlighted in yellow.

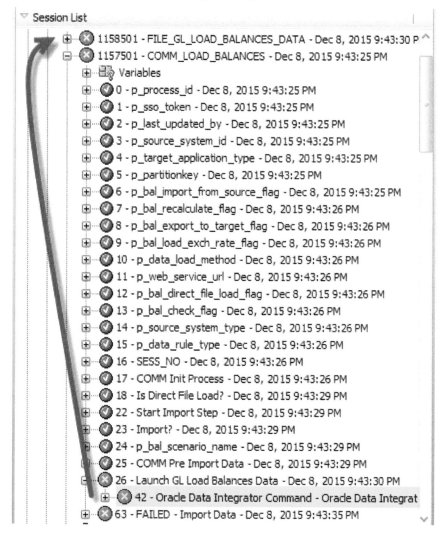

Figure 9-11B: Parent Session Launch Details

The below image shows the detailed information logged during step 42 of the parent process 1157501. The child process has an ODI session number of 1158501. This information is critical since session numbers associated with a single FDMEE process will not always be sequentially ordered especially when considering concurrent users and/or parallel processors.

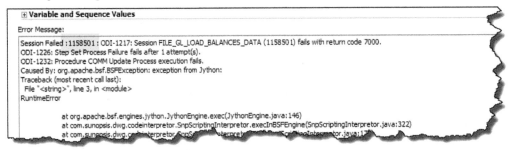

Figure 9-11C:

The below image shows the step (46) in the child process that failed. The error detail is highlighted in pink.

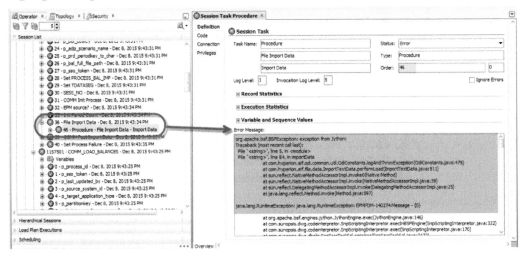

Often the information logged in the failed child process step will provide enough information to identify and resolve the issues. However, there are instances when the error message provides limited insight and additional troubleshooting efforts are required. In these cases, the FDMEE web application services log can be leveraged.

FDMEE Web Application Log

The FDM Web Application log captures very technical information about a number of events in the application. Unlike the process logs, the web application log is cumulative meaning that it contains events across multiple time periods and multiple executions.

The FDMEE Web application log is named `aif-WebApp.log` and is stored on the server where the FDMEE service is deployed. The path to the log is:

```
Oracle\Middleware\user_projects\domains\EPMSystem\servers\EPMServer0\logs
```

Figure 9-12:

The below image shows the web application log and the additional information related to the cryptic error message (Error EPMFDM-140274 in yellow) discovered in the ODI operator in Figure 9-11C. In this example, the data file for the location was not found as highlighted in pink.

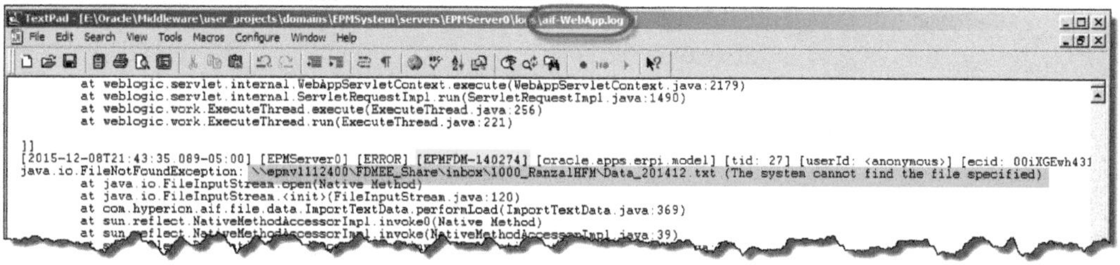

To find useful troubleshooting information in the web application log, start from the end of the log and search up for the error code. This will bring you to the section of the log that contains the error. Additional information related to the error can be found in the blocks below this error code. Be sure to pay attention to the date and time stamp of each entry in the log to ensure that the block being analysed corresponds to the time around which the error was encountered.

While the web application log can be daunting initially, eventually you will find it extremely useful when either process log or ODI Operator analyses are unable to be used to identify the root cause of the error encountered.

Oracle Knowledge Base and Support

For the purpose of this chapter, we assume that a valid login exists to access the Oracle support website. More information about obtaining a valid login to Oracle support can be provided by your Oracle sales representative.

The Oracle Knowledge Base (KB) is incredibly powerful as it is continually updated with information about product defects, resolutions and workarounds. Leveraging the KB properly can help an administrator quickly resolve issues that are related to product defects or improperly configured application components.

To access Oracle support, navigate to https://support.oracle.com and enter your access credentials. On the Knowledge tab there is a widget for the Knowledge Base. Select Hyperion Financial Data Quality Management, Enterprise Edition from the product list. In the search term field, enter the text that will be used to search the Oracle KB.

Figure 9-13: Oracle Knowledge Base

The below image shows where to access and search the Oracle Knowledge Base within the Oracle Support website. Be sure to select FDMEE as the product. The search term (highlighted in pink) is critical to finding relevant information.

When leveraging the KB, the search terms used will be critical to finding appropriate resolutions. You can search using errors codes – FDMEE or ODI – but in my experience this sometimes fails to locate a KB article containing the information needed to correct the problem. Many of the KB articles that exist are a result of other users creating Oracle support tickets. Tickets often contain more text information rather than error codes. That's not to say that a ticket and/or KB article will not contain an error code upon which a search can be performed but, more often than not, text-based searches will be more fruitful.

When performing a text search of the KB, it is recommended to use the exact error description contained in the process log, ODI session or web application log. Similar to an effective search against a search engine like Google, avoid a search that contains superfluous information or terms.

Figure 9-14: Example KB Article

The below image shows an example KB article. The versions (yellow) for which the article is applicable are specified. The error codes (pink) are contained in the symptoms section. The cause is highlighted in blue. The solution (circled in red) section which contains the information needed to correct the issues is truncated to adhere to Oracle's licensing of KB articles.

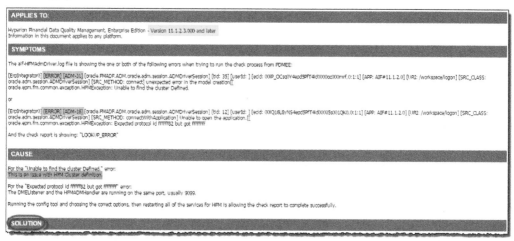

Service Requests

Once all of the troubleshooting methods which have been outlined in this chapter have been exhausted and the issue remains unresolved, then the creation of a service request (SR) with Oracle support is the next logical step. If the issue being encountered cannot be addressed using any of the methods outlined in this chapter, there is a chance that you have discovered a defect (bug) in the application.

Logging an SR is the most efficient way to engage Oracle and validate that the issue being encountered is either a result of an improper configuration, a misunderstanding of the expected application functionality or an actual known or unknown software defect. In the event of a bug, an SR provides Oracle support with a formal mechanism to engage the development team and provide them with a notification of a potential defect.

If the development team formally recognizes a defect, then a bug is logged. The development team will then evaluate the bug for severity, impact to number of customers and possible workarounds until the defect can be corrected. Once this is determined, the correction of the defect is prioritized in terms of other defects, future application functionality and level of effort. A defect may be addressed by a Patch Set Exception (PSE), by a patch set (e.g., 11.1.2.4.**100**) or by an upgrade. Oracle support can provide additional information about which of these methods will address the defect in the application.

Logging a Service Request

To log a service request, select the Service Requests tab in the Oracle support website. Click the Create SR button.

Figure 9-15: Creating a Service Request

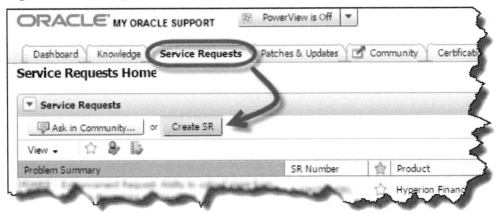

The SR will ask for a Problem Summary, Problem Description as well as information about the application and its deployment (O/S and RDBMS). A good practice when creating the problem summary is to begin with the product name, in this case FDMEE. This allows you in the future to search within your organization's service requests for all SRs related to a given product. The problem description should include as much information as possible for support to understand the issue and attempt to replicate the problem. I also include the exact version number (including patch set level) in the problem description. I have found that this is helpful because the product version is sometimes overlooked by the technical support analyst.

Figure 9-16A: SR Details

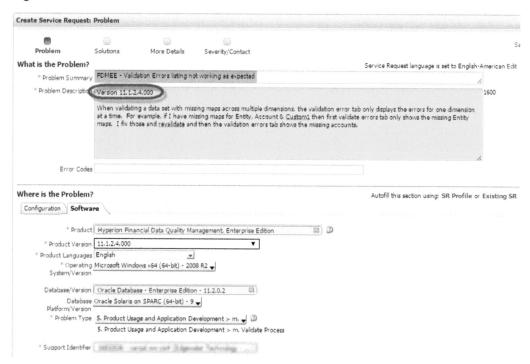

On the More Details section of the service request, attach the process log, an XML export of the ODI session (see figure 9-10), the web application log and any screenshots that may help support better understand the issue through a visual context.

Figure 9-16B: Service Request Attachments

On the Severity page, select the severity that corresponds to the problem. Understand that a severity level one (1) is reserved for production issues and if an SR is logged as severity one, then a contact will need to be available on a 24x7 basis to accept Oracle support assistance. In my experience, most service requests related to FDMEE do not require a severity one rating as often a workaround can be utilized until application functionality is restored.

Once you have provided all of the information for the service request, click Submit and a service request identifier will be generated. The status of a service request can be found at any time by clicking on the service request identifier in the Service Requests tab of the Oracle Support website.

A service request is also a method to log enhancement requests for the application. Enhancement requests are logged as service requests. When logging the SR, specify that request is for an enhancement and include as much detailed information including mock ups in MS Word that explain the requested enhancement as fully as possible. The more information and justification that is provided for an enhancement, the better the chance that Oracle development will be able to understand the request and evaluate it fully.

I will close this section with a thought about Oracle Support. I understand the frustration that can come with logging a service request when facing a critical issue and waiting for a response. I watched the FDM team set the standard for customer service and product knowledge. I watched the organization experience a significant transition resulting from turnover and adding new staff to support an ever-growing product. And I have watched as this new and expanded team has continued to grow. Throughout all of these phases, the Oracle support organization has remained committed to customers and ensured that issues are resolved in as timely a manner as possible. I assure you that your newly found knowledge of troubleshooting FDMEE errors will only enhance your Oracle support experience as you are now empowered to provide them with better and more thorough information which is critical for them to support you and your usage of the FDMEE.

Summary

In this chapter we explored troubleshooting in FDMEE. We learned how the process logs, ODI sessions and web application log are critical tools in this activity. We highlighted how the Oracle Knowledge Base is a powerful tool to help you find resolutions to known issues. And finally we discussed how to effectively log a service request to get assistance from the Oracle Support, and when applicable, Development organizations.

In the next chapter, we will explore the software development lifecycle of FDMEE. We will discuss the different phases of the software development lifecycle for FDMEE and highlight the critical outputs of each phase. Finally we will explore the primary tool – lifecycle management – which can be used to support the software development lifecycle of FDMEE.

10
Software Development Life Cycle

In this chapter, we will explore the software development lifecycle, and learn the different phases of the software development lifecycle for FDMEE. We will highlight the critical outputs of each phase. Finally, we will review the primary tool – lifecycle management – which is used in different phases of the software development lifecycle of FDMEE.

What is SDLC?

Software development lifecycle (SDLC) is yet another acronym in the world of Information Technology (IT). But one might ask, what exactly does SDLC mean? According to Wikipedia, SDLC describes a process for planning, creating, testing and deploying an information system. When you consider an FDMEE project, you have five phases – requirements, design, build, test and rollout. A well designed project, regardless of the scope, should include each of these phases.

Planning

"He who fails to plan is planning to fail." – Winston Churchill

The planning phase of SDLC encompasses the activities required to determine the scope of the project as well as the expected functional and technical design of the application. While the level of effort dedicated to these activities can vary depending on the size, scope and timeline of a project, this activity is critical to the overall success of a project and one that should not be forsaken.

The requirements phase incorporates gathering the needs of the users, while the design phase translates those needs into a functional and technical plan. Together, these steps represent the planning phase of SDLC.

Requirements

The requirements phase should capture all of the user needs and requests. The output of this phase is often a requirements matrix that includes requested functionality as well as the person or business unit submitting the request, the level of effort, the complexity, the prioritization and the phasing of the request.

I have sometimes observed user requirements being excluded from the requirements matrix because they are not in the scope, timeline, budget or some combination thereof of the project. I caution against this. The requirements matrix is simply a wish list of the functionality that an end user would like to have available in the application. Documenting these requests ensures that the end user understands that their request has been heard and understood. The challenge of an effective project execution is to prioritize the requirements and communicate to the end users what will be addressed within the scope, budget and timeline of the project.

Design

The design phase of an effective SDLC cycle transforms the agreed upon requirements into a technical and functional design of the application. The output of this phase is usually a design document which highlights how the application's functionality will be used to address requirements. An effective design document will represent a combination of the functional and technical architecture that is used to address the various requirements.

For example, when designing an integration to Oracle eBusiness Suite (eBS), the design document could highlight that an FDMEE Location will be created for each eBS Ledger to address the need to apply data security. The design decision to create a location for each eBS Ledger represents the functional requirement since (technically) all ledgers could process through a single location. The naming convention for the locations that will be used represents the technical design. The combination of both of these design elements ensures that an end user can more fully understand the design for which he or she is asked to provide approval.

I would like to offer a word of caution. The design phase can be very protracted. There is sometimes a belief that capturing extremely granular information about each component that will be deployed – including mapping – will ensure project success. In reality, especially with FDMEE, I have found the opposite to be true. Data often has hidden nuances that – without actually integrating the data to a target application – are unknown or simply forgotten by the end users.

Additionally, the actual deployment of a solution may require multiple iterations to achieve optimal performance and maintainability which is often unknown until integrating actual data sets and cannot be accounted for in the design phase. Finally, by creating an overly detailed design document, the project is unnecessarily constrained and could result in a system that adheres to the design document but which fails to deliver functionality that is valuable to the end user community.

Instead of spending valuable project time, budget and resources attempting to capture granular and sometimes obscure information, focus on documenting a design that captures the key requirements and design elements that are required for the project to be considered a success. I define project success as one that delivers the agreed upon requirements (scope) within the timeline and budget. Additionally, a key success criterion to any IT project is whether the end user community recognizes any benefits from the new application/functionality. A design phase that addresses functional requirements by striking a balance between documenting functional design and the technical components needed to deliver that design is often the most successful.

Creating

The creating process – also referred to as the build phase – represents the portion of the project where the design is transformed into an application and/or application functionality. This is the portion of the project where import formats, locations, maps, and scripts – to name but a few – are created. For an administrator or consultant, this is usually the exciting portion of the project. This is the part of the project where your knowledge and creativity can shine.

During the build phase, an FDMEE developer should also be unit testing his or her components and processes. A developer would be remiss to simply create FDMEE components and fail to ensure that they are working – using a small sample data set – as expected. Moreover, failure to unit test could have a potentially disastrous effect on the testing phase of the project.

Consider the potential impact to end user acceptance testing if a developer simply loaded a set of maps but never imported and validated the dataset to ensure that maps properly transformed the source segments to the target dimensions. There is the potential that the import format is improperly defined, or that the maps fail to capture a significant number of source segment values or simply produce poor results. Failure to unit test would mean that these issues are surfaced to the end users during formal testing. This could result in a failed testing cycle as well as end user loss of confidence in the application. Unit testing is a critical component of the build phase and should not be overlooked.

Testing

Once the creating (build) stage is complete, an application moves into the testing phase. The testing phase is critical to ensure application functionality, performance, and end user acceptance of the solution. There are multiple types of testing that can be applied to an FDMEE development cycle.

Integration Testing

Integration testing represents the testing protocol that confirms not only the functionality built within FDMEE but also FDMEE as a component of the entire Oracle EPM solution. Integration testing proves that data moved from a source system functions as expected and that the target application is receiving the appropriate data needed to provide the functionality for which the target application was designed and built.

Informal integration testing occurs throughout the build phase of a project since data movement into a target application is a lynchpin activity of any EPM project. More formal integration testing with formal test scripts and documented results is generally reserved for larger projects or organizations that follow strict SDLC procedures as often defined by Information Technology policies and procedures.

Performance Testing

Performance testing measures the responsiveness and/or scalability of the application and is multifaceted. Performance testing will capture metrics like how much time is required for the workflow process to complete with a full data set for one or more periods, how long the workflow process takes to complete if multiple users are executing the process concurrently, or how long it takes to perform identical functions when accessing the application using local and remote connections.

There are multiple software tools that can be utilized – such as HP LoadRunner – to facilitate performance testing. Additionally, analysis of FDMEE process logs can be a useful way to gather performance statistics to identify areas for potential performance improvement.

Functional Testing

I consider functional testing, for an FDMEE project, to be simply a more robust integration test. As noted in the integration testing section, informal integration testing naturally occurs as part of the build cycle including unit testing. Functional testing, in comparison, is usually far more formal. Functional test scripts track each step of a business process – including those up and downstream from FDMEE – to ensure that an end to end business process can be completed successfully with the application(s).

Functional testing is often also referred to as user acceptance or parallel testing. The delineation of these terms is often driven by the target application with which FDMEE is integrated. User acceptance testing is more common when integrating with Essbase or Planning since end users are generally testing reporting and functionality capabilities for which FDMEE supplies data.

Parallel testing is more common when integrating with HFM. A parallel close cycle is one in which the existing system and the newly developed system are used concurrently (or serially) to close the books. The goal of a parallel cycle is to produce financial results in the new application that match the existing application (or where differences are able to be explained). Several parallel close cycles are generally recommended for an HFM application before determining that the risk of going live is minimized and that financial results are accurate.

The difference between parallel and user acceptance testing is generally whether the existing process is duplicated (parallel) or if a new application/functionality is being introduced (user acceptance).

It is critical to educate users that functional testing – for full implementations, not simple enhancements – is, especially in the first iteration, intended to surface errors and possible areas for future improvement in the application design and build. A functional test that fails to uncover either of these is not likely to be as robust as it could or should have been.

Training – The Key to Success

A successful project hinges on a robust test phase. In an ideal world, the testing phase would include each of the aforementioned testing phases. Not only would each of these phases be included but adequate time between each cycle would be given to identify and remediate issues surfaced during testing. At a minimum, every FDMEE project should include functional testing.

In order for functional testing to be meaningful, the end users of the application must understand how to properly use the applications. This learning is usually imparted through some training methodology. The different training approaches available and the benefits/costs of each are outside the scope of this chapter and book; however, it is important to understand that a successful project is heavily dictated by how well users understand not only the application interface but also the application's functionality and how it can be used to address their needs.

Every testing phase should ensure end user education to help drive adoption of the application and ensure that testing is meaningful.

Deploying

In the deployment phase, the application is deemed production ready. During this phase, documentation of the application's components and processes is prepared and the application is migrated to production hardware. This latter step is the technical focus of this chapter as we will explore how the Oracle Hyperion Life Cycle Management (LCM) feature can be used to promote applications across different hardware environments.

Once 'going live' is completed successfully, the application then enters a sustaining and, eventually, enhancing cycle. We will discuss the sustaining activities in Chapter 11. The enhancement cycle is natural as the application must change to adapt to new and changing business requirements. Additionally, as most projects lack an unlimited budget and timeline, enhancements or next steps are often planned at the planning stage or uncovered during the testing stage. In either event, the application life cycle repeats and the process described herein is applied once again.

Life Cycle Management

Oracle Hyperion Life Cycle Management (LCM) is a feature of the Oracle Hyperion Enterprise Performance Management suite of products. LCM is used as part of the Test and Deploy software development lifecycle phases to migrate applications or individual application artifacts (including data for some EPM applications) across different hardware environments. Moreover, LCM can be used to backup applications within a given environment. LCM provides a common interface for the management of these migration and/or backup activities across multiple applications within the EPM suite including FDMEE.

Figure 10-1: Accessing Life Cycle Management

The below image shows how LCM is accessed through Oracle Hyperion Shared Services by selecting Navigate → Administer → Shared Services Console.

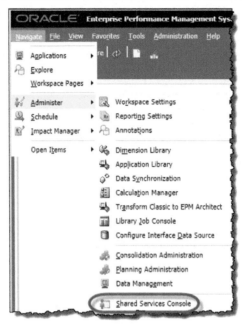

An FDMEE migration is enabled via an LCM generated export and subsequent import to the target hardware environment. While LCM enables application components to be migrated, FDMEE data and workflow process status cannot be migrated using this functionality. In order to migrate FDMEE data and workflow status, a database migration would be required. This is currently not supported by Oracle and is a rare requirement. As such, this chapter will not explore migrating FDMEE at the relational tier. It should be noted that LCM does not migrate any FDMEE components stored at the file system level including report templates (.rtf) or scripts. These items must be migrated using standard file system functionality.

Life Cycle Management Export

The LCM export feature allows FDMEE application components to be extracted from the source environment for migration or backup purposes. An entire FDMEE application, as well as select application components, can be selected for export.

Figure 10-2: Access LCM Export

The below image displays the path to access the FDMEE application components for LCM exporting. Expand the FDM folder and click on the FDM Enterprise Edition link.

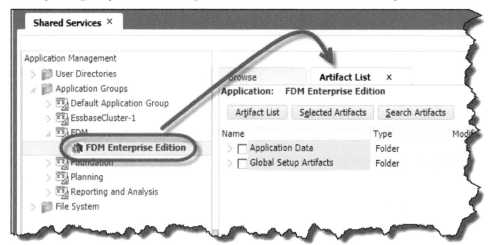

The registered applications – both source and target – as well as the global application components can be selected for export.

Figure 10-3: Application Components

The below image shows applications available for export. Each application type (circled in red) contains the applications (yellow) which are registered. The individual components for the registered application (green) are displayed below each application.

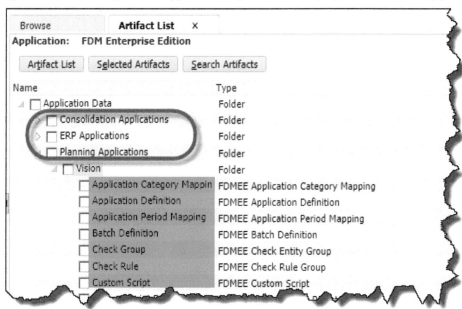

Figure 10-4: Global Components

The below image shows the global application components that are available for LCM export.

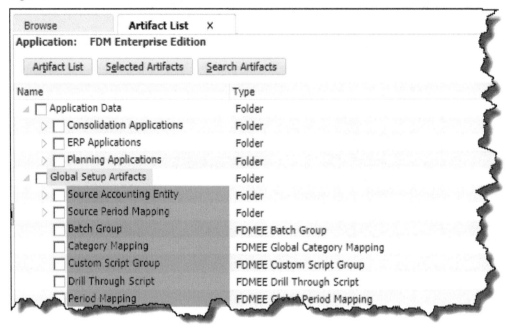

While LCM will allow individual application components (e.g., Locations, Import Formats, Maps) to be selected for export, the individual items within that application component (e.g., Location A, Import Format C, Maps for just the Entity dimension) cannot be selected.

LCM Export Output

When an export process is executed, a directory is created by Lifecycle Management that contains a number of files and subdirectories. This directory is created in the `import_export` directory of `\Oracle\Middleware\user_projects\epmsystemx` where x is the deployment – often one (1).

Figure 10-5A: Export

The below image shows the directory that is created based on the export file system folder specified.

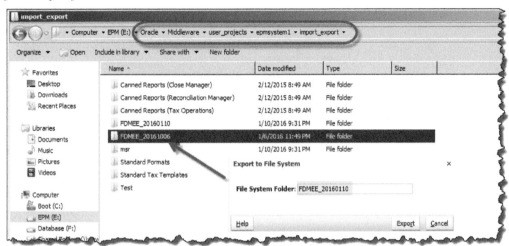

There are a series of subdirectories within the root directory created by the LCM export. Application and global artifacts are found in subdirectories of \FDMEE-FDM Enterprise Edition\resource.

Figure 10-6: Artifact Directories

The below image shows Application and Global artifact subdirectories.

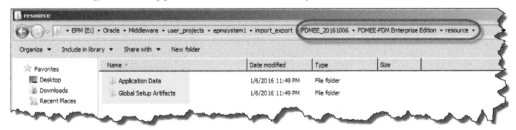

Each of the application or global artifacts selected for export is outputted to an XML file. This XML file can be modified or appended as needed; however, it is strongly recommended to create a backup of the file or entire output directory before modifications are made to ensure that any changes which yield unexpected results can be overwritten using the original export result.

Figure 10-7: Example Artifact

The below image shows the global period mapping that was outputted to XML.

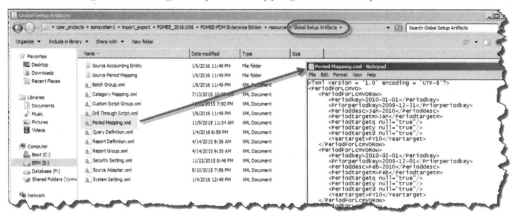

LCM Import

FDMEE application components can be imported into a target environment. The import of application artifacts can be utilized to create objects, as well as update existing objects. An LCM import can be executed against an existing application or be used to create a new application.

For example, for a new deployment of FDMEE, following a robust SDLC process, one would develop the application in a development hardware environment. Once application unit testing is complete and more formal integration, performance or functional testing is ready to begin, the application would be migrated to the test hardware using LCM. Following successful testing, the application would then be migrated to production hardware, again using LCM.

Lifecycle management empowers an administrator to perform this migration through the web interface – assuming security access to lifecycle management has been provided. Once the export of application artifacts is complete, the output needs to be imported into the target environment.

As discussed in the LCM Export section, FDMEE application components are outputted to a file system directory as a series of subdirectories and XML files. In earlier versions of LCM, access to the server import_export directory was required to move this directory from the source hardware environment to the target hardware environment into which the application was to be imported. Now, the LCM-generated export directory can simply be downloaded as a zip file.

Figure 10-8A: Download LCM Export

The below image shows how right clicking on the export directory name and selecting download allows the output directory to be downloaded as a zip file.

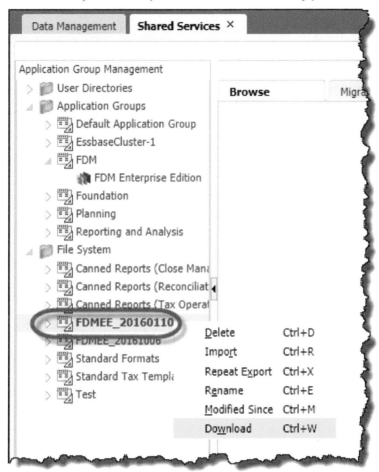

Once the LCM output directory is downloaded as a zipped archive, the file can simply be uploaded and imported into the target environment.

Figure 10-9A: Upload Source Environment Export

The below image displays how right clicking the File System folder in LCM allows you to select the Upload option. Browse to select a zipped archive saved locally or on a network folder and click Finish.

Figure 10-9B: Import Directory

The below image shows how – after an upload – a new import directory is available from which application artifacts can be imported.

Expand the group name from which the application artifacts should be imported and click on the FDMEE-FDM Enterprise Edition link. This action allows the individual components which should be imported to be individually selected.

Figure 10-10: Artifact List

The below image shows how individual artifacts can be selected for import for a target application as well as the global setup. In this example, the period and category mapping, data load rule, import format and location for the Vision planning application will be imported. Also, the category mapping for the global setup will be imported.

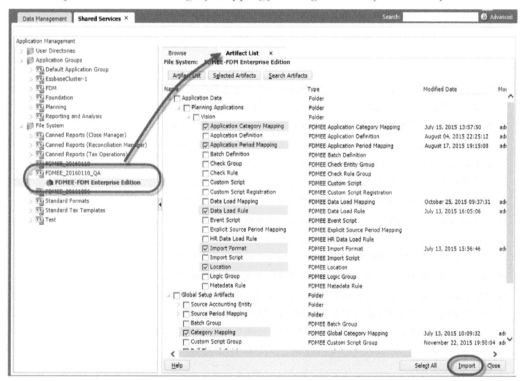

The import results can be tracked utilizing the migration status report. When a migration completes successfully, the status is simply Completed. When an error is encountered, the status will show as Failed.

Figure 10-11: Migration Status

The below image shows the migration status report.

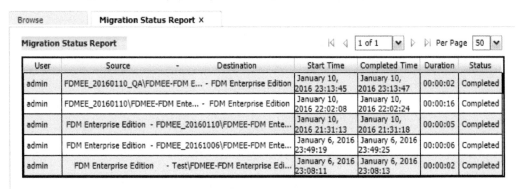

In the event that an import encounters an error, clicking on the status text Failed will display the migration details which will provide additional information about the errors encountered.

Figure 10-12A: Failed Status

The below image shows a failed migration. The Failed status can be clicked to display migration details.

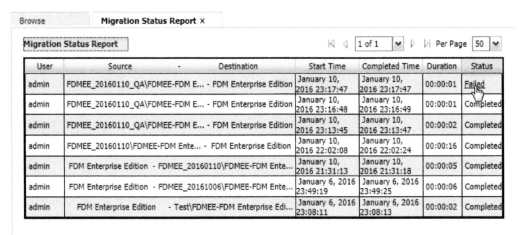

Figure 10-12B: Migration Details

The below image shows that the import failed because the target application (Vision8) for location 1000_Vision does not exist in FDMEE and the location could not be imported. In this instance, the target application either needs to be registered or the location XML needs to be modified to associate the 1000_Vision application to a valid registered target application.

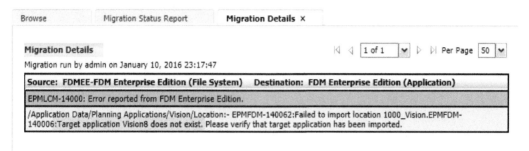

LCM Leading Practices

There are several leading practices to consider when utilizing Lifecycle Management. These recommendations will enable you to more meaningfully leverage the LCM module to support the SDLC process.

Import Validation

The Lifecycle Management module provides an option to validate the XML contents as part of the import process. This option is powerful as it can prevent maps that specify invalid or non-existent target members from being imported into the target environment.

However, this validation can be extremely detrimental to import performance. When enabled, each mapping item being imported needs to be confirmed against the target application's metadata. Depending on the volume of mapping, this can be a very lengthy process.

It is a good practice to import all target application artifacts except data load mapping with the import validation option disabled. Once these items are imported successfully, then the data load mapping can be imported individually. This allows the import validation to be selectively turned on or off depending on the need.

Figure 10-13: LCM Migration Options

The below image shows how the Skip Validation option can be toggled in Migration Options. The migration options are accessed from the Administration menu.

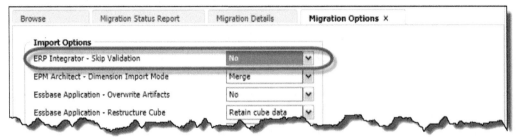

During an initial or final migration, it is a good practice to enable the validation. With interim/iterative migrations, which can be common during the creating and testing phases, the need to validate during each migration is usually not as critical. During an interim migration, the performance gains associated with disabling validation are usually worth the incremental risk of loading an invalid mapping.

Avoid Blind Imports

Often, as developers or administrators, we need to remind ourselves to pause and evaluate the actions we are about to undertake. An LCM import is no exception to this idea. Rather than blindly importing all of the file contents within an LCM directory, one should review the artifacts contained in the directory and ensure that importing each is appropriate.

Figure 10-14A: Import from File System

The below image shows the import option that is available when right clicking an archive from the file system folder of LCM. This option should not be utilized as all artifacts contained in the directory will be imported.

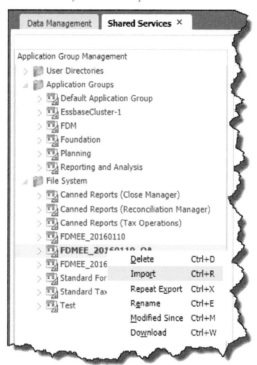

Figure 10-14B: Import All Artifacts

The below image shows how simply selecting the top level Application Data or Global Artifacts folders selects all of the items below that group. As such, an administrator should evaluate individually which artifacts to import.

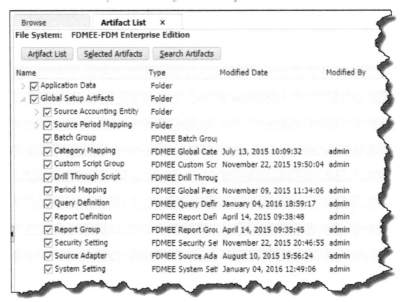

Artifacts Not to Migrate

There are certain application components/artifacts that simply should not be migrated. Instead, these items should be configured within each environment to reflect the information specific to that environment. This leading practice is derived from the fact that these elements contain information that is specific to one hardware environment.

Migration of these artifacts from one hardware environment to another environment will require modification to said elements post migration. Additionally, an inadvertent import of those artifacts (see blind import section above) would overwrite information that has been configured for the current hardware environment with information related to the source's hardware environment. This action can render a system inoperable or inadvertently expose source environment artifacts to changes from the target hardware environment. Moreover, if this were to occur, the changes expected in the target application would not be effected and would potentially cause FDMEE to produce unexpected or incorrect results.

The following global setup artifacts should not be migrated using LCM:

Artifact	Reason
System Setting	Contains application path and ODI connection information that is specific to a single hardware environment.
Source Adaptor	Contains configuration information that is specific to a single hardware environment.
Security Setting	May be migrated if security configuration is equivalent across environments; user access is migrated when the Hyperion Shared Services module is migrated.

Summary

In this chapter, we explored the software development lifecycle of not only an FDMEE application but of the entire Oracle Hyperion EPM application suite. We learned the different phases of SDLC and the core outputs of each. Lastly, we highlighted the capabilities of Oracle's Lifecycle Management (LCM) component and how it can assist in the software development lifecycle.

In the next and final chapter we will discuss application care and feeding. This chapter is fundamental in understanding how to keep an application performing well over time while maintaining the right amount of historical information to support reporting and audit requirements.

11

Application Care and Feeding

In this chapter, we will explore application care and feeding. We will discuss how to keep an application performing well over time while maintaining the right amount of historical information to support reporting and audit requirements. We will highlight the application layers that require maintenance and components from which information can be purged. We will outline the impact to application functionality from purging information from any of these layers. Finally, we will highlight the scripts that Oracle introduced in 11.1.2.4.100 that streamline and systematize the purging process.

What is Application Care and Feeding?

The term "application care and feeding" is not a technical term like SDLC with which one may (or should have been) familiar. Application care and feeding is a term I apply to the routine maintenance that should be considered for not only an FDMEE application but for any information technology application and/or platform. As with a child, plant or pet, you care for it constantly; you feed it, you give it water to keep it healthy and growing. The same analogy can be made for an FDMEE application.

Why is Application Maintenance Important?

The process of maintaining an Oracle Hyperion EPM application is often one of the most overlooked functions of an administrator. Too often, an administrator is consumed with the daily activities of simply keeping the application running. An administrator is constantly responding to the neverending flow of enhancement requests for his/her user community. This is actually very positive as Oracle Hyperion EPM applications exist because they can rapidly respond to the everchanging needs of the business. When an application administrator is fielding constant enhancement requests, this is a great sign of an application that has been widely adopted by the organization and is providing a great return on investment.

That said, it is important not to overlook a series of standard maintenance procedures that are critical to ensuring an application continues to perform well and prove a stable platform. An FDMEE application can grow substantially over time. A tremendous amount of information is stored within the RDBMS as well as at the file system level and – as with any application that leverages an RDBMS – the more data stored in the database, the longer it will take to access, add and update information stored in those tables.

Additionally, removing data from either the RDBMS or file system layers is good not only for application performance but also for stability. While disk storage has become incredibly economical, it still is not unlimited. This applies not only to the RDBMS layer but also to the file system layer. The application generates a tremendous number of log and archive files as well as data files depending on target system integration. Over time, between the RDBMS and file system layers, hundreds of gigabytes (or more) of data can be housed in an FDMEE application. If the disk space allocated to either of these tiers is fully exhausted, the application will cease to function.

Finally, a more efficient upgrade cycle is an ancillary benefit of removing data and/or metadata from an application. The Oracle EPM application suite has continuous improvements and updates. Some of these are offered as patches to the current version while others require an upgrade to the newest release.

When an upgrade to a newer release is required, there is usually an upgrade process that Oracle provides that brings the applications from the current release to the new release. Often, as part of this upgrade, the applications, including FDMEE, are run through a migration utility. These utilities will often affect the data tier (RDBMS in the case of FDMEE) to apply the new data storage standards and definitions. This process can be incredibly time-consuming when an application contains a significant amount of data.

For these reasons, it is critical to develop a strategy for a periodic purging of information from the FDMEE application. Since FDMEE is an application that is used in support of financial reporting and planning applications, it is critical that this activity and its schedule should be reviewed by internal and/or external audit to ensure compliance with data retention policies and procedures. As such, this chapter does not provide any recommendation of the objects to purge or the frequency thereof.

The information that follows simply highlights the objects that tend to grow over time and are available for purging. Any comments contained in the following are meant to educate the reader as to the impact of removing an object and should not be misconstrued as a recommendation – explicit or implied – to remove any of these objects. Finally, any comments regarding the impact, or lack thereof, to application functionality ignores the idea that purging application elements removes the ability to audit previously executed processes. The need for this capability should also be considered when developing a purging strategy.

Lastly, any purging strategy should include a robust and fully-tested backup process. The backup should encompass both the RDBMS and file system layers. In the event of an inadvertent purge of critical information, a backup may be required to restore application functionality and/or critical data.

Oracle Provided Scripts

This book was first envisioned and authored when the 11.1.2.4.000 release was the most current. Over the course of writing this book, the 11.1.2.4.100 patch set has been released. With this patch set, Oracle introduced a series of System Maintenance scripts which can be used to systematically remove data from the RBDMS and file system layers of the FDMEE application. This chapter will highlight these scripts but it should be noted by the reader that they are only available in the 11.1.2.4.100 or greater release. Additional information about each script is provided in the 11.1.2.4.100 FDMEE Administrator guide as an appendix called Purge Scripts.

Each of the Oracle-provided scripts except `MaintainODISesssions` can be run in a testing mode simply by toggling the `dryRun` variable from `False` to `True`.

Figure 11-1: Dry Run

The below image shows the dryRun Boolean variable that can allow the maintenance script to run without actually impacting the RDBMS or file system layers. This is useful to assess the impact of the script before running it.

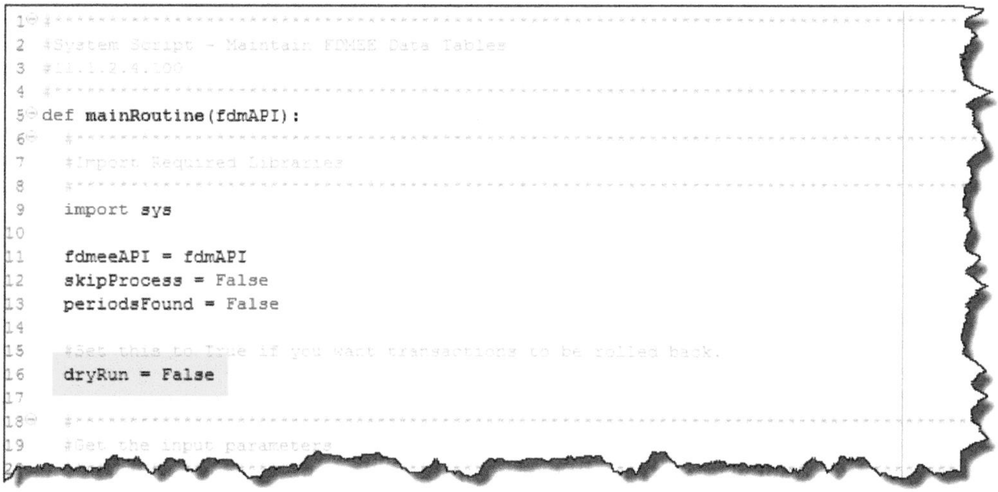

File System Layer

The file system layer contains log, archive and data files. In Chapter 1, we discussed the application root folder. This is the file system directory in which FDMEE will store these various files. The application root directory has three immediate subdirectories – data, inbox and outbox. This applies not only for the root folder specified in the System settings but also for any application specific folders specified in the Application settings.

Data Folder

In Chapter 1, we explained how the Archive Mode setting can result in a source data file being duplicated or moved to the `data` folder of the application. Whenever a data file is archived – either through a Move or Copy setting – this is the directory to which the file is copied. Depending on the file size and the number of time periods processed through

Chapter 11

the application, this directory can consume a significant amount of disk space. However, removing data files from this directory will prevent drill through to the source data file from functioning.

Figure 11-2: Data Folder Purge Impact

The below image shows the impact to application functionality when purging the data folder. Open Source Document cannot be used since the data file being opened is retrieved from the data folder with an archive mode of copy or move.

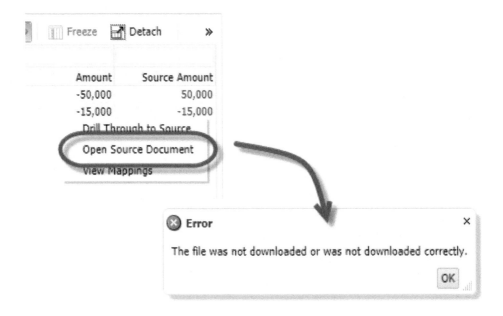

Instead of a wholesale purging of this directory, one could develop a process to remove only the data files that were generated as a result of an iterative load of a given point of view. For example, if processing data to HFM on day one through day six of the close, only the day six information would persist in the application at the end of the current close cycle. Any of the data files associated with the earlier executions could be purged without impacting open source document functionality.

Scripts Folder

The `scripts` folder is a subdirectory of the `data` folder. This is where any script registered in the application – except the System Maintenance scripts provided by Oracle – gets stored. Files should not be removed from this directory unless it is determined that they are no longer in use.

Inbox Folder

The `inbox` folder often contains the original data file processed through the FDMEE workflow since end users without administrator rights must upload the file to this directory or their location specific subdirectory (depending on the `Create Location` Folder setting). Purging data files from this directory has no impact upon application functionality.

Batches Folder

The `batches` folder is a subdirectory of the `inbox` folder. Within the batches folder are two subdirectories – `openbatch` and `openbatchml`. These are the folders from which data files (i.e., non-direct integration) can be processed in a 'lights out' fashion. Each time a file-based batch process is executed, a new folder corresponding to the process ID is generated in the `openbatch` folder corresponding to the execution type. A single period execution generates a new folder in the `openbatch` directory while a multiperiod execution generates a new folder in the `openbatchml` folder.

The batch folders and file contents within the `openbatch` and `openbatchml` directories can be purged without any impact upon application functionality.

Outbox Folder

The `outbox` directory is where the application generates a data file for loading to a target application. These data files represent an export of the mapped/transformed data for a specific POV within the FDMEE application. Data files (.dat) are always generated during the Export workflow step when integrating with HFM. As discussed in Chapter 2, data files are only generated for Essbase and custom applications when the application settings dictate. Additionally, the intersection validation XML and drill region definitions are outputted by the application to this directory.

Figure 11-3: Outbox Directory Contents

The below image shows example files contained in the outbox directory. The .dat files are the data exported for a given FDMEE POV. The XML file is the HFM intersection validation report. The .drl files are the drill through region definitions. The .log files that correspond to each .dat or .drl file are the log files that capture the log information generated by the target application.

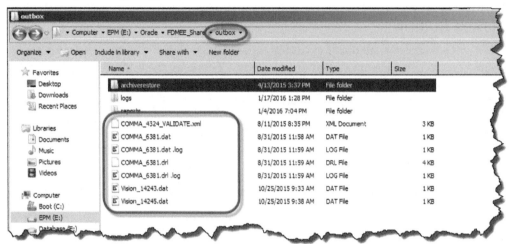

Files contained in the outbox directory can be purged without impact upon application functionality. Moreover, these files can be regenerated by simply re-executing the Export workflow process.

Logs Directory

The `logs` folder is a subdirectory of the `outbox` folder. As we discussed in Chapter 9, a log file is generated for each process executed in FDMEE. The information captured during these executions is written to a log file that is stored within this directory.

Figure 11-4: Logs Directory

The below image shows example log files contained in the logs directory.

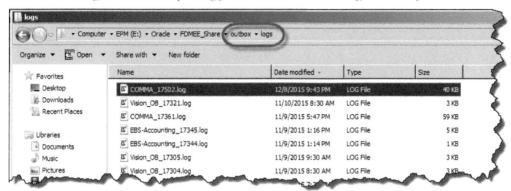

Purging log files from this directory prevents the use of the Show function within the Process Details. While the link can still be clicked, the downloaded file will be blank.

Figure 11-5A: Process Details

The below image shows Process Details. Clicking on the Show hyperlink (yellow highlight) for process ID 17743 (circled in red) will open the log file for execution.

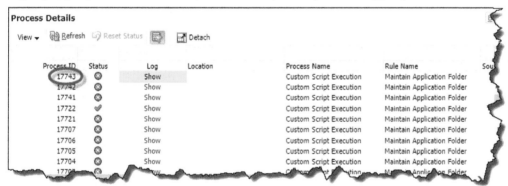

Figure 11-5B: Process Log

The below image shows the blank log file for execution 17743. This file is blank because the log file was deleted from the logs directory.

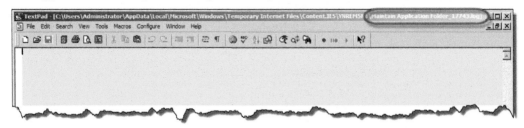

Reports Directory

The `reports` folder is a subdirectory of the `outbox` directory. Starting with the 11.1.2.4.100 patch set, when any location is assigned a check rule, the application will generate a copy of the check report anytime the Check workflow is executed. This file is generated in the reports folder.

Files contained in the reports directory can be purged without any impact upon application functionality. Like the outbox directory's contents, Check workflow generated output can be regenerated simply by re-executing the Check workflow.

Oracle Provided Maintain Application Folder Script

As previously noted, Oracle introduced this script in 11.1.2.4.100. The script will purge data files from the data, inbox and outbox folders as well as the relevant subdirectories.

There are several things to consider when leveraging this script. First, the script prompts for the target application upon which the purge should occur. This assumes that application folders are created for each target application. As we discussed in Chapter 1, one may or may not choose to utilize this functionality. When the FDMEE application does not utilize application-specific folders, the script will purge files from the application root folder, specified in the system settings, according to the time period parameter specified in the script prompts.

Second, this script will purge all files in the directory and subdirectory. The impact of this purging should be considered carefully, especially as it relates to aforementioned application functionality. To skip a root directory and its subdirectories, simply enter a non-numeric value like the word Skip and the directory will not be purged.

Figure 11-6: Maintain Application Folder Prompts

The below image shows the prompts for the Maintain Application Folder script that is executed from the System Maintenance Tasks script group. The Target Application – Vision (in yellow) – is only applicable when using application-specific folders. The 'Days to keep' parameters will delete any files older than the threshold specified for each primary subdirectory. Any non-numeric value (green) entered will result in the folder being skipped.

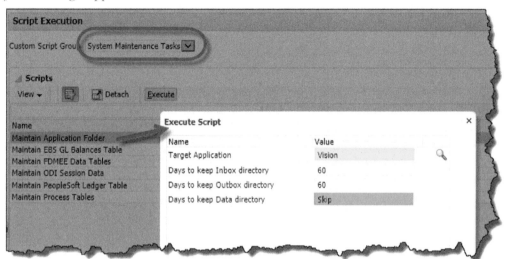

Database Layer

Like the file system layer, the RDBMS layer of the FDMEE application contains log, archive and data information. The database layer is generally far larger than the file system since the database contains not only the data files but a significant number of records that define application metadata and track executions. Purging information from the RDBMS tier should be done with great caution. Deleting records can have unexpected results especially in the event of not knowing the interdependency of different database objects. As an example, you notice that the TDATAMAPSEG table has grown significantly and decide that the table can be cleared since maps are stored on the TDATAMAP table. However, what you may not realize is that this table is used to enable View Mappings functionality.

The maintenance of the database layer can be grouped into two primary categories – process information and data. For the maintenance of the database layer, using Oracle provided scripts is highly recommended. Since Oracle authors the scripts they will also provide support.

One final consideration when purging information from the RDBMS layer is reclaiming the unused space. I am not a database administrator but my understanding is that simply deleting rows from a table will not shrink the database size. There are certain shrink procedures that need to be executed to reduce the size of the database. After purging information from the database, you should work with the DBA to reclaim the unused space of the database.

Process Information

Every execution of an FDMEE process results in records being generated in one or more FDMEE database tables. All executions are tracked in the AIF_PROCESSES, AIF_PROCESS_DETAILS, AIF_PROCESS_LOGS, AIF_PROCESS_PARAMETERS, AIF_PROCESS_PERIODS, AIF_PROCESS_STEPS tables. Any execution of a data load rule generates records in the AIF_BAL_RULE_LOADS and AIF_BAL_RULE_LOAD_PARAMS tables. And finally any execution of a batch generates records in the AIF_BATCH_JOBS and AIF_BATCH_LOAD_AUDIT tables. The AIF_APPL_LOAD_AUDIT and AIF_APPL_LOAD_PRD_AUDIT tables are also impacted for certain workflow events.

In addition to the FDMEE application process tables (those denoted by AIF) there is also ODI execution information stored within the FDMEE RDBMS. Each of the scenarios executed as part of the FDMEE process are logged including the process steps of the scenario. A scenario can contain dozens of steps. As a result, the ODI process information logged to the RDBMS is significant.

When considering hundreds or thousands of executions of different data load rules over the course of a single year, the data explosion that can occur on each of these tables is significant. It is not unreasonable to have hundreds of thousands if not millions (or more) of rows across all of these tables. Periodic purging of data from these tables will ensure that the database size does not continue to perpetually grow unchecked.

In addition to the performance and stability benefits that can be gained by purging information from these tables, there is the additional benefit that systematic database backups will be processed in a more timely fashion and as such will be more reliable.

Oracle Provided Scripts

Oracle has provided two scripts to enable the purging of process information. The Maintain Process Tables script is used to purge records from the database layer that are related to the FDMEE process information – i.e., AIF tables noted previously. The Maintain ODI Session Data script is used to purge records from the database layer that are related to the ODI scenario executions which are launched when FDMEE processes are executed.

Figure 11-7: Oracle Process Purge Scripts

The below image shows the two Oracle scripts that can be used to purge process information from the FDMEE database layer. Both of these scripts prompt for the number of days of history to maintain within the database.

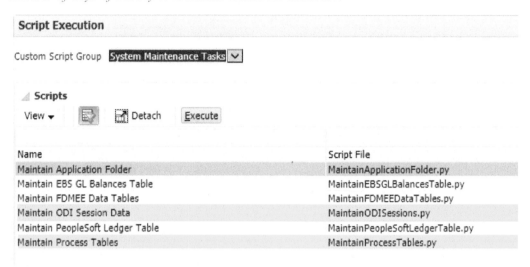

In general, it is a good practice to execute these scripts in concert with one another. If process information is being purged then it would be difficult to associate ODI scenario execution information with an FDMEE process execution. Likewise, purging ODI information while maintaining process information would prevent any additional analysis on an FDMEE process ID since the ODI scenario execution information would no longer exist.

Data

Data for each point of view processed in FDMEE is stored in the RDBMS. This is one of the key benefits of FDMEE as a data integration tool that allows it to distinguish itself from other ETL tools since most ETL tools do not maintain the data that they transform. However, this differentiator also means that the FDMEE database layer will grow continually as more data is processed through the application.

Let's consider a very basic example. Imagine an FDMEE application that processes 15,000 data records on a monthly basis. After one year, the database will contain 180,000 rows just for the data. There are also entries for the mapping tables applied as well as the process status. For simplicity, let's assume those add an additional 20,000 records over the course of a year. After five years, the application will have one million rows just related to the data.

While the application can certainly support this data volume, whenever any point of view that has been previously processed is reprocessed, the application must query and delete from the data table before importing the new dataset. Any time that tables grow significantly, performance of this query operation can be impacted, especially if no indexing has been done on the table. Moreover, this cost is encountered whenever data is queried from the FDMEE database for loading to the target application.

The majority of data and information related to the workflow process is stored on the following tables:

Table Name	Data Contained
TDATASEG	Data processed through FDMEE.
TDATAMAPSEG	Mapping records actually applied when processing a dataset for a given POV. Each unique combination of location, time period, category, and data load rule(s) processed will have a set of records.
TLOGPROCESS	Workflow status for each POV processed.
TDATACHECK	Check rule results for any location assigned a Check rule and for which the Check workflow step has been executed.
TDATAARCHIVE	Information about the flat files processed for each POV. Will contain multiple records for a single POV if the POV was processed multiple times.
AIF_EBS_GL_BALANCES_STG AIF_EBS_GL_DAILY_BAL_STG	Only applicable when directly integrating with Oracle eBusiness Suite. Contains financial data from EBS.
AIF_PS_LEDGER_STG	Only applicable when directly integrating with Oracle PeopleSoft. Contains financial data from PeopleSoft.
AIF_OPEN_INTERFACE	Only applicable when using the Open Interface adaptor. Contains data sourced from a relational repository when the Open Interface data load rule parameter to delete data after execution is set to No.

Purging data from these tables can certainly reduce the size of the database and thereby improve overall performance and stability; however, the cost of this action is that FDMEE reporting, including auditing mapping, will be unavailable for any data that was removed from the application. Additionally, drill through from a target application like HFM or Planning will also be unavailable for the points of view for which data was purged.

As I stated at the beginning of this chapter, one needs to consider the purging action as it relates to data retention policies and procedures. An administrator should also consider the impact to users of the application and their ability to utilize the FDMEE application for analysis purposes. Even when confirming that a purge operation adheres to data retention policies, an administrator should not perform this action in a vacuum. He/she should communicate with the user community and strike a balance of ensuring that adequate data is preserved in concert with maintaining an efficient application.

Oracle Provided Scripts

Oracle has provided three scripts for data purging. The primary script is the `Maintain FDMEE Data Tables` and the secondary scripts are `Maintain EBS GL Balances Table` and `Maintain PeopleSoft Ledger Table`. The latter two are only applicable if using the prebuilt direct integration capability of FDMEE to EBS and/or PeopleSoft.

The Maintain FDMEE Data Tables purges information from the `TDATASEG`, `TDATAMAPSEG` and `TLOGPROCESS` tables.

Figure 11-8: Data Purge Script

The below image shows the script parameters for the Maintain FDMEE Data Tables script. When executed, data is cleared from the tables for <u>all</u> locations associated to the target application selected for the range of periods and category specified.

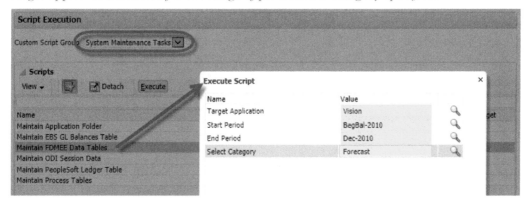

The remaining scripts for EBS and PeopleSoft maintenance will prompt for the source system name and the range of periods to clear from the staging tables.

Summary

In this chapter, we explored the concept of application care and feeding. We discussed the two primary layers of an FDMEE application – the file system and the RDBMS. We outlined the different components within each layer and how purging can affect application functionality and usability. We highlighted how maintenance of these items is critical to ensuring performance and stability. We also reinforced the importance of developing a purging process that adheres to organizational data retention policies and procedures. Finally, we highlighted the scripts that Oracle has provided starting in the 11.1.2.4.100 release to streamline the purging process.

Throughout this book, we have explored a variety of topics. We have discussed the fundamentals of data integration including defining key terminology such as source systems and mapping. We have outlined leading practices for application and new integration setup. We discussed the mapping capabilities of FDMEE. We explored the scripting capabilities of the application as well as provided detailed instructions on configuring an IDE for script development. We shared information about the security model of FDMEE and how to configure it to meet your organizational needs. We highlighted the application user interface and exposed key functionality that allows end users to do more with the application. We shared troubleshooting methods and techniques to empower an administrator. We outlined the software development lifecycle and showed how Life Cycle Management (LCM) is a critical component to this process and we closed with essential information about maintaining an application over the years of ownership.

Throughout these chapters I have shared leading practices, technical information and simply, knowledge that I have developed from years of implementing FDMEE as well as FDM Classic. I sincerely hope that you have found this book to be useful and will continue to unlock the power of FDMEE based on your new and expanded knowledge.

Index

Other P8 Titles

Oracle Siebel Open UI Developer's Handbook

The Oracle Data Relationship Management 11 Guide
Successful Implementation Essentials

Jeff Flak
Edward J. Cody

Oracle Hyperion Financial Reporting 11
A Practical Guide

Edward J. Cody
Eric M. Somers

WHERE DATA IS WEALTH
Profiting from data storage in a digital society

In our society you can't be too thin, too rich, or have too much data. This book won't help you lose weight, but it will help you with the other two.
Dave Sutton, CEO and Author

J. BRUCE DALEY

Java 8 New Features
A Practical Heads-Up Guide

Richard Reese

Java Masterclass
Java Exceptions, Assertions and Logging

Sam Alapati

CPSIA information can be obtained
at www.ICGtesting.com
Printed in the USA
LVOW05s0509150216

475123LV00022B/329/P